A HOUSE WITHOUT WINDOWS

MARC ELLISON & DIDIER KASSAÏ

Life Drawn
by Humanoids

MARC ELLISON
Writer, Photographer,
Videographer

DIDIER KASSAÏ
Artist

AMANDA LUCIDO
US Edition Editor

NANETTE MCGUINNESS
Assistant Editor & Translator (pp. 157–158)

VINCENT HENRY
Original Edition Editor

JERRY FRISSEN
Senior Art Director

MARK WAID
Publisher

Rights and Licensing - licensing@humanoids.com
Press and Social Media - pr@humanoids.com

A HOUSE WITHOUT WINDOWS.
This title is a publication of Humanoids, Inc. 8033 Sunset Blvd. #628, Los Angeles, CA 90046. Copyright © 2021 Humanoids, Inc., Los Angeles (USA). All rights reserved.
Humanoids and its logos are ® and © 2021 Humanoids, Inc. Library of Congress Control Number: 2020903454

Life Drawn is an imprint of Humanoids, Inc.

First published in France under the title "Maison sans fenêtres" Copyright © 2018 La Boîte à Bulles & Marc Ellison, Didier Kassaï. All rights reserved.
All characters, the distinctive likenesses thereof and all related indicia are trademarks of La Boîte à Bulles Sarl and / or of Marc Ellison, Didier Kassaï.

No portion of this book may be reproduced by any means without the express written consent of the copyright holder except for artwork used for review purposes. Printed in Latvia.

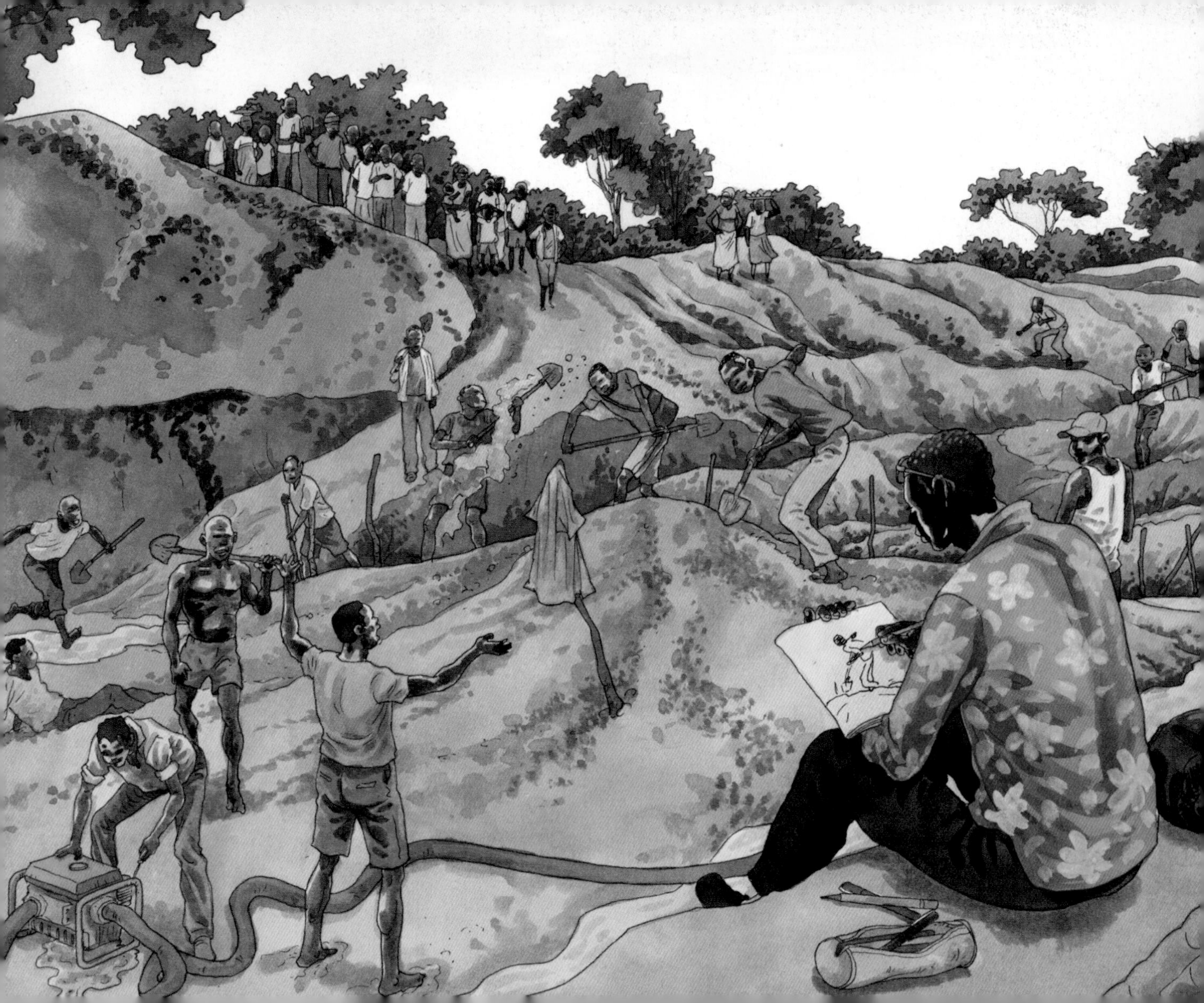

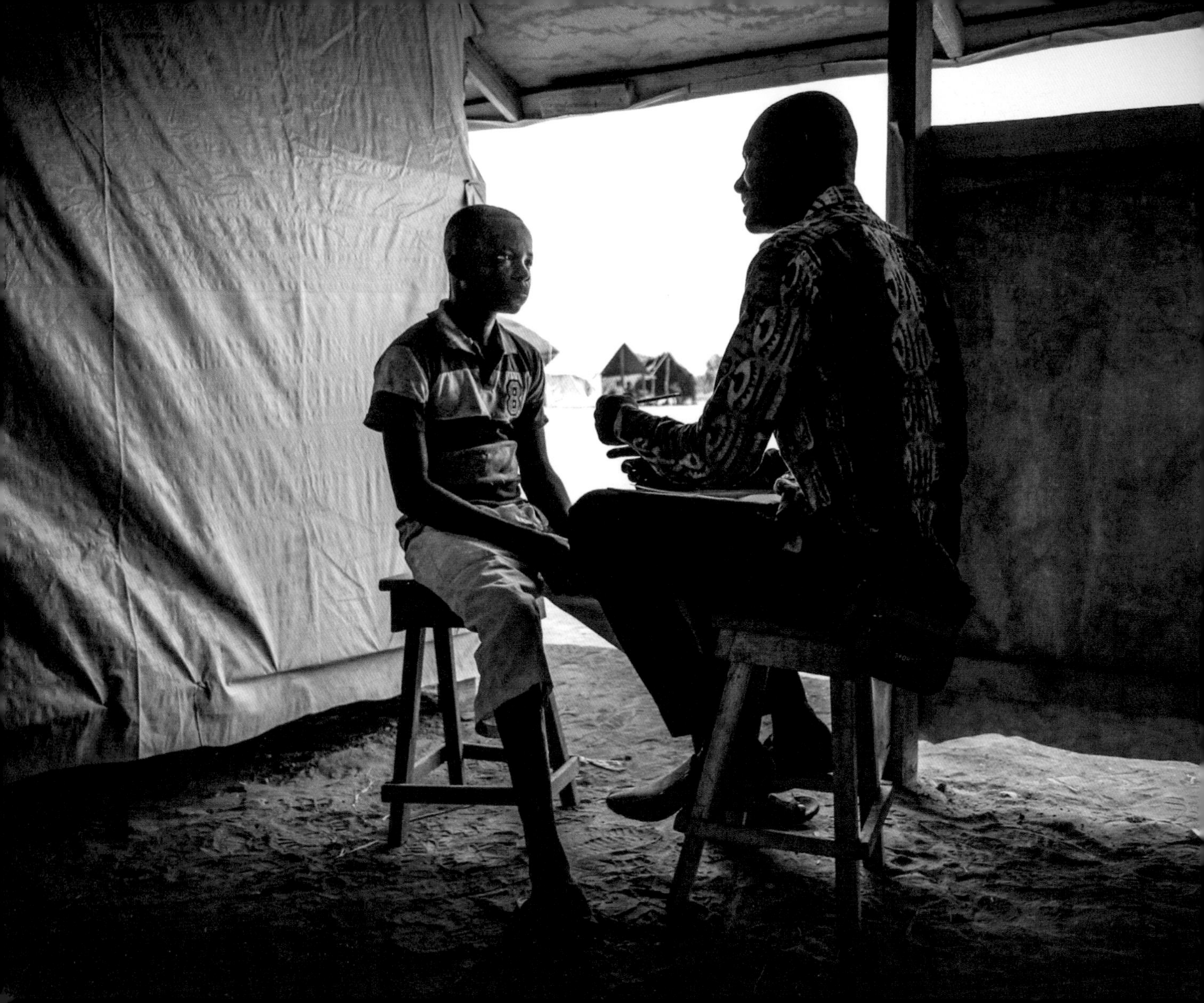

PREFACE

The Central African Republic is one of the worst countries in the world to be a child.

Sitting second only to Niger at the bottom of the UN's human development index, the children in this former French colony grow up with an infrastructure crippled by decades of misrule, corruption, and countless coups. As a result, the country is beset by poverty, food insecurity, and malnutrition. The armed conflict in 2013-14 exacerbated this situation, and ongoing insecurity has hamstrung humanitarian efforts. Years later, many schools remain closed and few children are enrolled. Many still live in sprawling camps for the internally displaced, with minimal access to healthcare or an education.

Theirs is a childhood interrupted, a childhood lost.

It's been three years since I first sat down to write this foreword for the French edition—and, sadly, little has changed. Despite a recent peace deal, armed groups continue to commit serious human rights abuses against civilians country-wide, with more than seventy percent of the country remaining under their control. Over 600,000 people are now caught in the crossfire and have been displaced from their homes—many of them children.

But as tragic as this situation is, the Central African Republic remains a house without windows. Media coverage of this ongoing crisis has been minimal, and the public's interest fleeting. The situation has often been billed by humanitarian actors as the "forgotten crisis," overshadowed by events in the neighbouring Democratic Republic of Congo and South Sudan.

This graphic novel follows me and Central African artist Didier Kassaï as we document the challenges facing youth in the country's streets, classrooms, camps, and hospitals. A father himself, Kassaï worries about the legacy his own children will inherit. Using illustration, photography, and immersive 360° video, this comic provides a virtual window through which an international audience can finally observe the problems facing this nation's most vulnerable demographic: its children.

—*Marc Ellison*
Glasgow, May 2020

THE 360° EXPERIENCE

A House Without Windows is the first graphic novel to use 360° video to transport its readers to the center of its story in an immersive virtual-reality experience.

Stand in a diamond mine, cycle around a refugee camp, and meet children living on the streets of Bangui.

Watch the full-length 360° video documentary by scanning the QR code below, or by visiting this link:
http://bit.ly/HWW-360

The video is best viewed on a desktop computer, or on your smartphone via the YouTube app, Google Cardboard, or a similar headset.

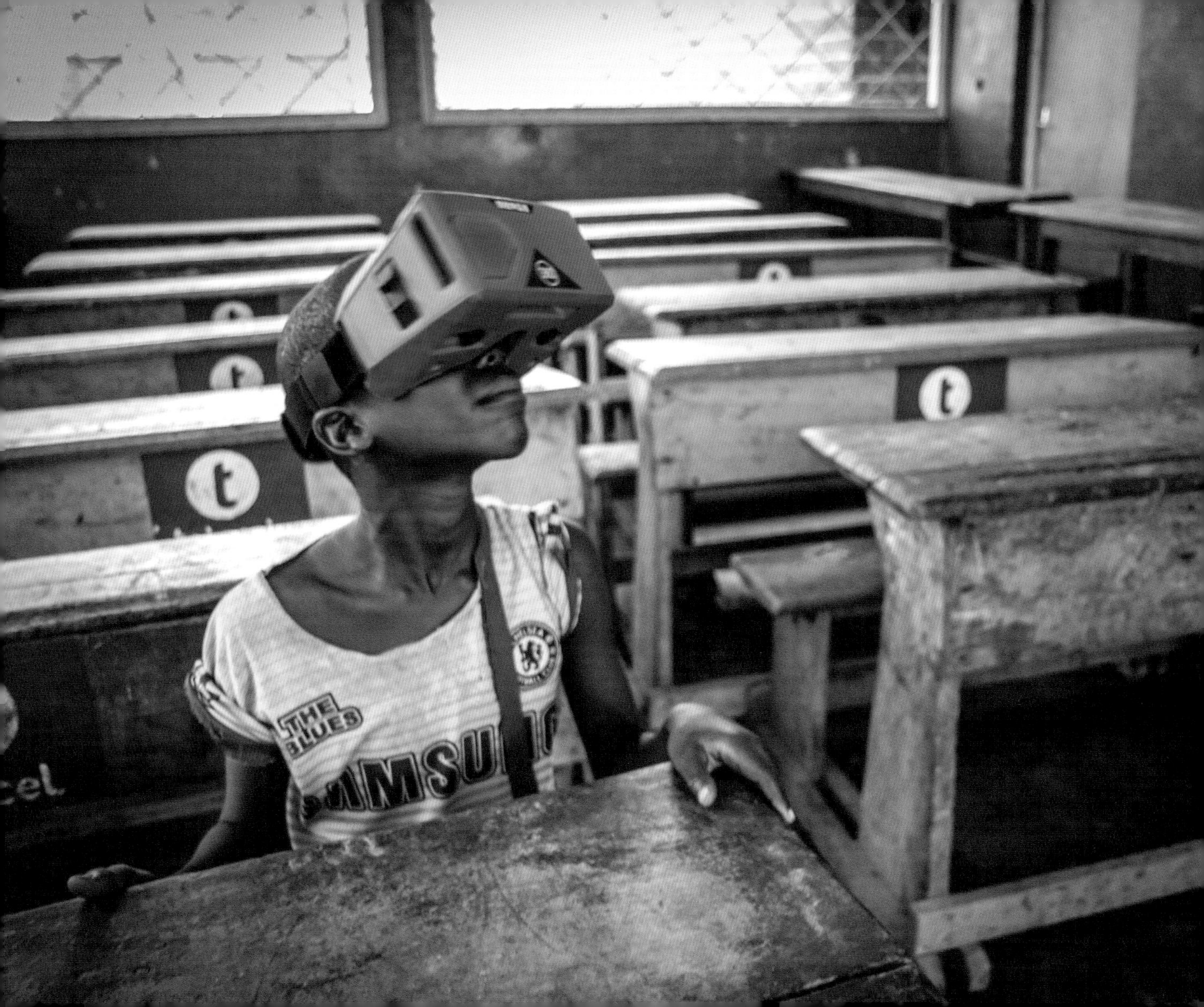
THE BLUES

BANGUI BOYS

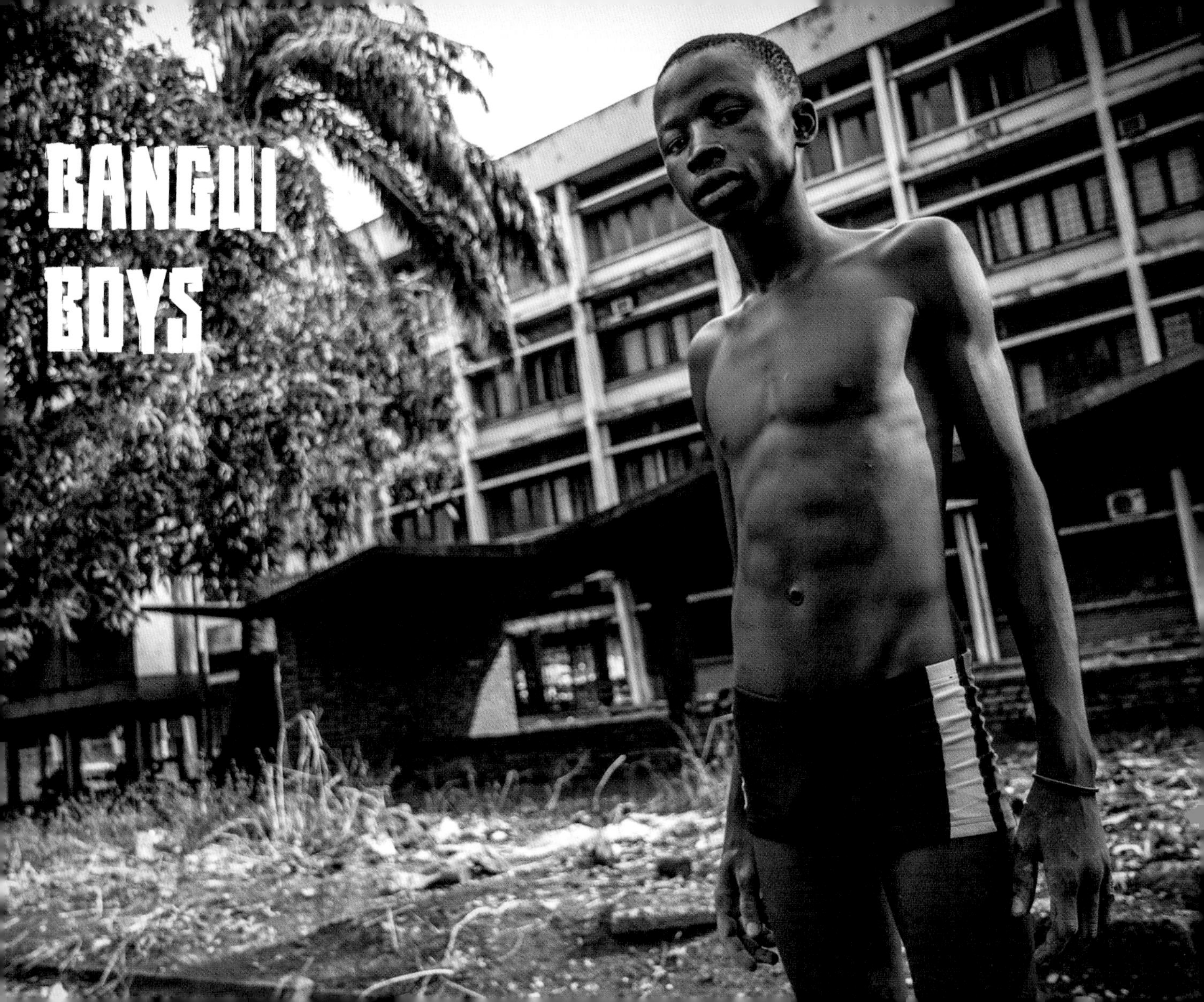

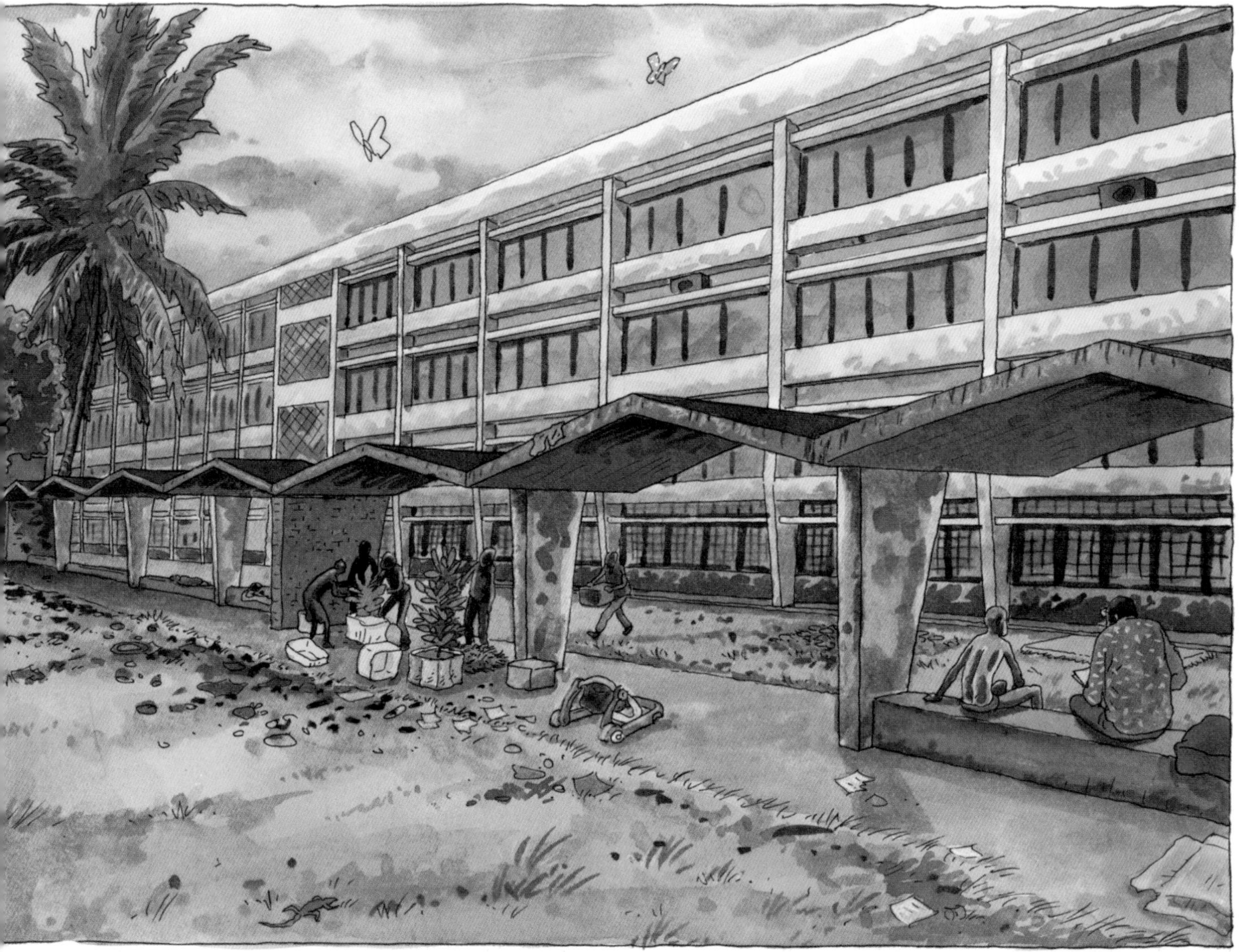

YOU CAN USE MY STREET NAME...CALL ME JACK BAUER.

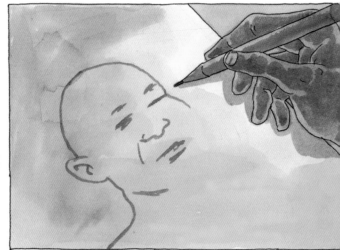

JACK BAUER?

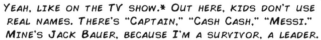

YEAH, LIKE ON THE TV SHOW.* OUT HERE, KIDS DON'T USE REAL NAMES. THERE'S "CAPTAIN," "CASH CASH," "MESSI." MINE'S JACK BAUER, BECAUSE I'M A SURVIVOR, A LEADER.

*THE HIT FOX TELEVISION SERIES "24" WITH KIEFER SUTHERLAND.

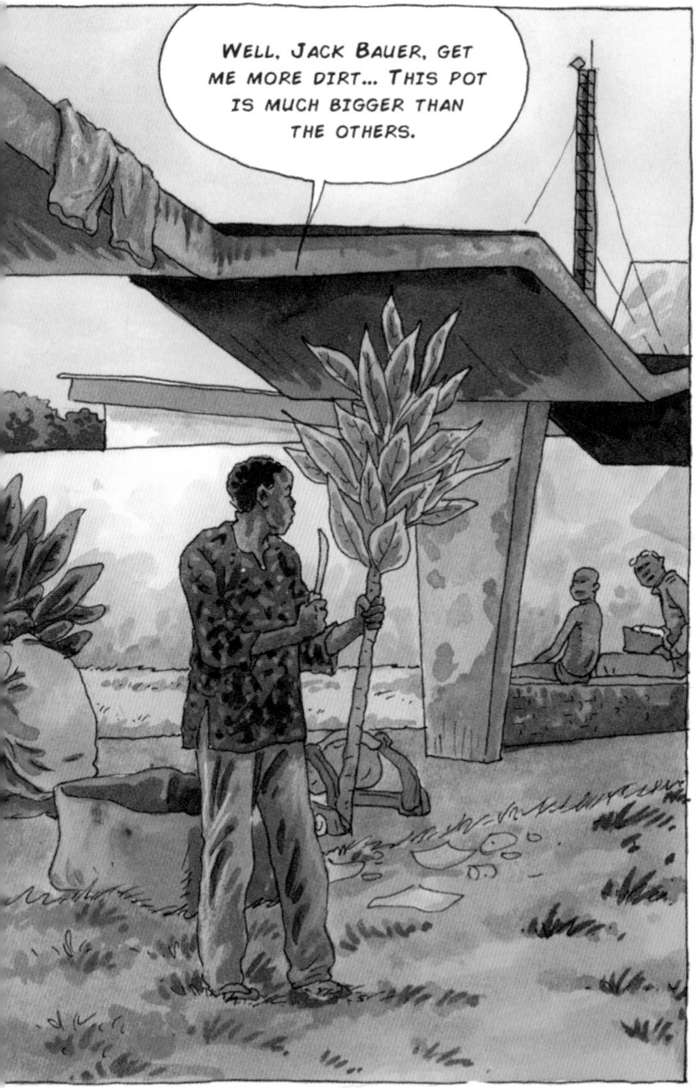
WELL, JACK BAUER, GET ME MORE DIRT… THIS POT IS MUCH BIGGER THAN THE OTHERS.

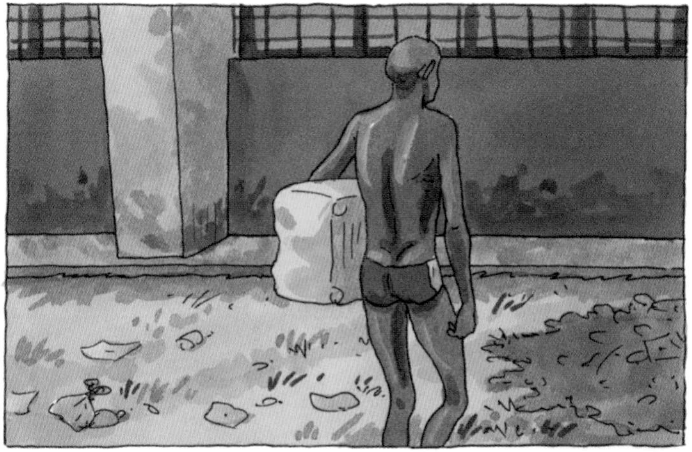

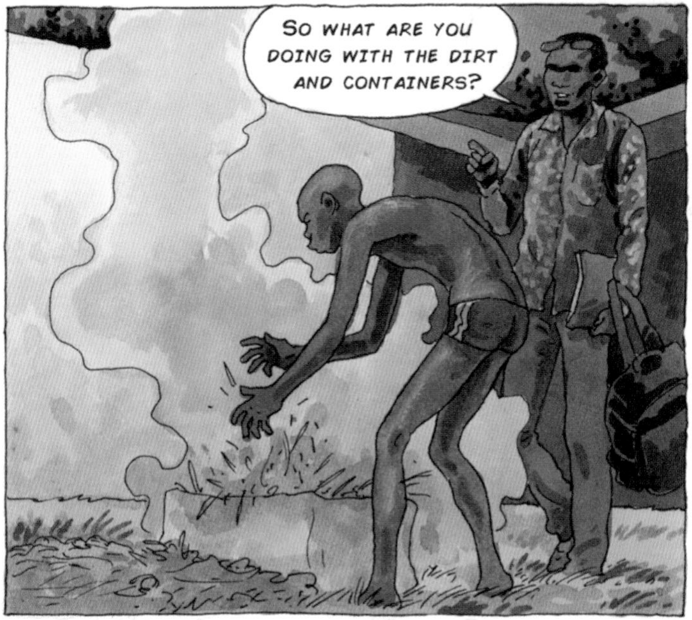
SO WHAT ARE YOU DOING WITH THE DIRT AND CONTAINERS?

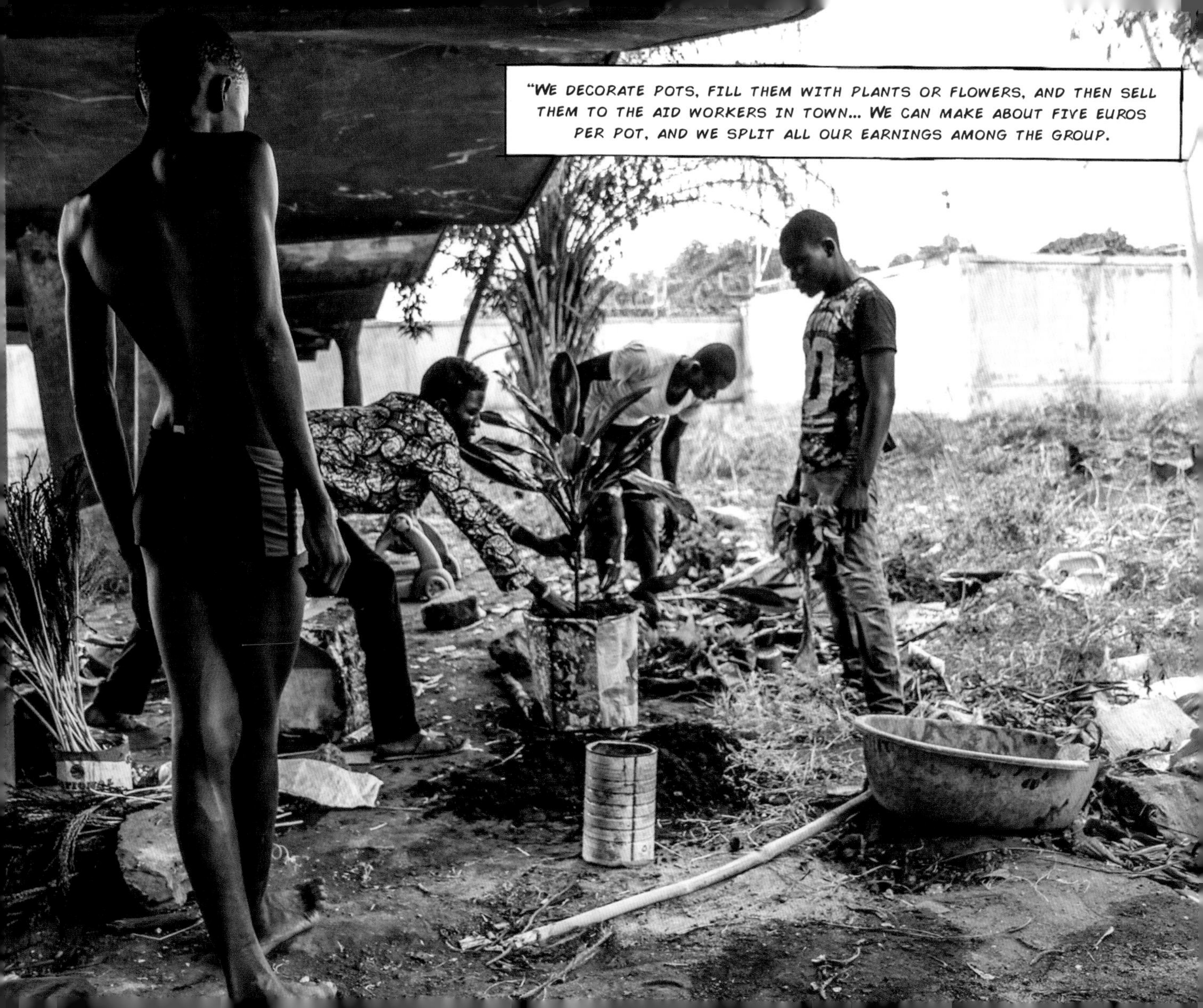
"WE DECORATE POTS, FILL THEM WITH PLANTS OR FLOWERS, AND THEN SELL THEM TO THE AID WORKERS IN TOWN... WE CAN MAKE ABOUT FIVE EUROS PER POT, AND WE SPLIT ALL OUR EARNINGS AMONG THE GROUP.

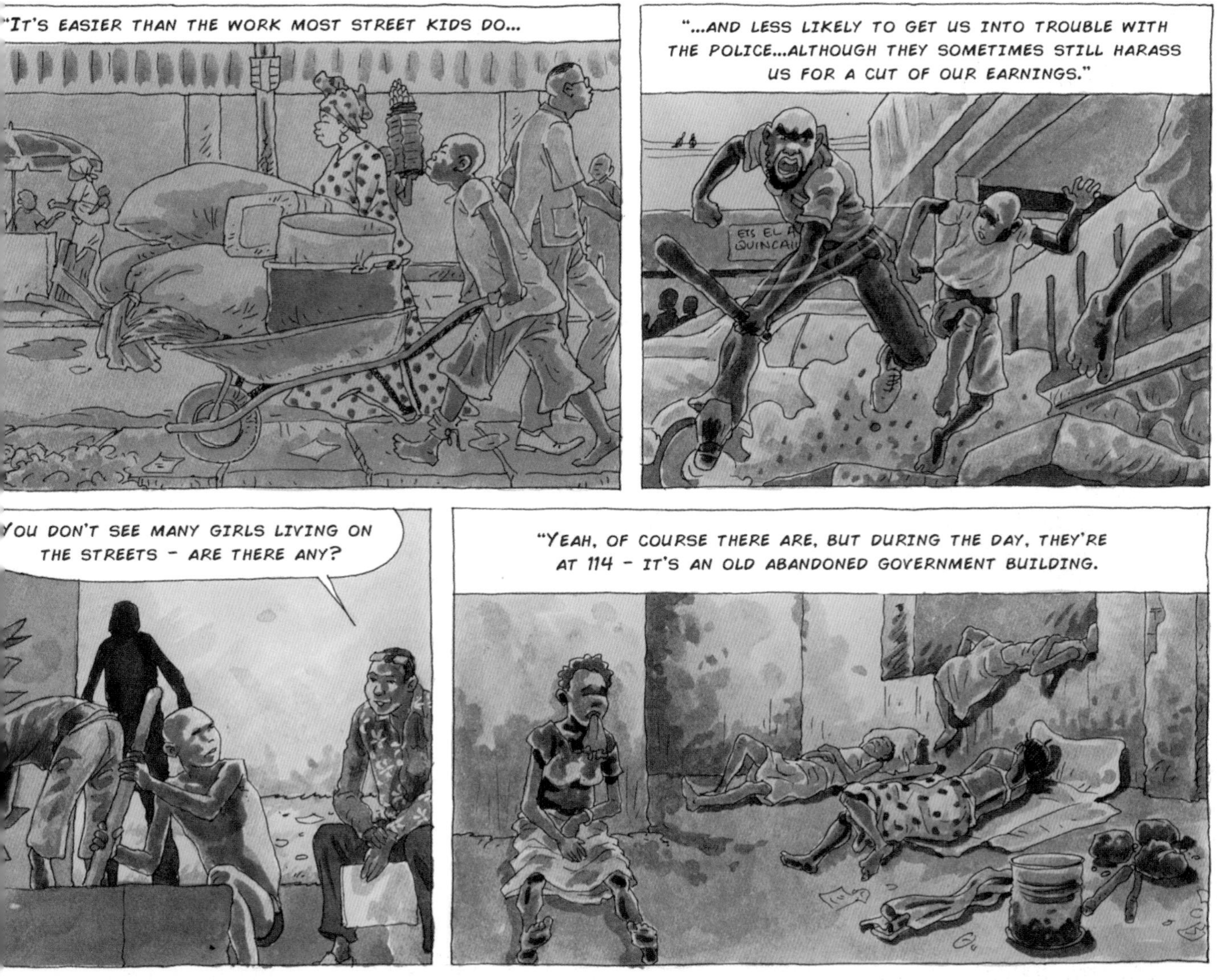
"IT'S EASIER THAN THE WORK MOST STREET KIDS DO...
"...AND LESS LIKELY TO GET US INTO TROUBLE WITH THE POLICE...ALTHOUGH THEY SOMETIMES STILL HARASS US FOR A CUT OF OUR EARNINGS."
YOU DON'T SEE MANY GIRLS LIVING ON THE STREETS - ARE THERE ANY?
"YEAH, OF COURSE THERE ARE, BUT DURING THE DAY, THEY'RE AT 114 - IT'S AN OLD ABANDONED GOVERNMENT BUILDING.

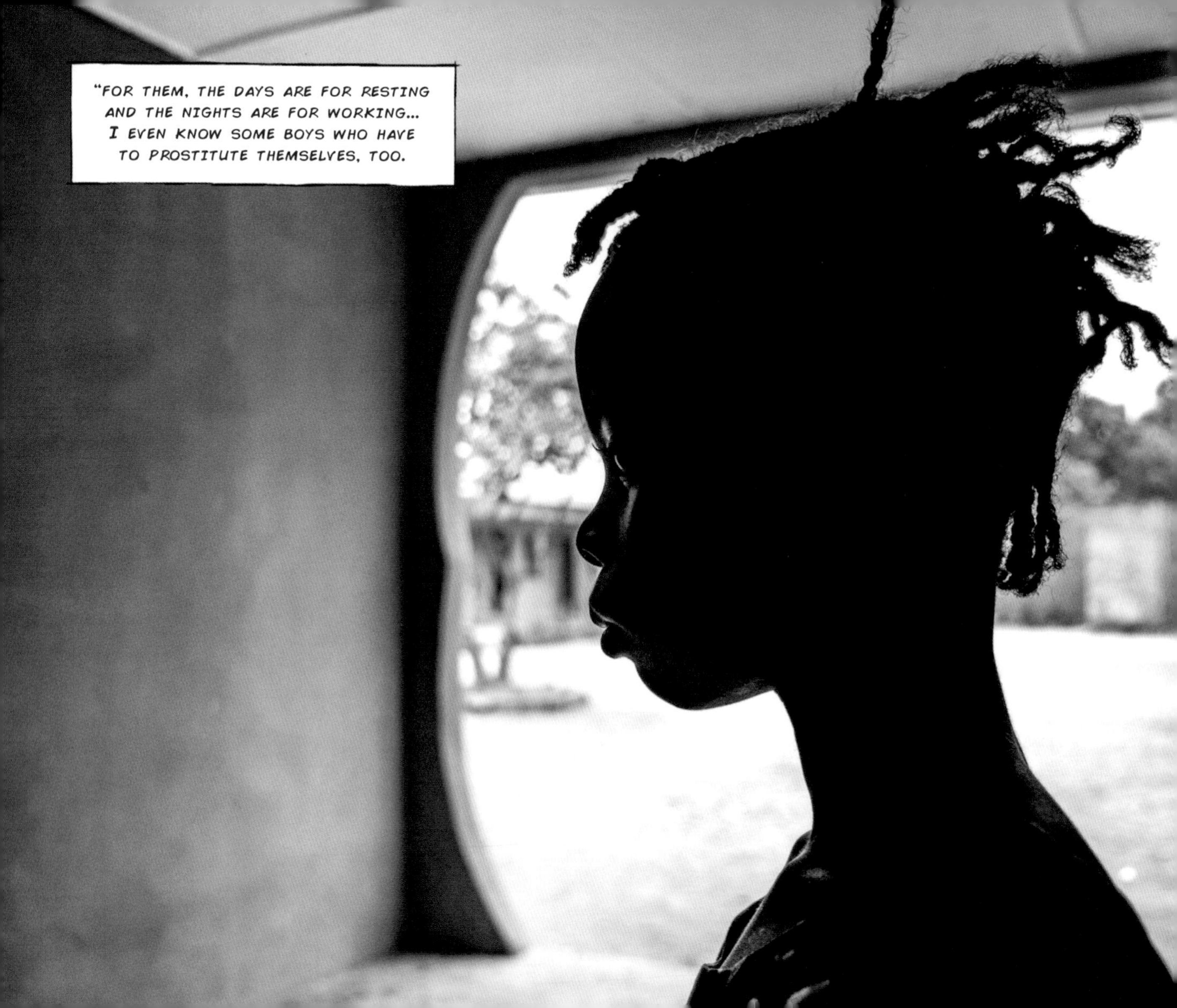
"FOR THEM, THE DAYS ARE FOR RESTING AND THE NIGHTS ARE FOR WORKING... I EVEN KNOW SOME BOYS WHO HAVE TO PROSTITUTE THEMSELVES, TOO.

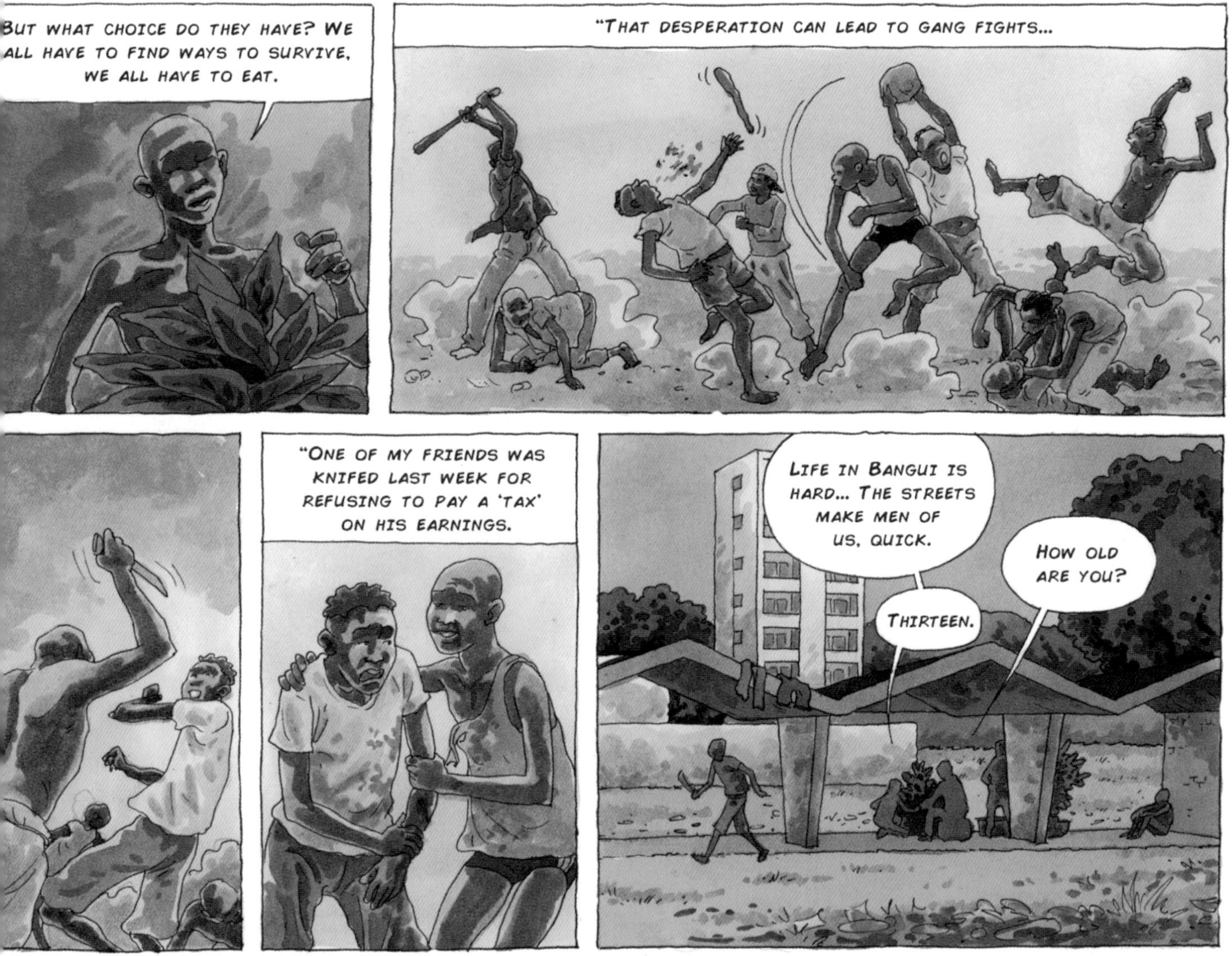

BUT WHAT CHOICE DO THEY HAVE? WE ALL HAVE TO FIND WAYS TO SURVIVE, WE ALL HAVE TO EAT.
"THAT DESPERATION CAN LEAD TO GANG FIGHTS...
"ONE OF MY FRIENDS WAS KNIFED LAST WEEK FOR REFUSING TO PAY A 'TAX' ON HIS EARNINGS.
LIFE IN BANGUI IS HARD... THE STREETS MAKE MEN OF US, QUICK.
HOW OLD ARE YOU?
THIRTEEN.

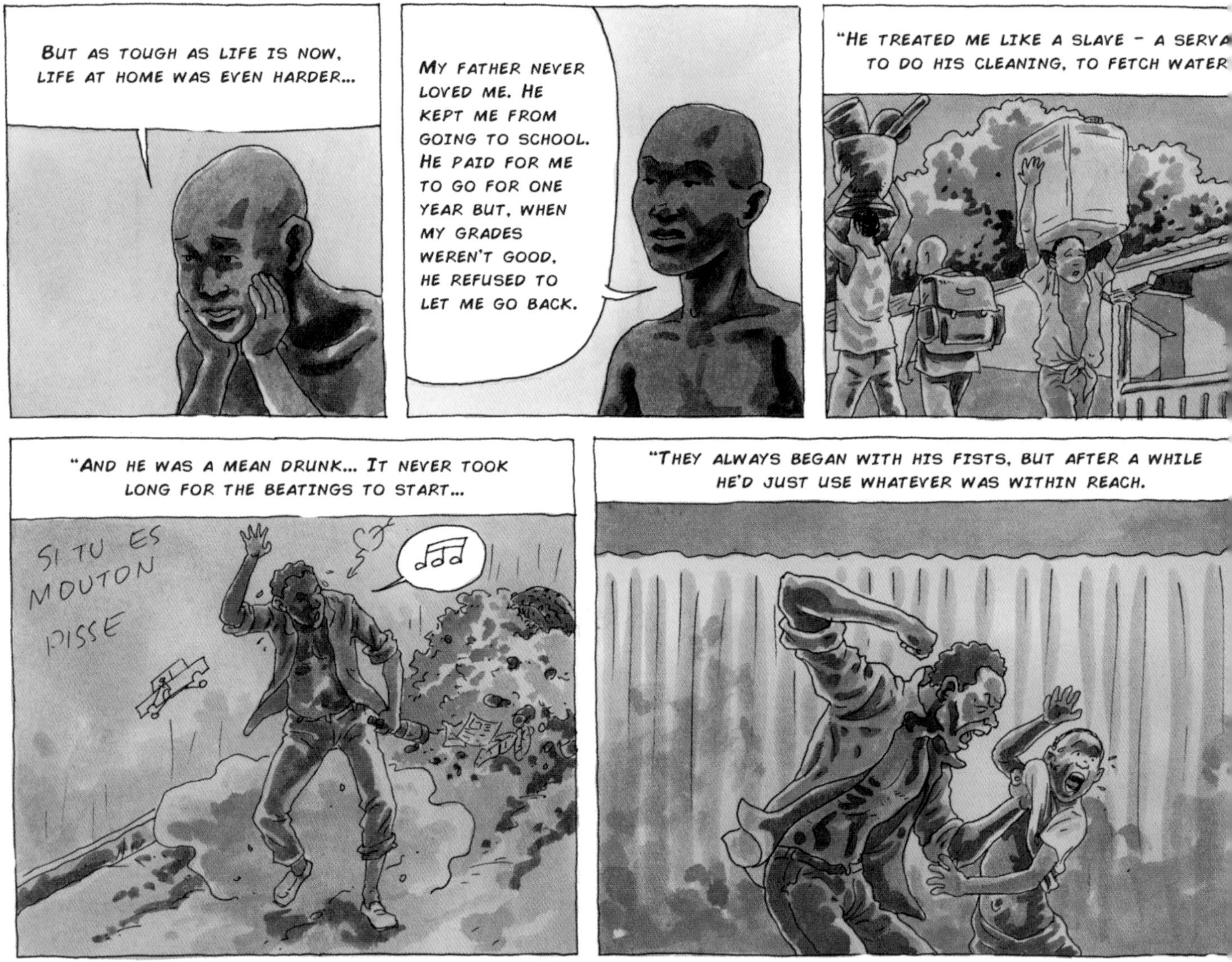

BUT AS TOUGH AS LIFE IS NOW, LIFE AT HOME WAS EVEN HARDER...
MY FATHER NEVER LOVED ME. HE KEPT ME FROM GOING TO SCHOOL. HE PAID FOR ME TO GO FOR ONE YEAR BUT, WHEN MY GRADES WEREN'T GOOD, HE REFUSED TO LET ME GO BACK.
"HE TREATED ME LIKE A SLAVE – A SERVA
TO DO HIS CLEANING, TO FETCH WATER
"AND HE WAS A MEAN DRUNK... IT NEVER TOOK LONG FOR THE BEATINGS TO START...
SI TU ES MOUTON PISSE
"THEY ALWAYS BEGAN WITH HIS FISTS, BUT AFTER A WHILE HE'D JUST USE WHATEVER WAS WITHIN REACH.

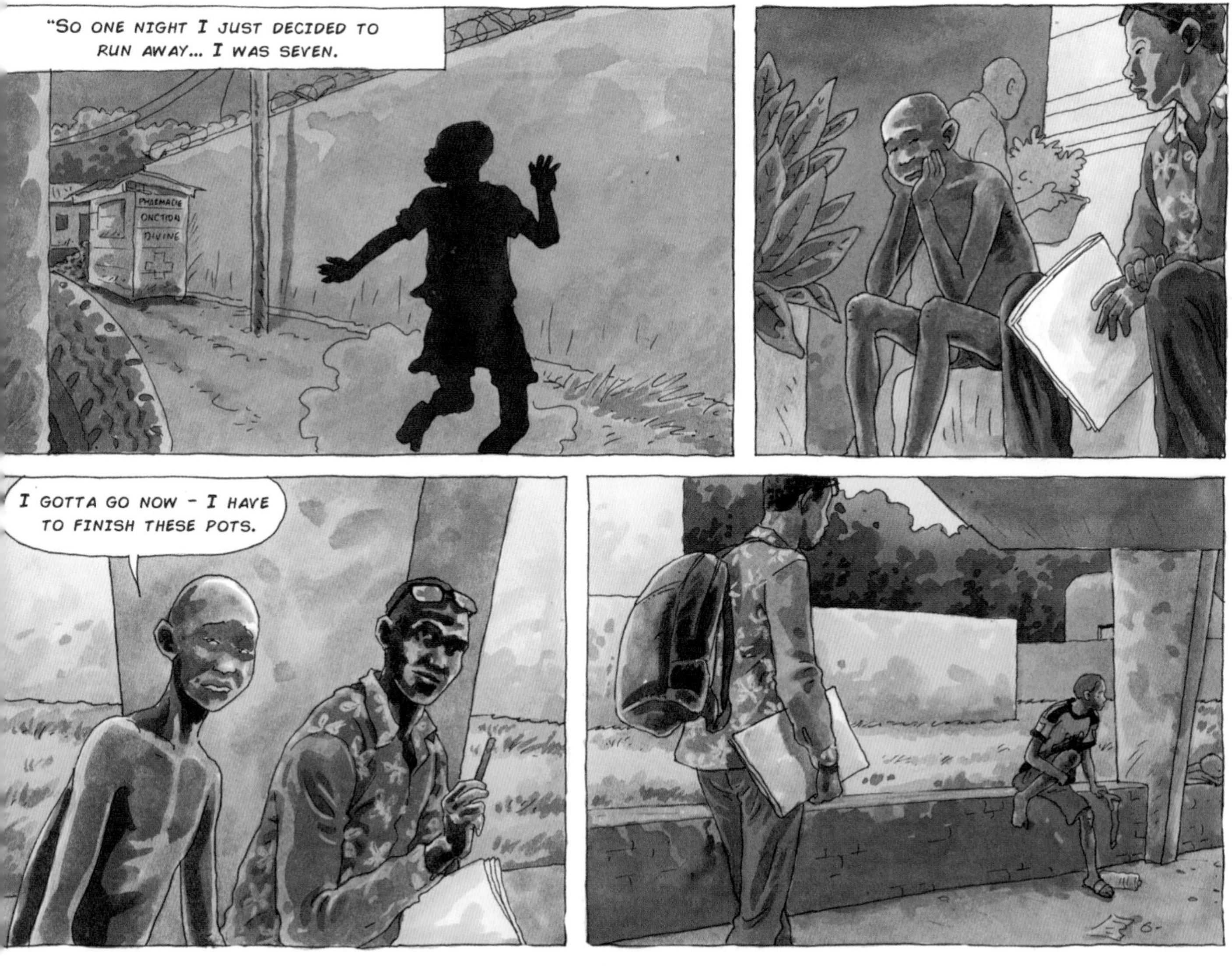
"SO ONE NIGHT I JUST DECIDED TO RUN AWAY... I WAS SEVEN.
PHARMACIE
ONCTION
DIVINE
I GOTTA GO NOW - I HAVE TO FINISH THESE POTS.

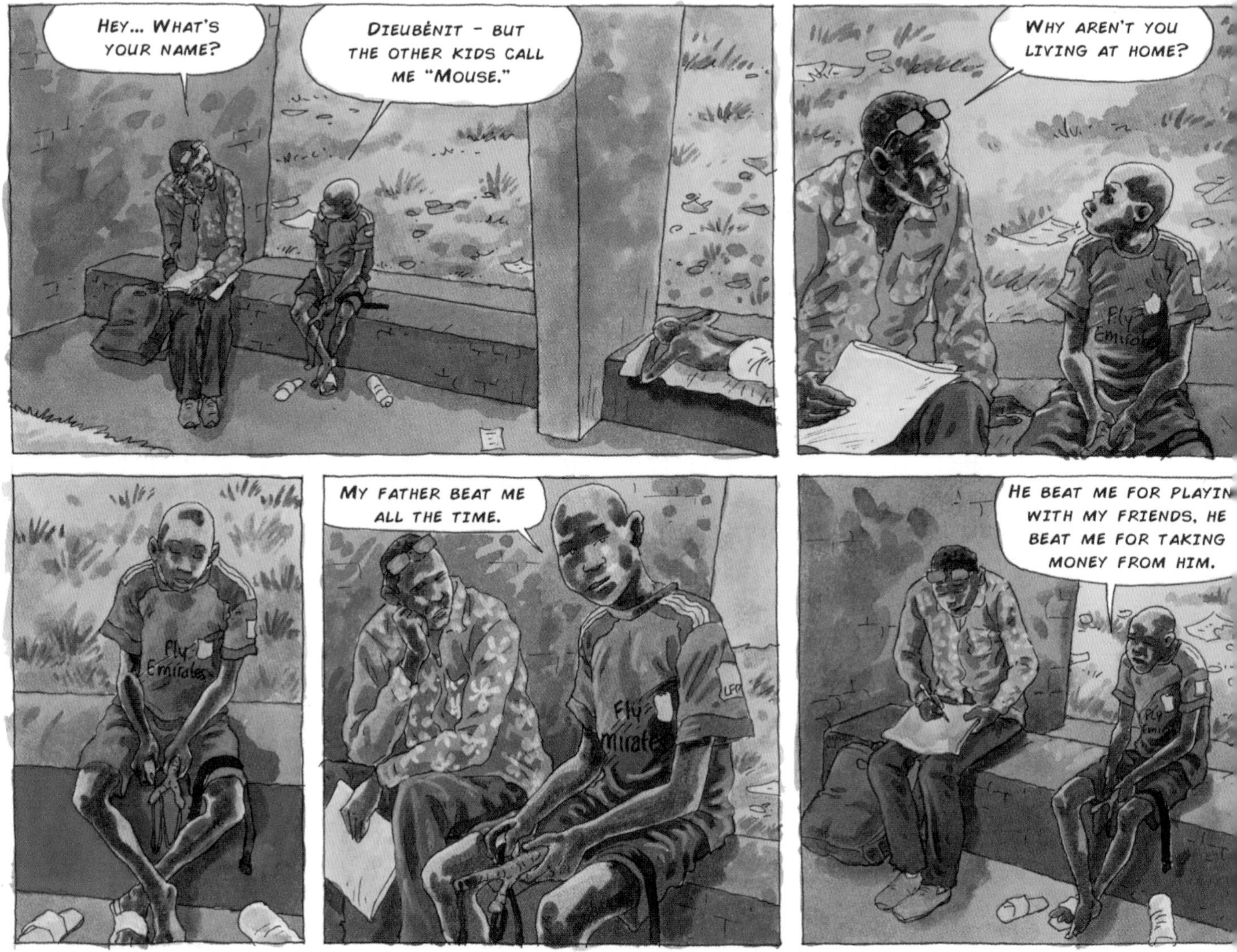
HEY... WHAT'S YOUR NAME?
DIEUBÉNIT - BUT THE OTHER KIDS CALL ME "MOUSE."
WHY AREN'T YOU LIVING AT HOME?
MY FATHER BEAT ME ALL THE TIME.
HE BEAT ME FOR PLAYIN WITH MY FRIENDS, HE BEAT ME FOR TAKING MONEY FROM HIM.

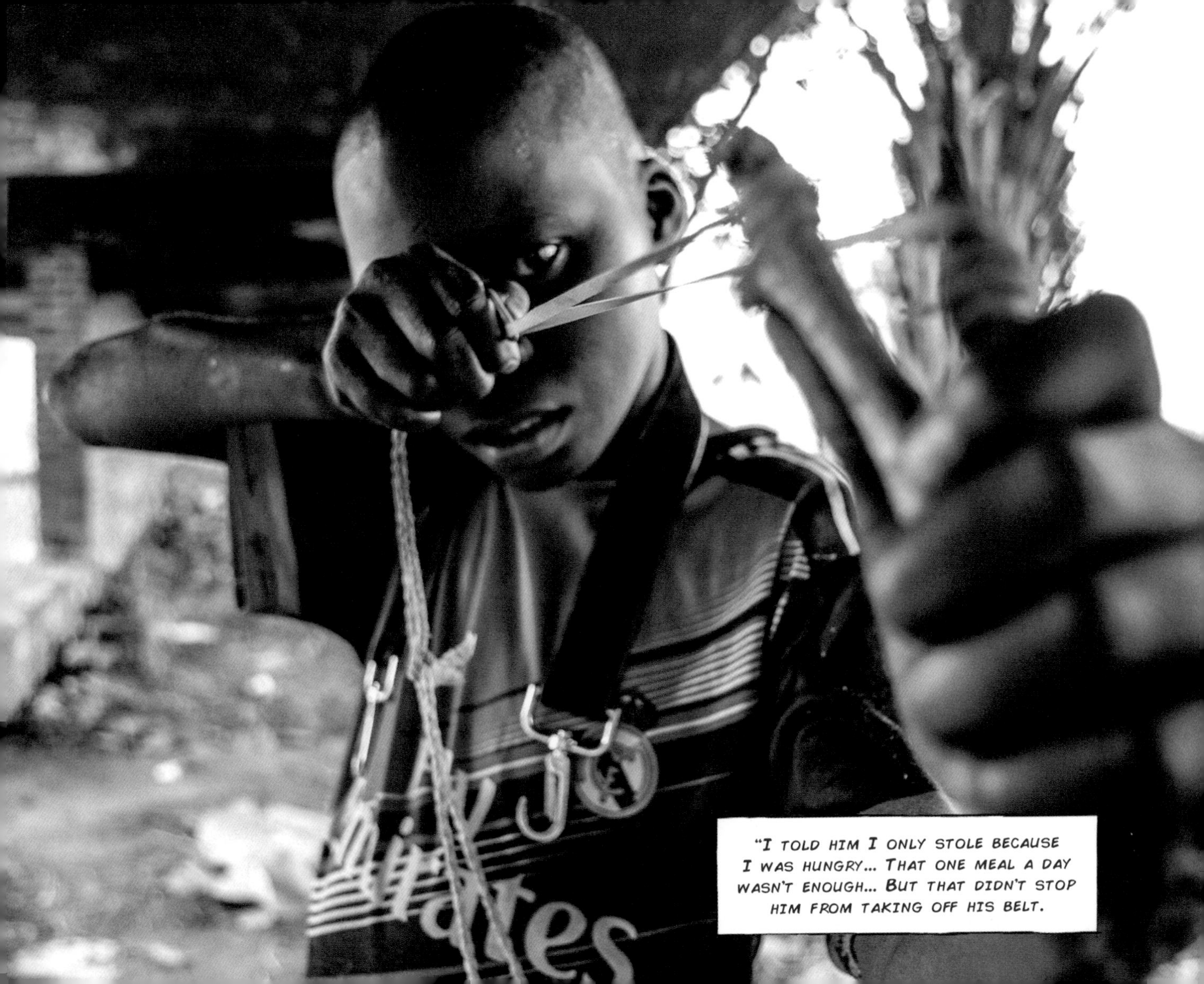
"I TOLD HIM I ONLY STOLE BECAUSE I WAS HUNGRY... THAT ONE MEAL A DAY WASN'T ENOUGH... BUT THAT DIDN'T STOP HIM FROM TAKING OFF HIS BELT.

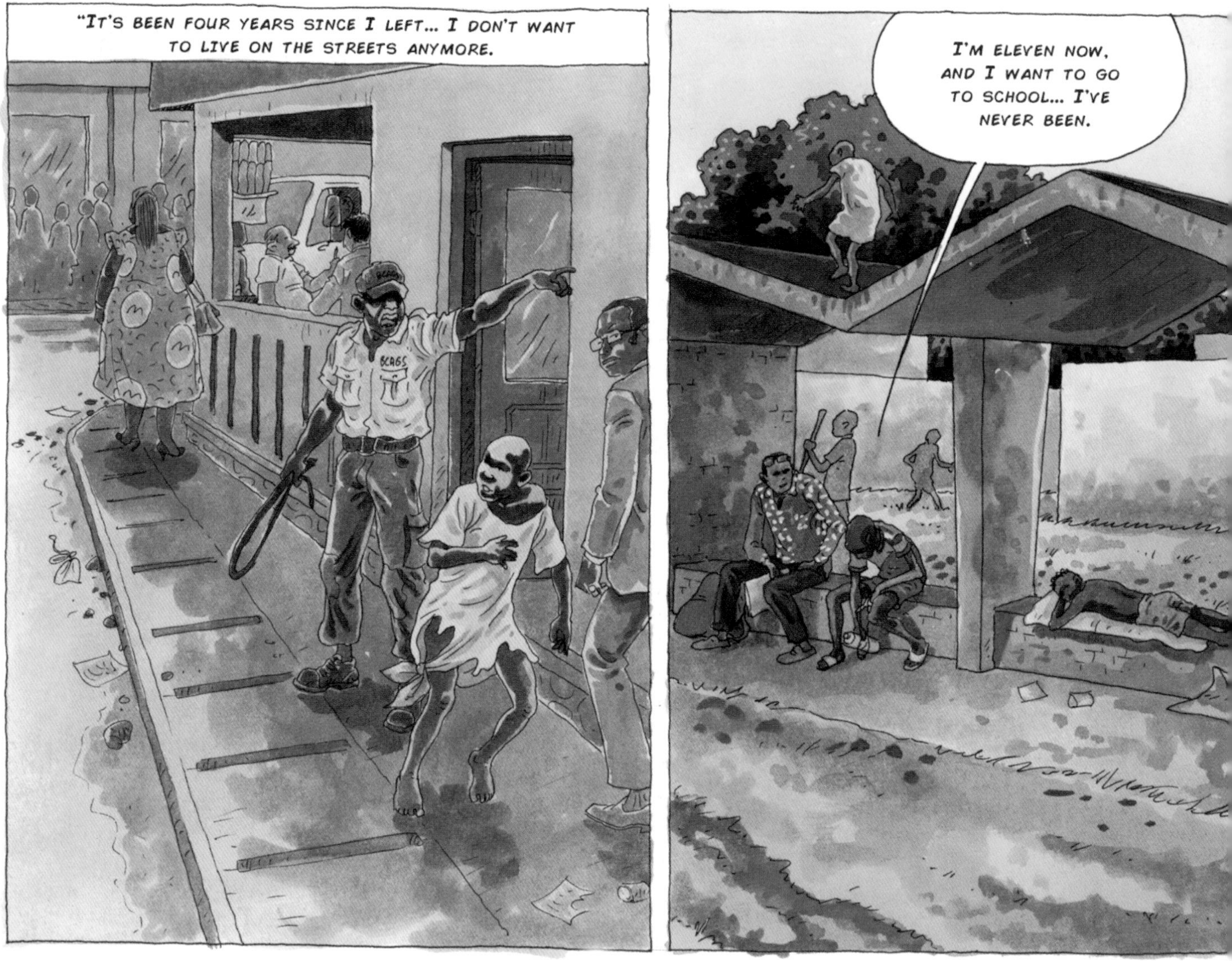
"IT'S BEEN FOUR YEARS SINCE I LEFT... I DON'T WANT TO LIVE ON THE STREETS ANYMORE.
I'M ELEVEN NOW, AND I WANT TO GO TO SCHOOL... I'VE NEVER BEEN.

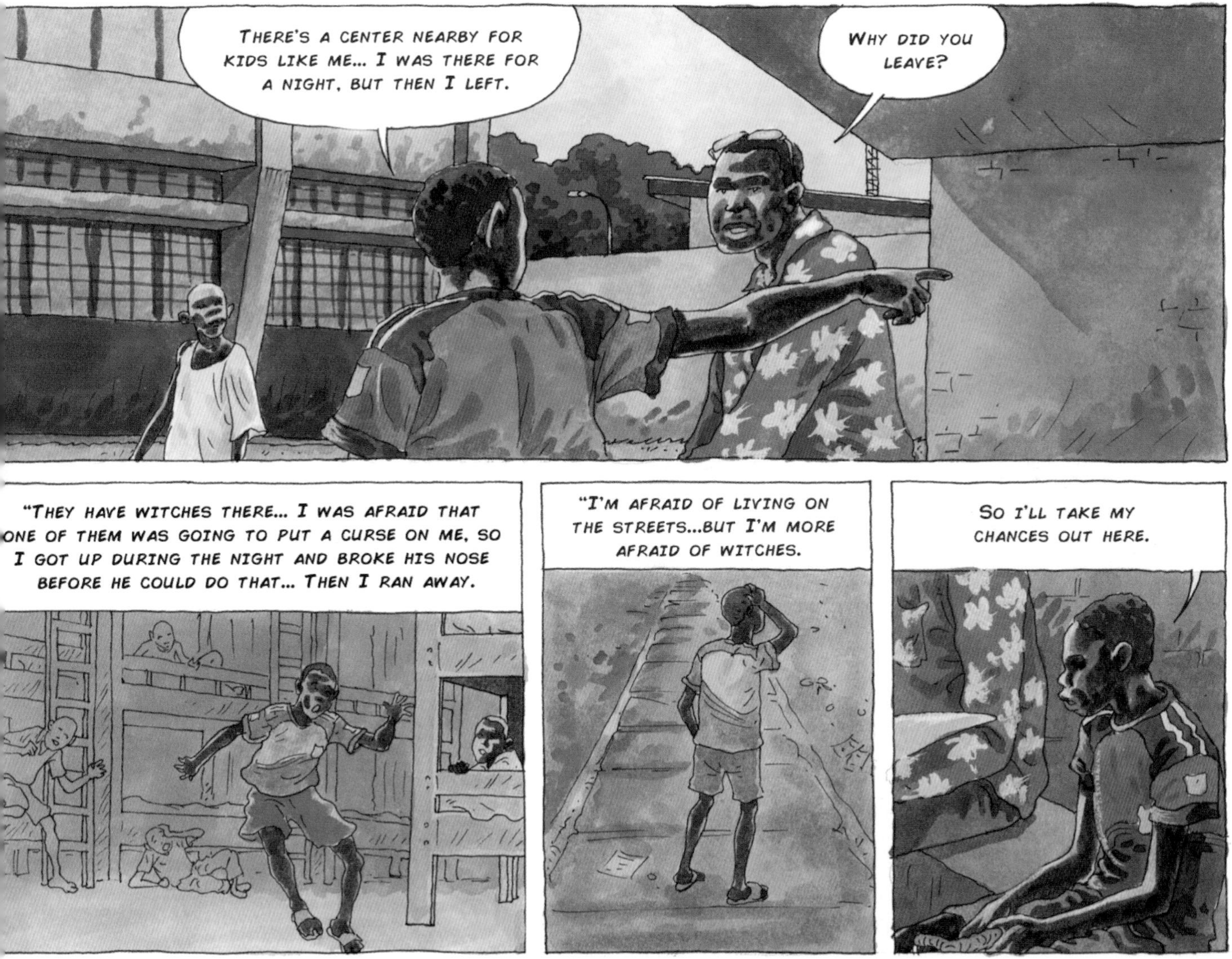
THERE'S A CENTER NEARBY FOR KIDS LIKE ME... I WAS THERE FOR A NIGHT, BUT THEN I LEFT.
WHY DID YOU LEAVE?
"THEY HAVE WITCHES THERE... I WAS AFRAID THAT ONE OF THEM WAS GOING TO PUT A CURSE ON ME, SO I GOT UP DURING THE NIGHT AND BROKE HIS NOSE BEFORE HE COULD DO THAT... THEN I RAN AWAY.
"I'M AFRAID OF LIVING ON THE STREETS...BUT I'M MORE AFRAID OF WITCHES.
SO I'LL TAKE MY CHANCES OUT HERE.

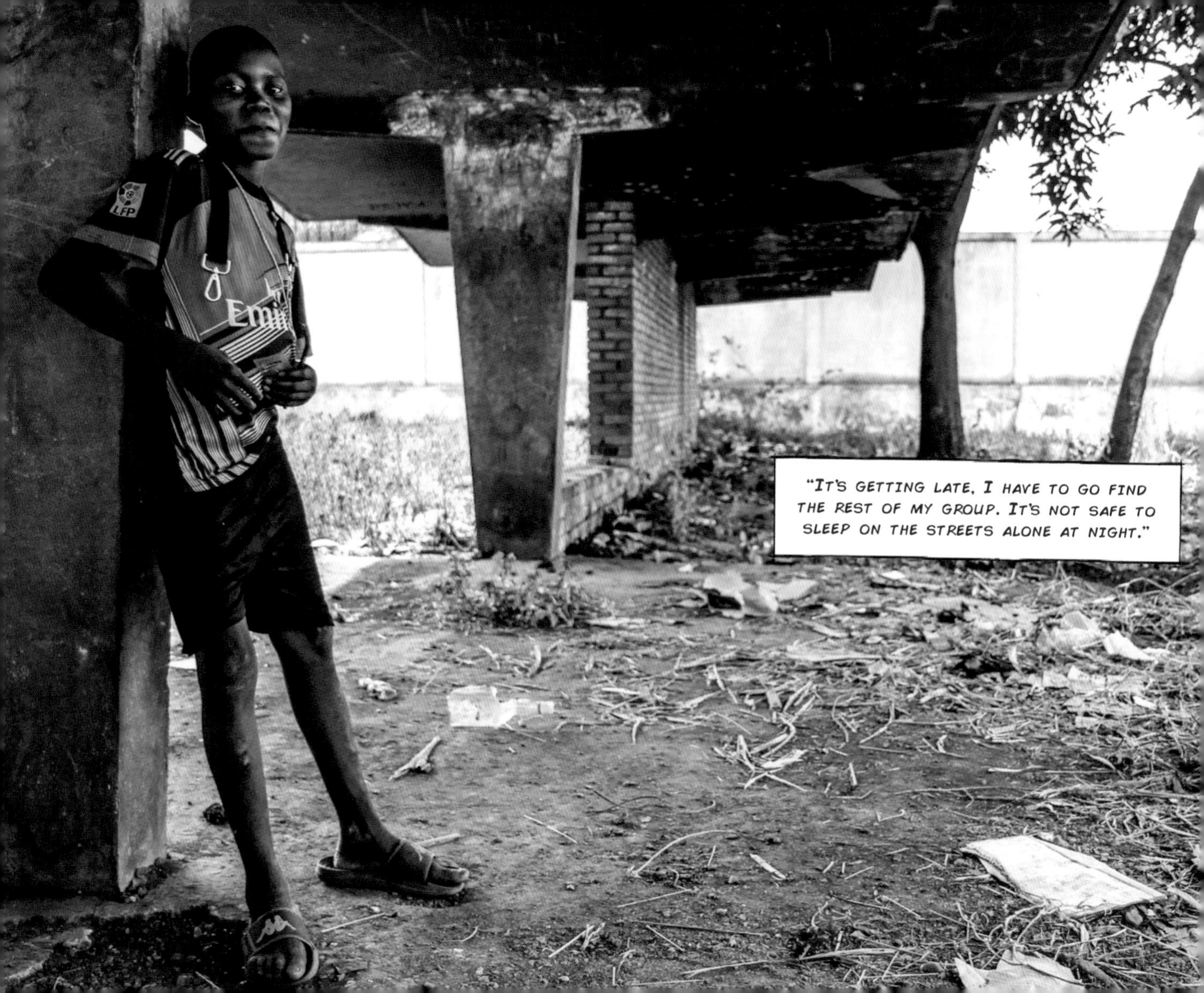
"IT'S GETTING LATE, I HAVE TO GO FIND THE REST OF MY GROUP. IT'S NOT SAFE TO SLEEP ON THE STREETS ALONE AT NIGHT."

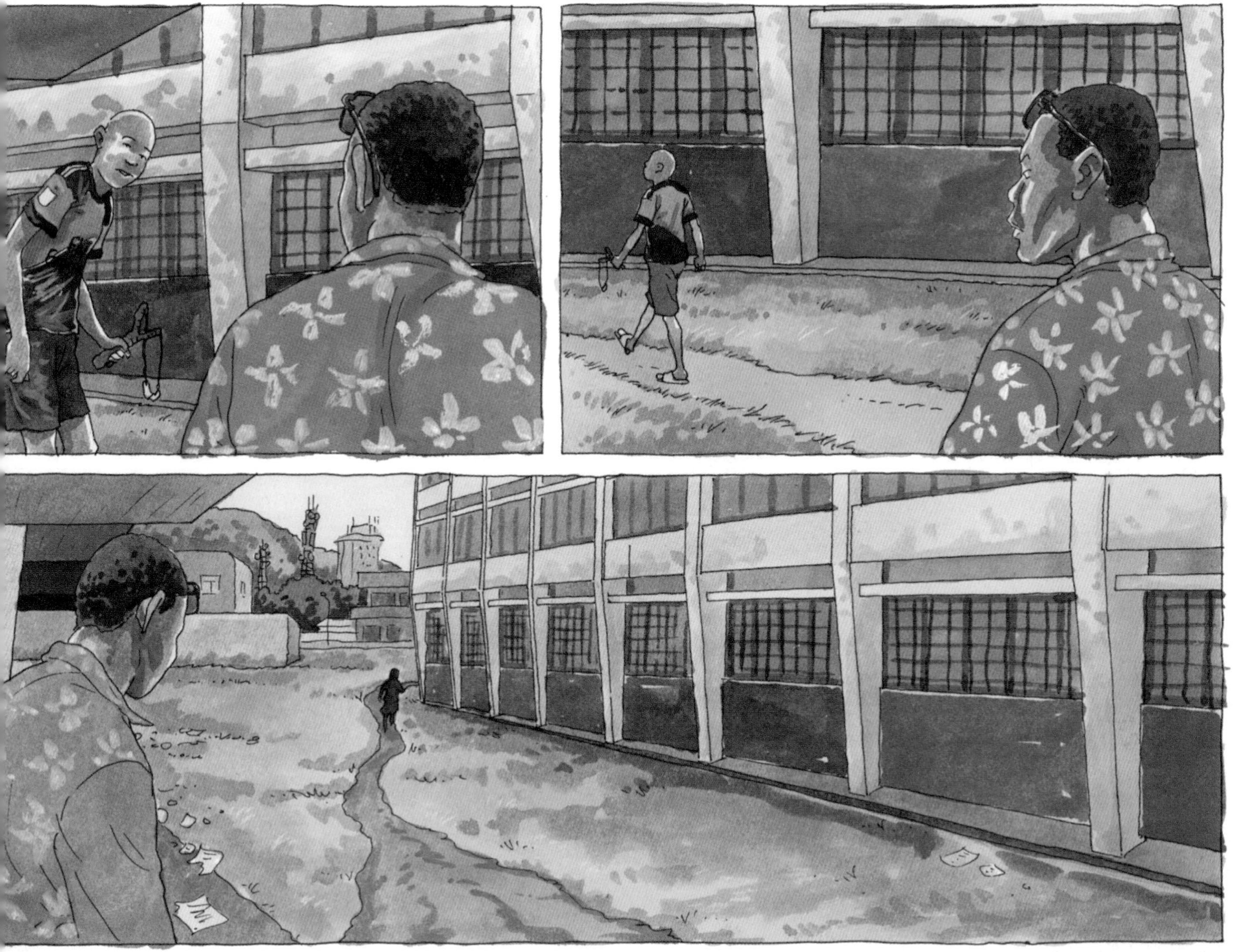

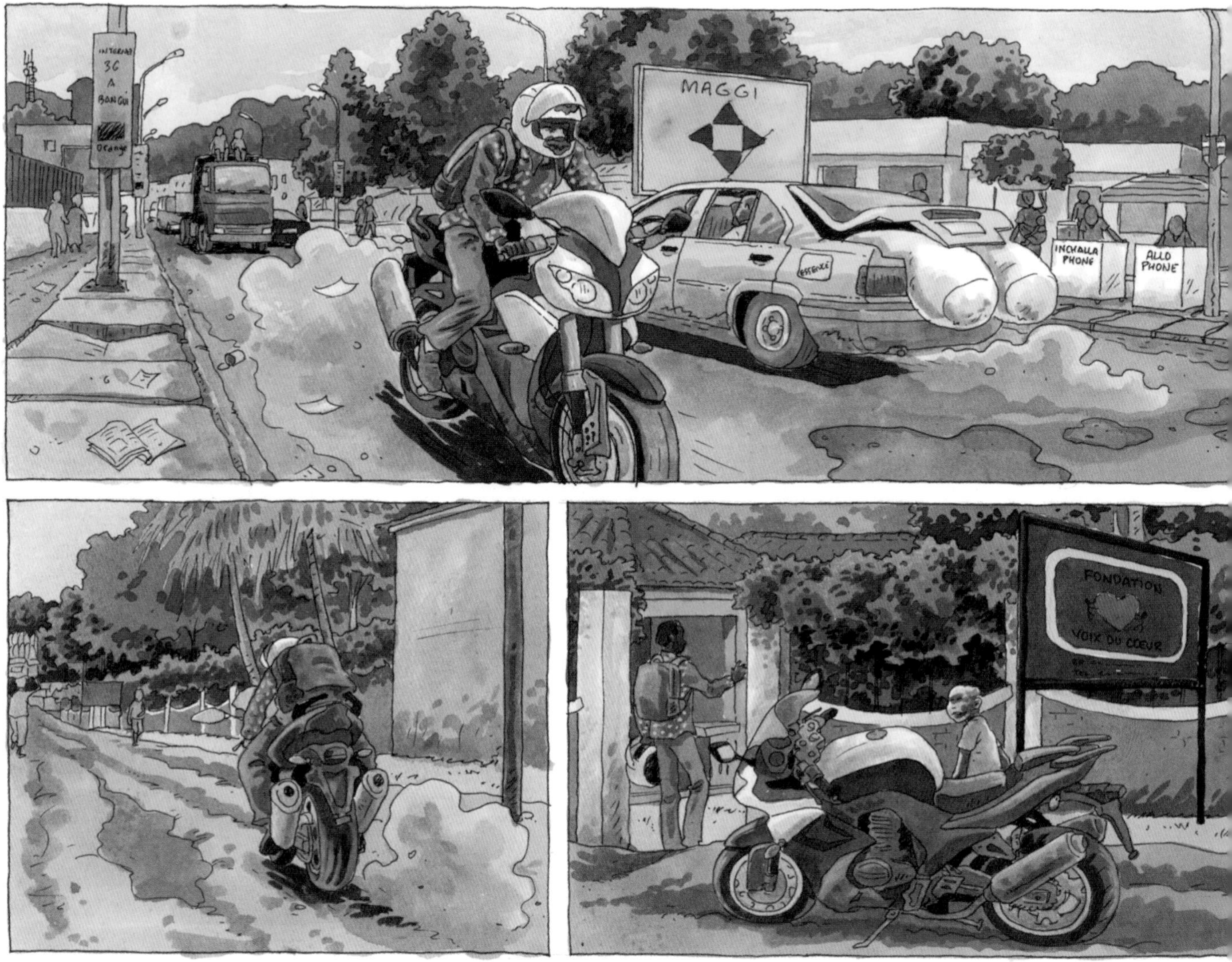
3G
A
BANGUI
Orange
MAGGI
ESSENCE
INCHALLA PHONE
ALLO PHONE
FONDATION
VOIX DU COEUR

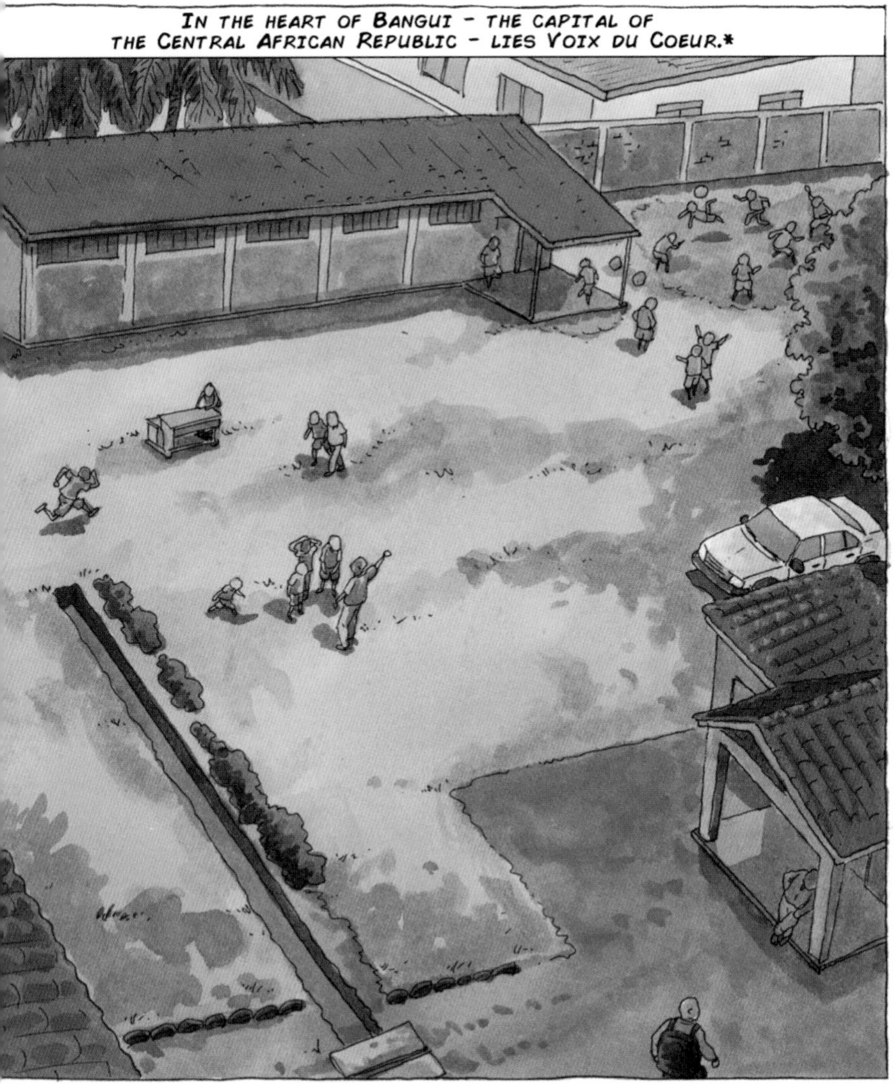
IN THE HEART OF BANGUI - THE CAPITAL OF THE CENTRAL AFRICAN REPUBLIC - LIES VOIX DU COEUR.*

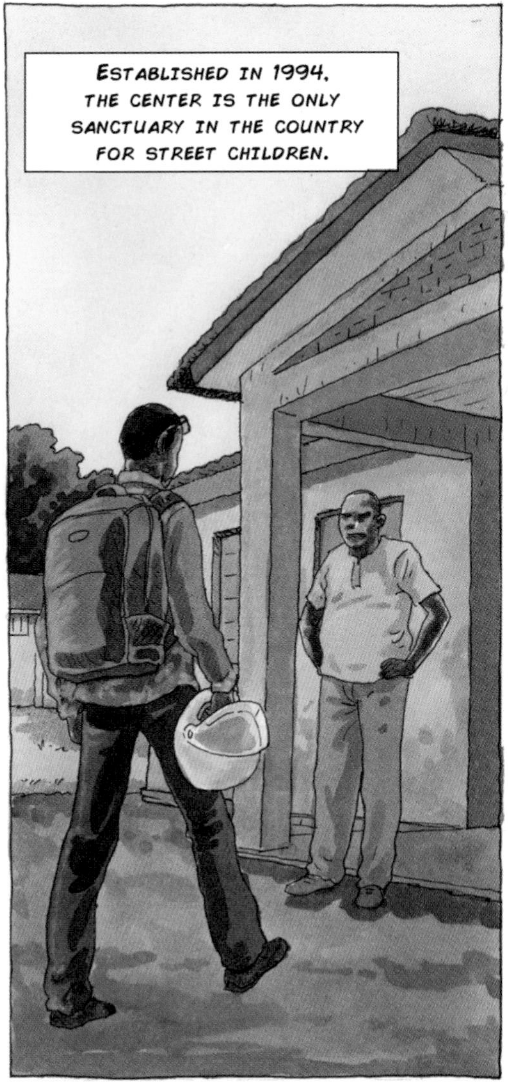
ESTABLISHED IN 1994, THE CENTER IS THE ONLY SANCTUARY IN THE COUNTRY FOR STREET CHILDREN.

*"VOICE OF THE HEART" IN ENGLISH.

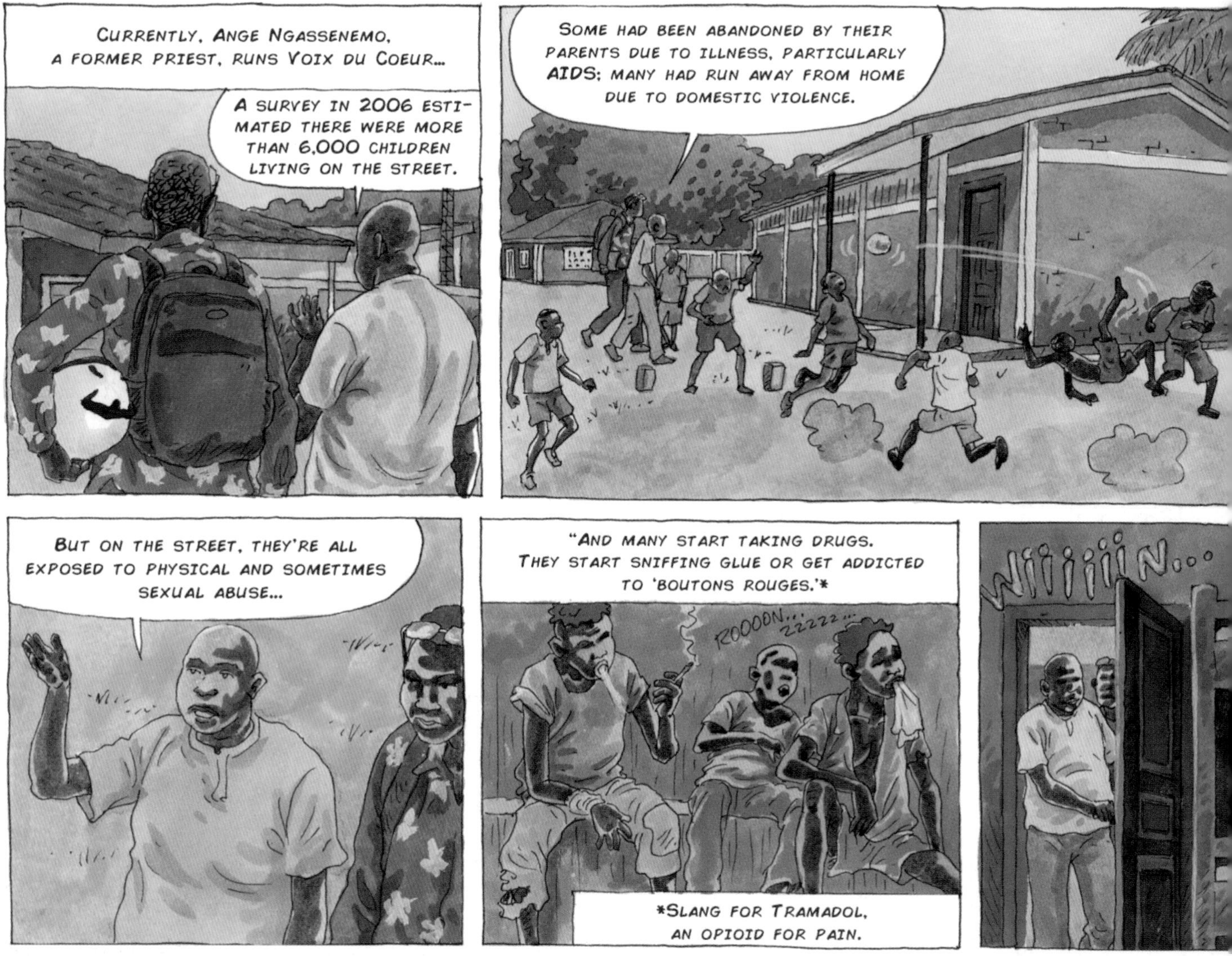
CURRENTLY, ANGE NGASSENEMO, A FORMER PRIEST, RUNS VOIX DU COEUR...
A SURVEY IN 2006 ESTIMATED THERE WERE MORE THAN 6,000 CHILDREN LIVING ON THE STREET.
SOME HAD BEEN ABANDONED BY THEIR PARENTS DUE TO ILLNESS, PARTICULARLY AIDS; MANY HAD RUN AWAY FROM HOME DUE TO DOMESTIC VIOLENCE.
BUT ON THE STREET, THEY'RE ALL EXPOSED TO PHYSICAL AND SOMETIMES SEXUAL ABUSE...
"AND MANY START TAKING DRUGS. THEY START SNIFFING GLUE OR GET ADDICTED TO 'BOUTONS ROUGES.'*
ROOOON... ZZZZZ...
*SLANG FOR TRAMADOL, AN OPIOID FOR PAIN.
WIIIIIIN...

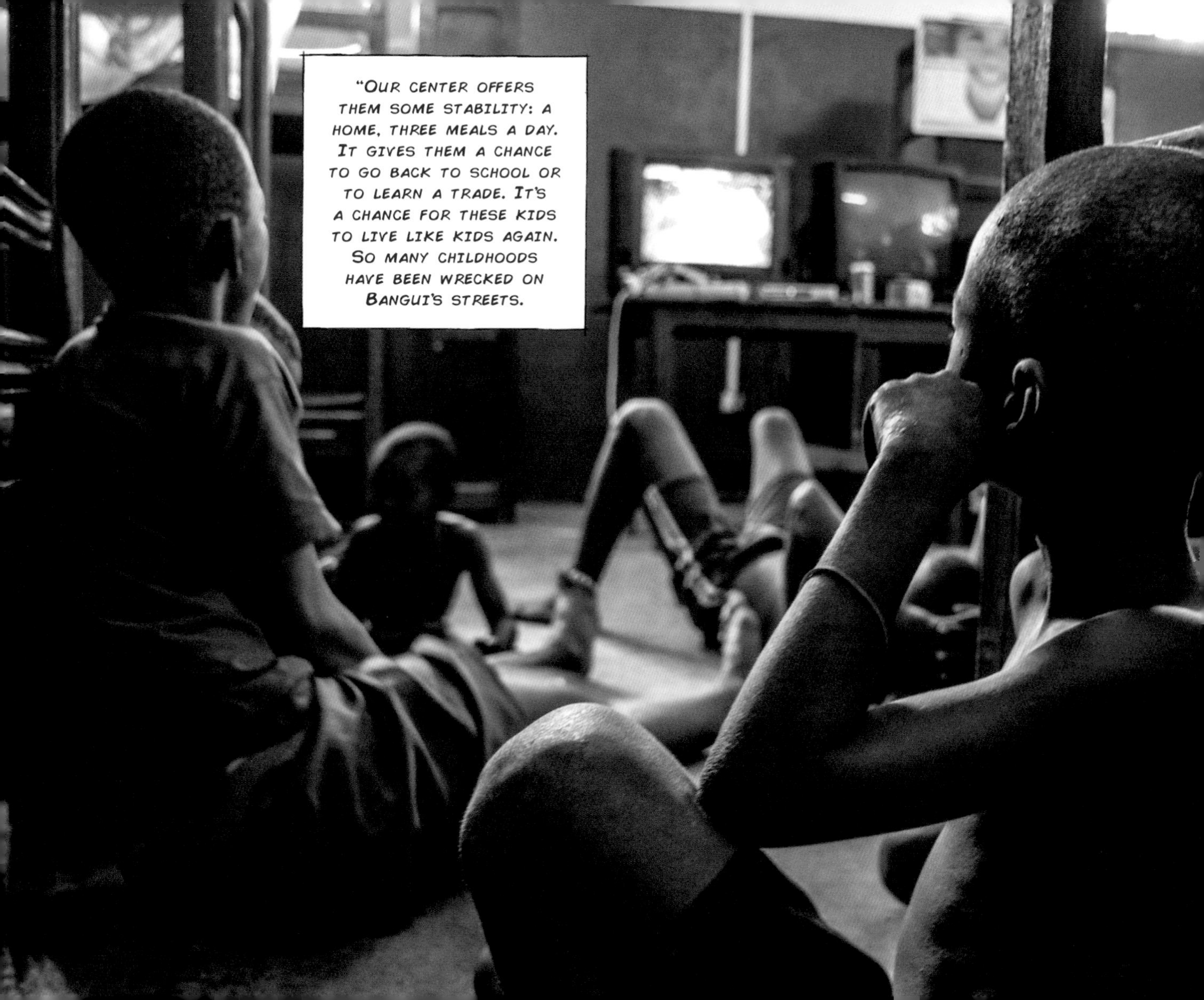
"Our center offers them some stability: a home, three meals a day. It gives them a chance to go back to school or to learn a trade. It's a chance for these kids to live like kids again. So many childhoods have been wrecked on Bangui's streets.

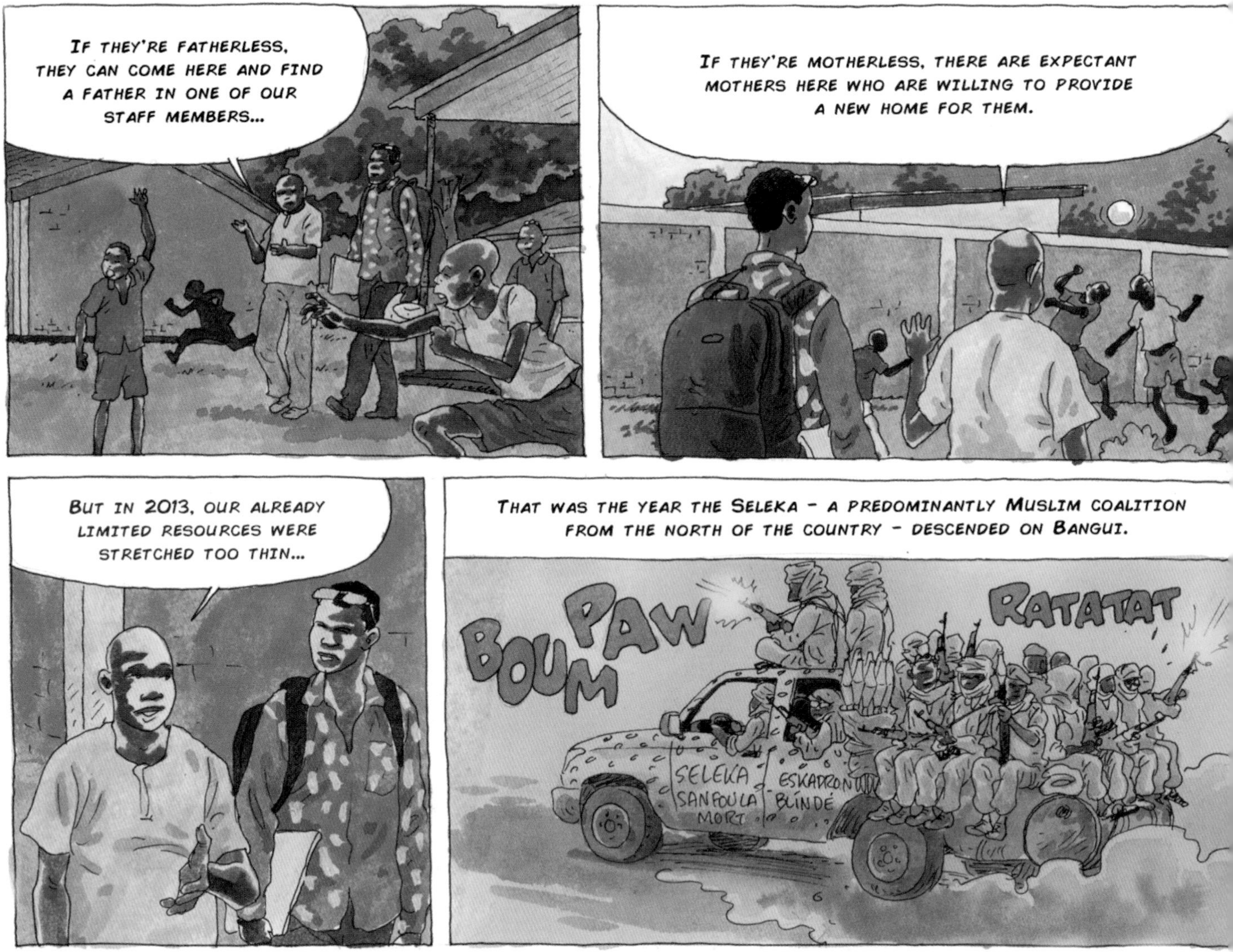
IF THEY'RE FATHERLESS, THEY CAN COME HERE AND FIND A FATHER IN ONE OF OUR STAFF MEMBERS...
IF THEY'RE MOTHERLESS, THERE ARE EXPECTANT MOTHERS HERE WHO ARE WILLING TO PROVIDE A NEW HOME FOR THEM.
BUT IN 2013, OUR ALREADY LIMITED RESOURCES WERE STRETCHED TOO THIN...
THAT WAS THE YEAR THE SELEKA - A PREDOMINANTLY MUSLIM COALITION FROM THE NORTH OF THE COUNTRY - DESCENDED ON BANGUI.
BOUM
PAW
RATATAT
SELEKA SANFOULA MORT
ESKADRON BLINDÉ

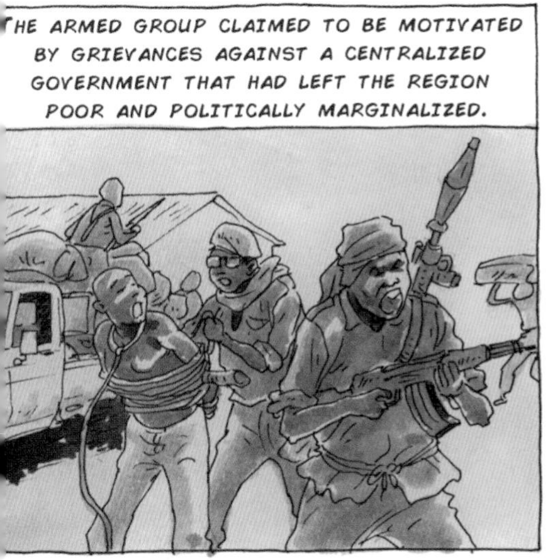
THE ARMED GROUP CLAIMED TO BE MOTIVATED BY GRIEVANCES AGAINST A CENTRALIZED GOVERNMENT THAT HAD LEFT THE REGION POOR AND POLITICALLY MARGINALIZED.

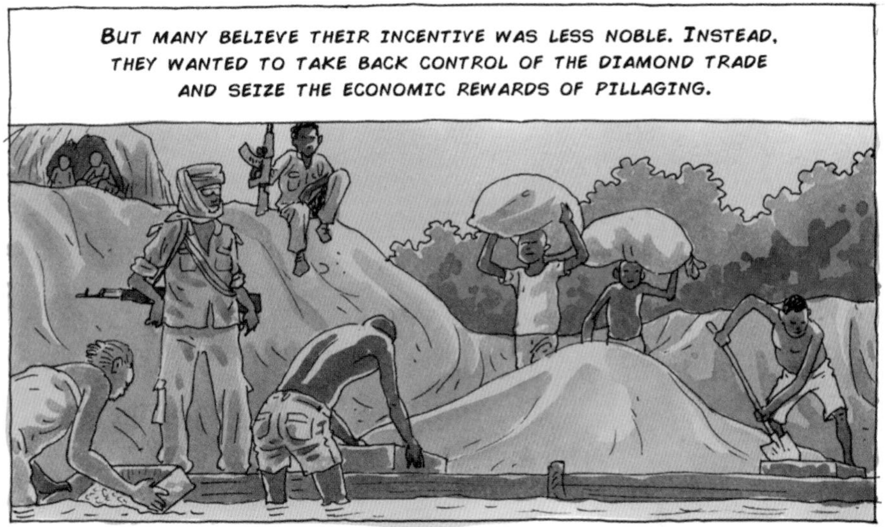
BUT MANY BELIEVE THEIR INCENTIVE WAS LESS NOBLE. INSTEAD, THEY WANTED TO TAKE BACK CONTROL OF THE DIAMOND TRADE AND SEIZE THE ECONOMIC REWARDS OF PILLAGING.

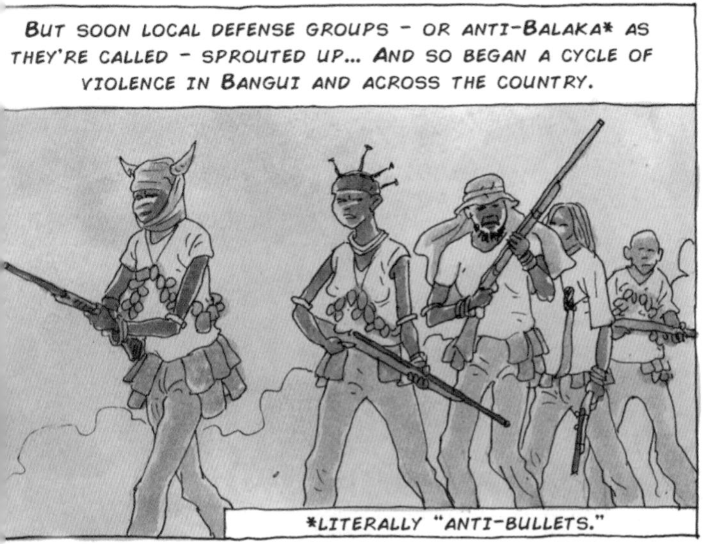
BUT SOON LOCAL DEFENSE GROUPS - OR ANTI-BALAKA* AS THEY'RE CALLED - SPROUTED UP... AND SO BEGAN A CYCLE OF VIOLENCE IN BANGUI AND ACROSS THE COUNTRY.
*LITERALLY "ANTI-BULLETS."

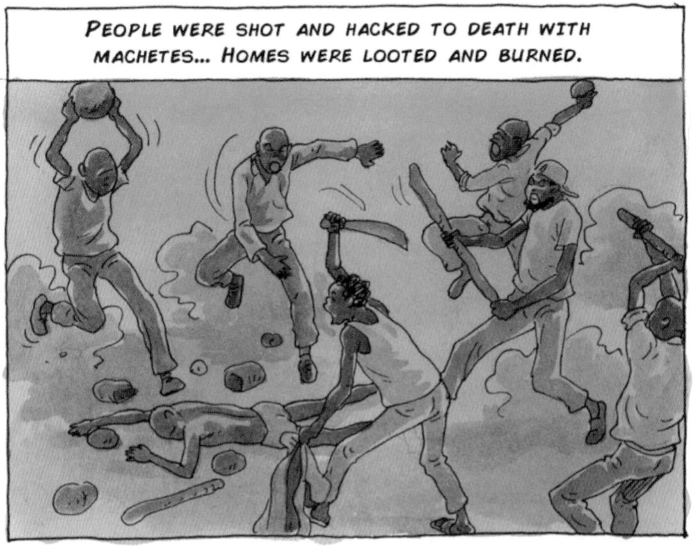
PEOPLE WERE SHOT AND HACKED TO DEATH WITH MACHETES... HOMES WERE LOOTED AND BURNED.

THE CRISIS IS LIKE AN ORPHAN FACTORY... I'VE SEEN THREE TIMES MORE KIDS LIVING ON THE STREETS SINCE.

"MOST OF THEM HAVE LOST BOTH PARENTS AND HAVE NO OTHER FAMILY WILLING TO TAKE THEM IN DURING THESE HARD TIMES...

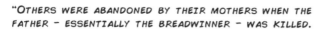

"OTHERS WERE ABANDONED BY THEIR MOTHERS WHEN THE FATHER — ESSENTIALLY THE BREADWINNER — WAS KILLED.

BUT WE CAN'T HELP THEM ALL — WE ONLY HAVE SIXTY BEDS, AND WE'VE HAD TO TURN MANY AWAY.

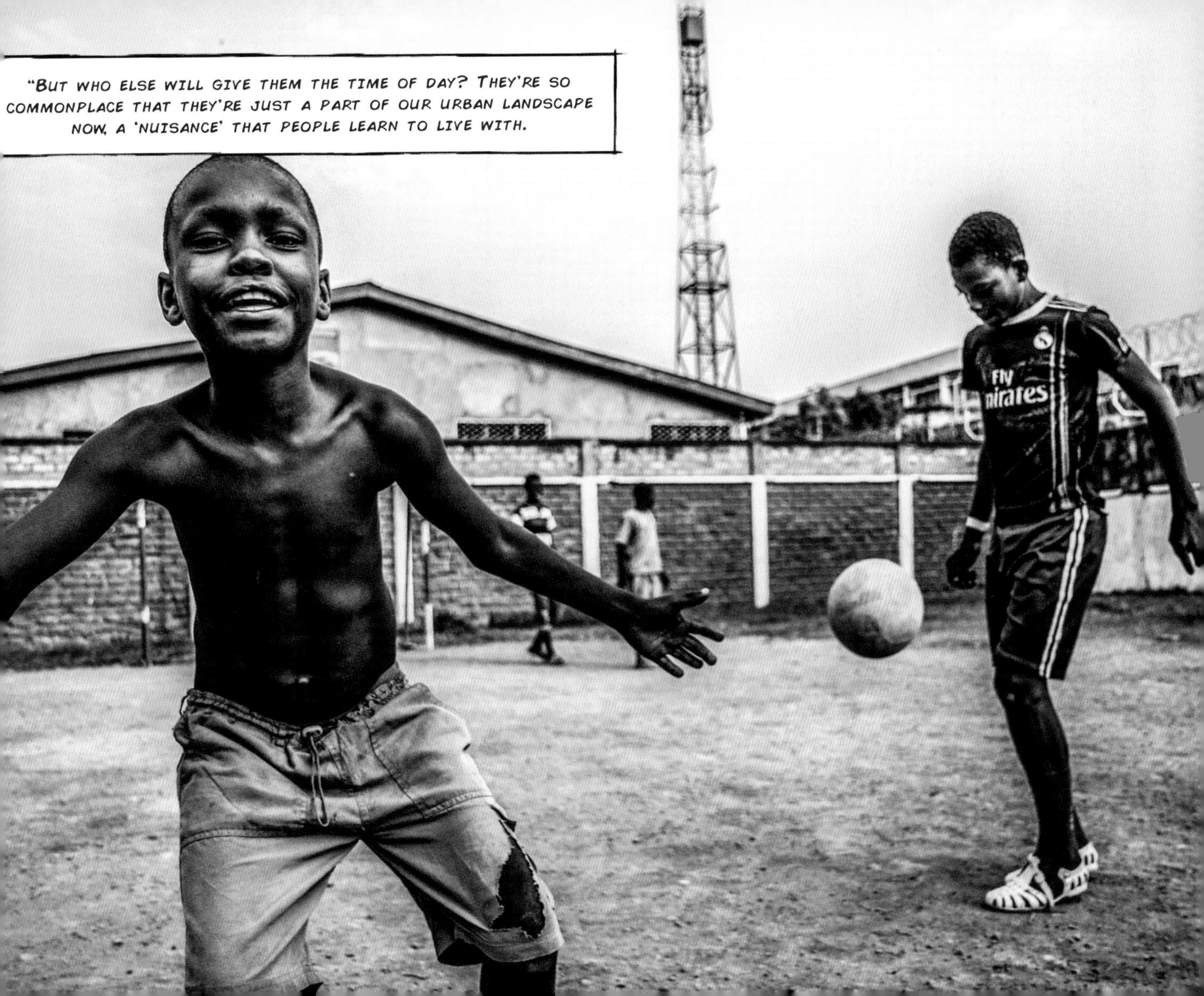
"BUT WHO ELSE WILL GIVE THEM THE TIME OF DAY? THEY'RE SO COMMONPLACE THAT THEY'RE JUST A PART OF OUR URBAN LANDSCAPE NOW, A 'NUISANCE' THAT PEOPLE LEARN TO LIVE WITH.

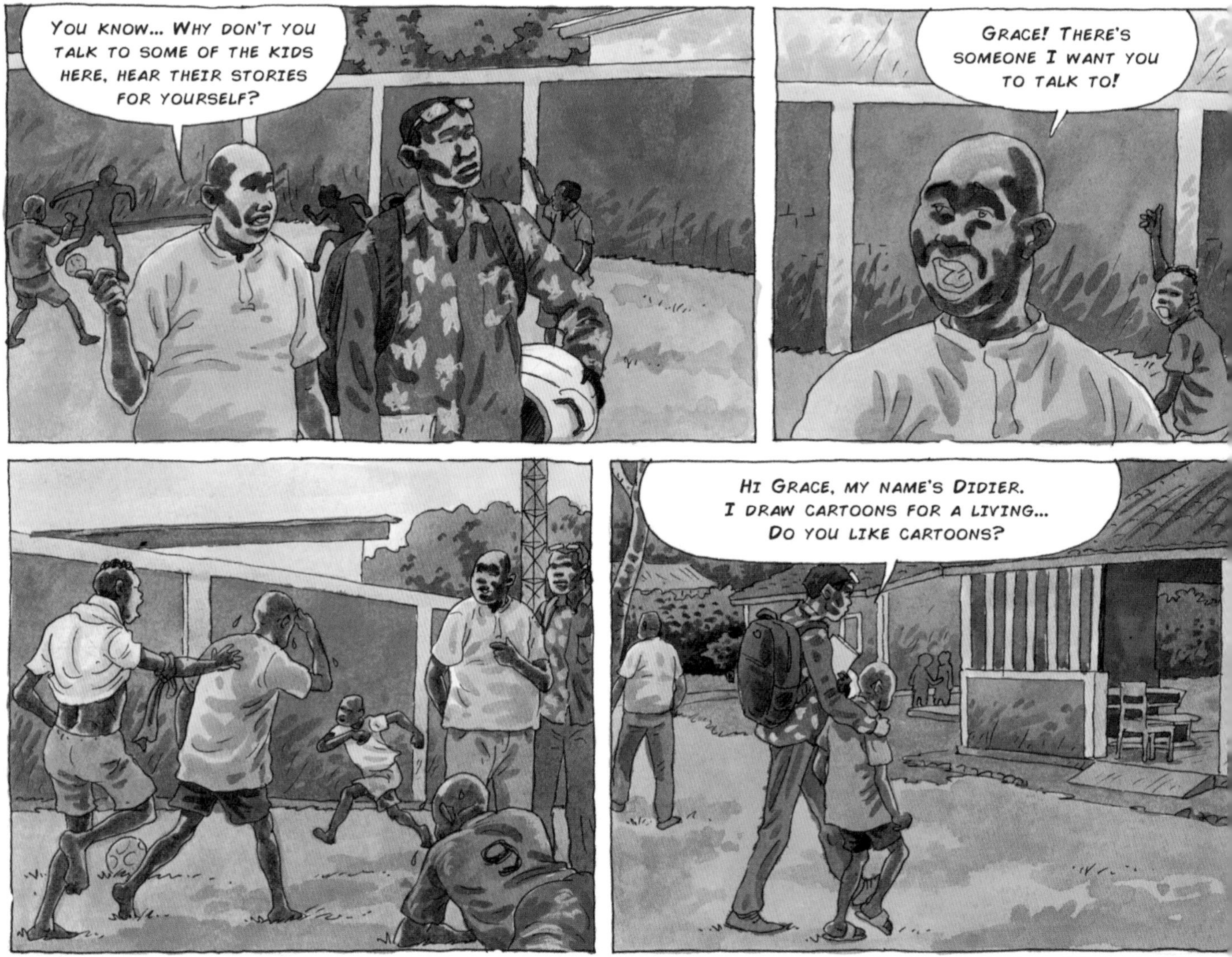
You know... Why don't you talk to some of the kids here, hear their stories for yourself?
Grace! There's someone I want you to talk to!
Hi Grace, my name's Didier. I draw cartoons for a living... Do you like cartoons?

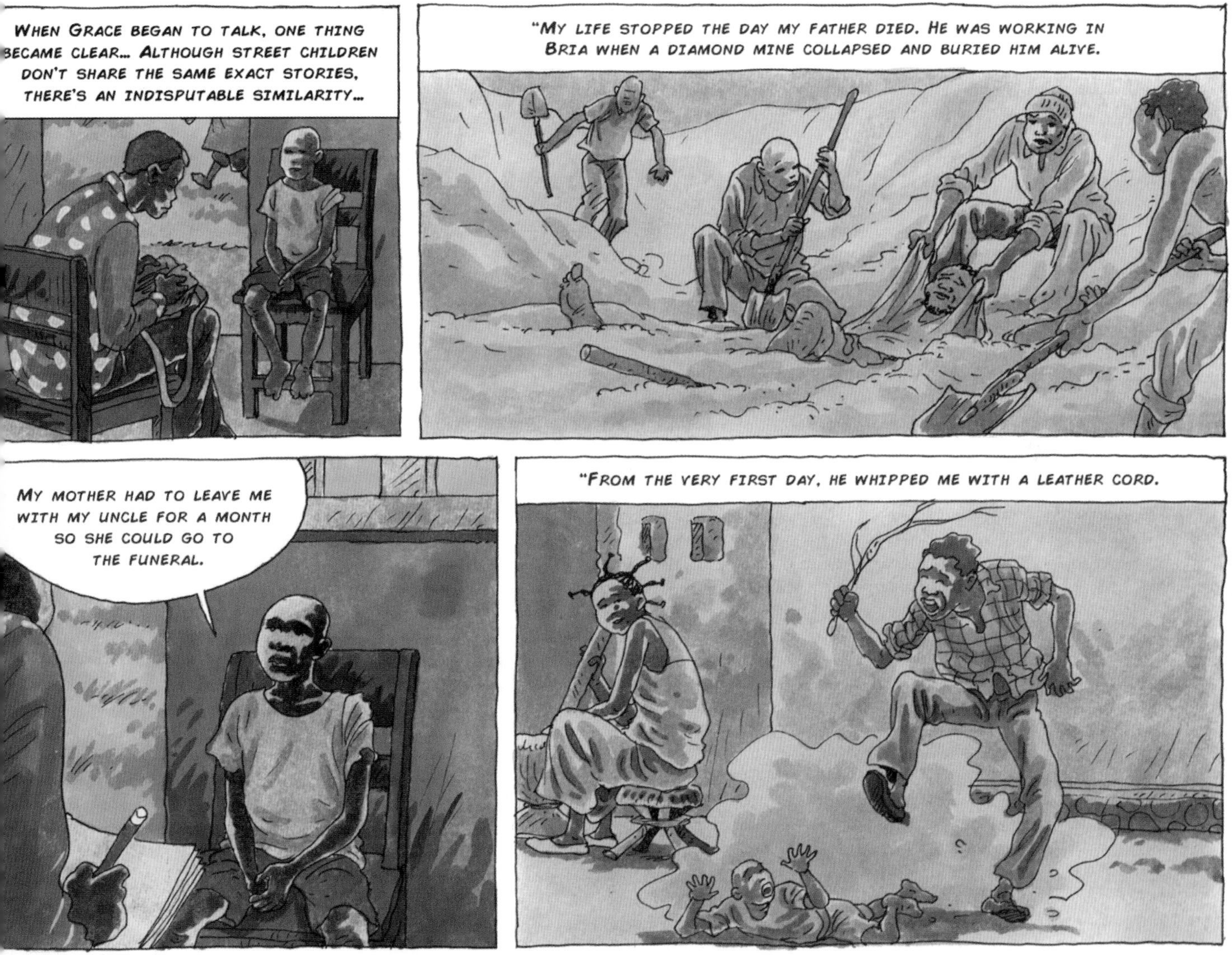
WHEN GRACE BEGAN TO TALK, ONE THING BECAME CLEAR... ALTHOUGH STREET CHILDREN DON'T SHARE THE SAME EXACT STORIES, THERE'S AN INDISPUTABLE SIMILARITY...
"MY LIFE STOPPED THE DAY MY FATHER DIED. HE WAS WORKING IN BRIA WHEN A DIAMOND MINE COLLAPSED AND BURIED HIM ALIVE.
MY MOTHER HAD TO LEAVE ME WITH MY UNCLE FOR A MONTH SO SHE COULD GO TO THE FUNERAL.
"FROM THE VERY FIRST DAY, HE WHIPPED ME WITH A LEATHER CORD.

IF I WAS HUNGRY AND TOOK FOOD WITHOUT ASKING, HE BEAT ME.

"IF I TRIED TO PLAY WITH MY FRIENDS, HE HIT ME AND FORCED ME TO DO WORK FOR HIM.

"IF I DIDN'T CLEAN THE HOUSE, HE USED HIS BELT.

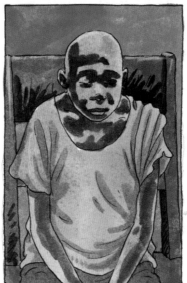

"THERE WASN'T A PART OF MY BODY THAT WASN'T BLACK AND BLUE.

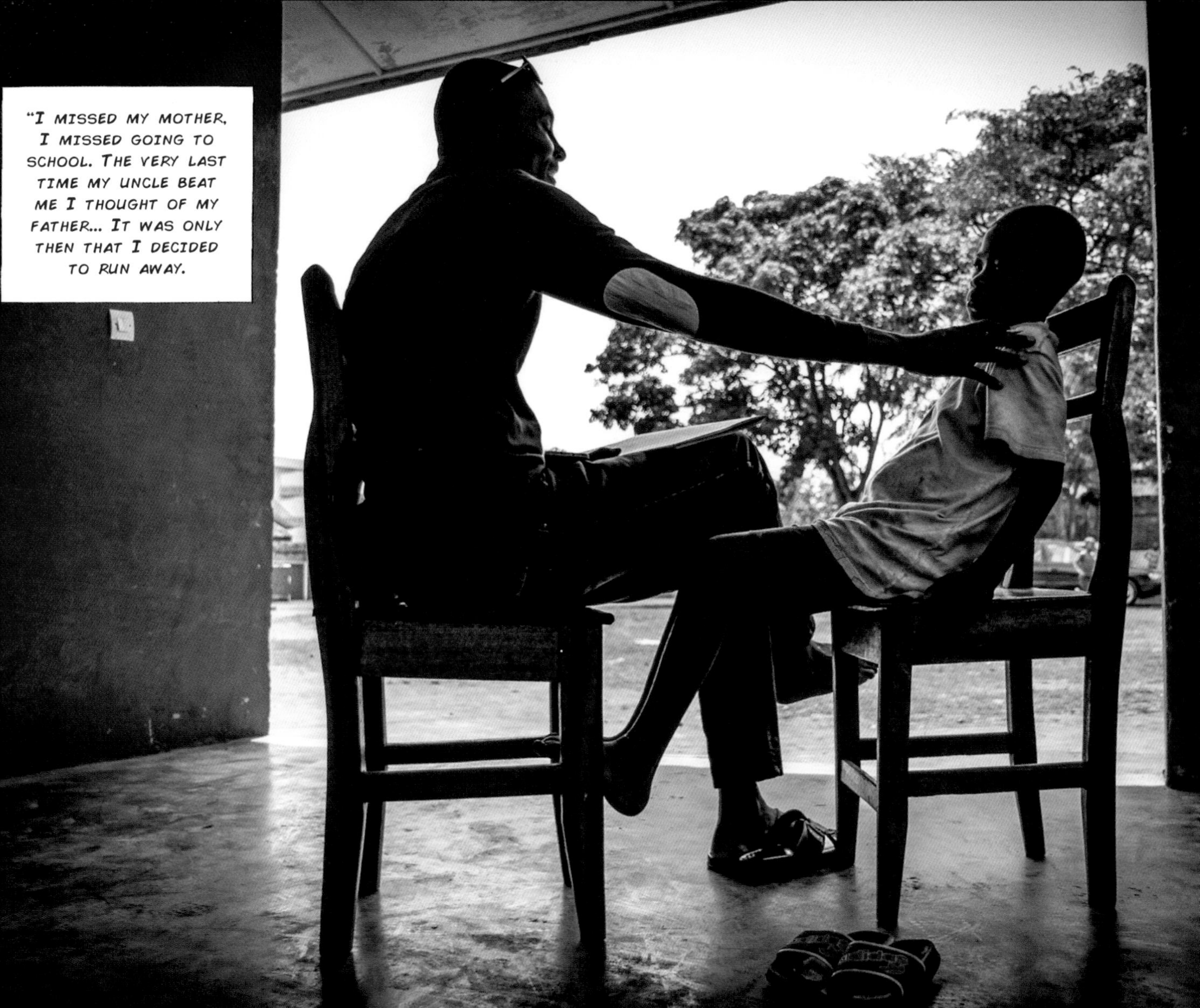

"I MISSED MY MOTHER, I MISSED GOING TO SCHOOL. THE VERY LAST TIME MY UNCLE BEAT ME I THOUGHT OF MY FATHER... IT WAS ONLY THEN THAT I DECIDED TO RUN AWAY.

"BY NIGHT, I SLEPT AT A STALL AT THE MARKET...

"...AND BY DAY, I WASHED PLATES AT A ROADSIDE RESTAURANT WHERE I MADE ABOUT A EURO A DAY.

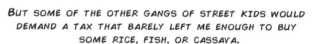

BUT SOME OF THE OTHER GANGS OF STREET KIDS WOULD DEMAND A TAX THAT BARELY LEFT ME ENOUGH TO BUY SOME RICE, FISH, OR CASSAVA.

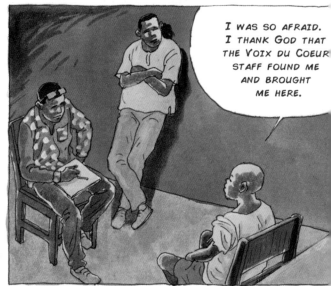

I WAS SO AFRAID. I THANK GOD THAT THE VOIX DU COEUR STAFF FOUND ME AND BROUGHT ME HERE.

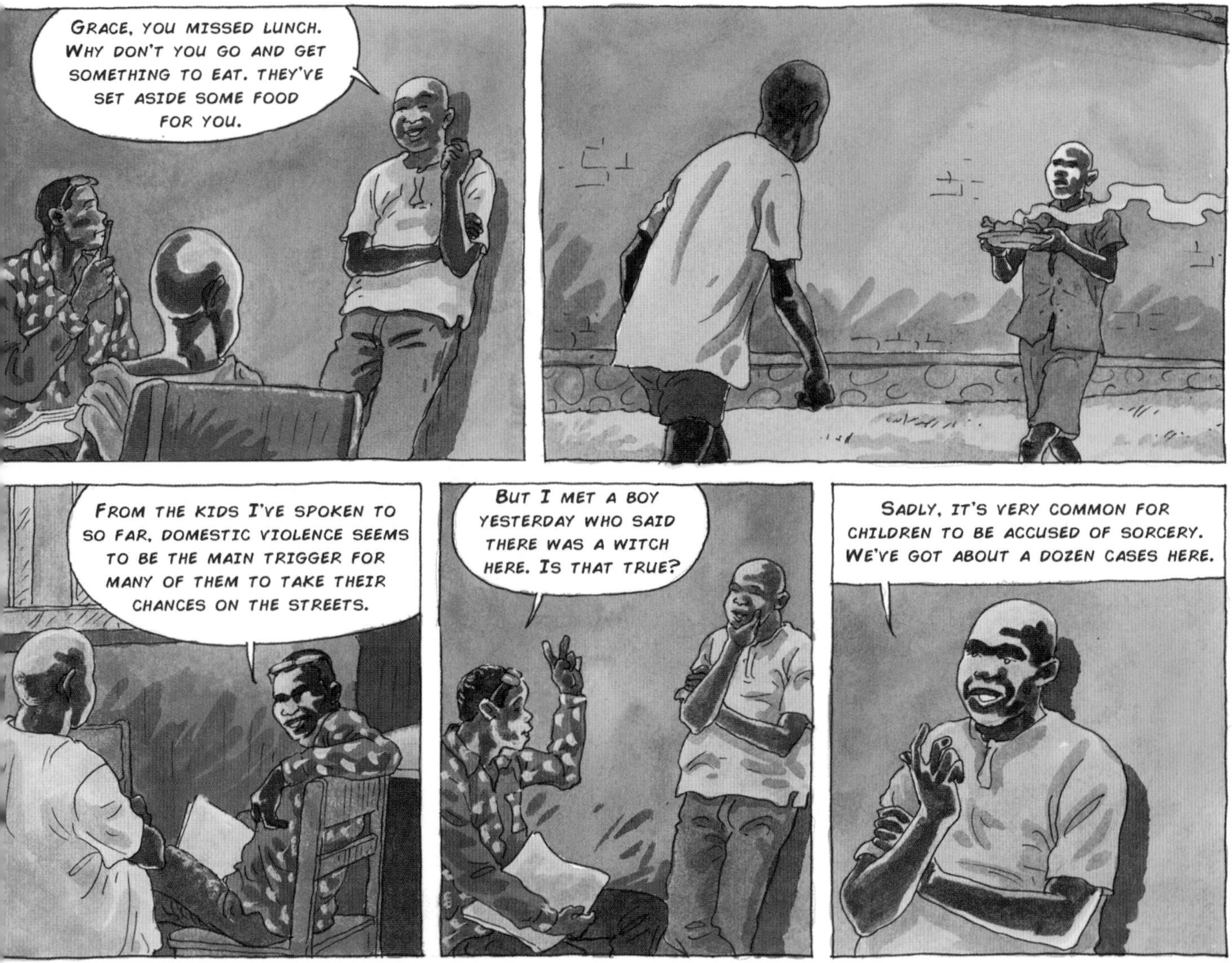
GRACE, YOU MISSED LUNCH. WHY DON'T YOU GO AND GET SOMETHING TO EAT. THEY'VE SET ASIDE SOME FOOD FOR YOU.
FROM THE KIDS I'VE SPOKEN TO SO FAR, DOMESTIC VIOLENCE SEEMS TO BE THE MAIN TRIGGER FOR MANY OF THEM TO TAKE THEIR CHANCES ON THE STREETS.
BUT I MET A BOY YESTERDAY WHO SAID THERE WAS A WITCH HERE. IS THAT TRUE?
SADLY, IT'S VERY COMMON FOR CHILDREN TO BE ACCUSED OF SORCERY. WE'VE GOT ABOUT A DOZEN CASES HERE.

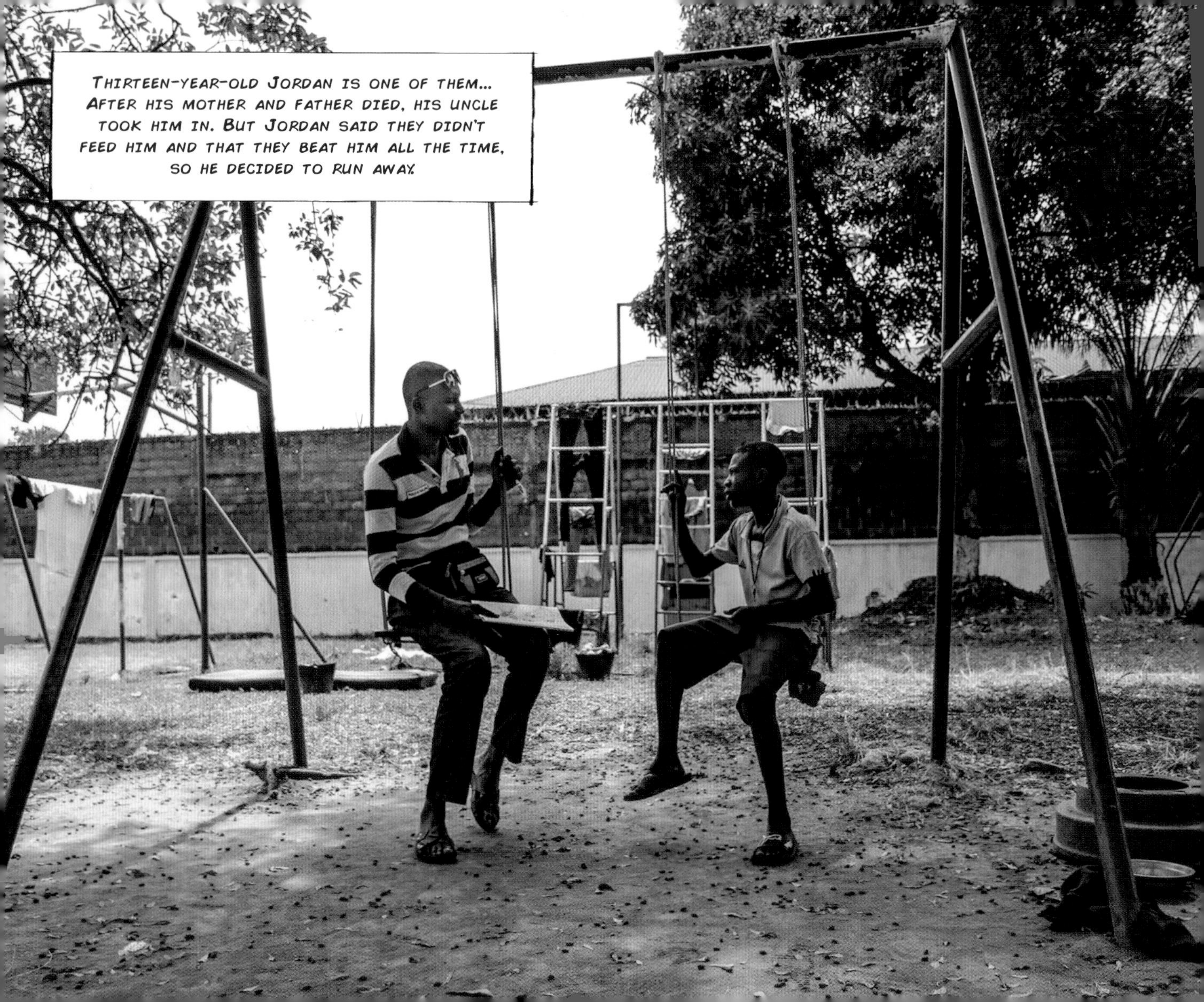
THIRTEEN-YEAR-OLD JORDAN IS ONE OF THEM... AFTER HIS MOTHER AND FATHER DIED, HIS UNCLE TOOK HIM IN. BUT JORDAN SAID THEY DIDN'T FEED HIM AND THAT THEY BEAT HIM ALL THE TIME, SO HE DECIDED TO RUN AWAY.

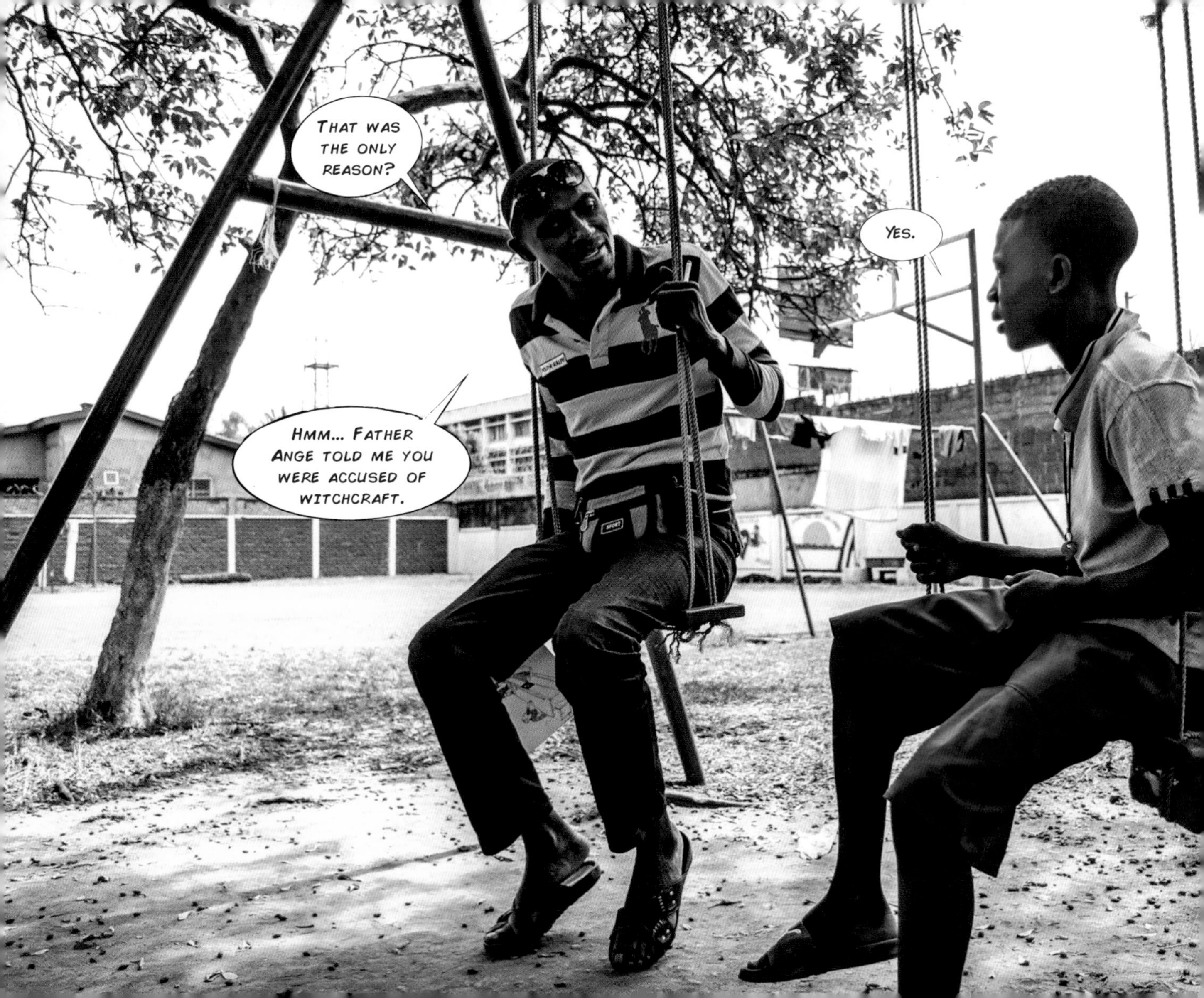
Hmm... Father Ange told me you were accused of witchcraft.
That was the only reason?
Yes.

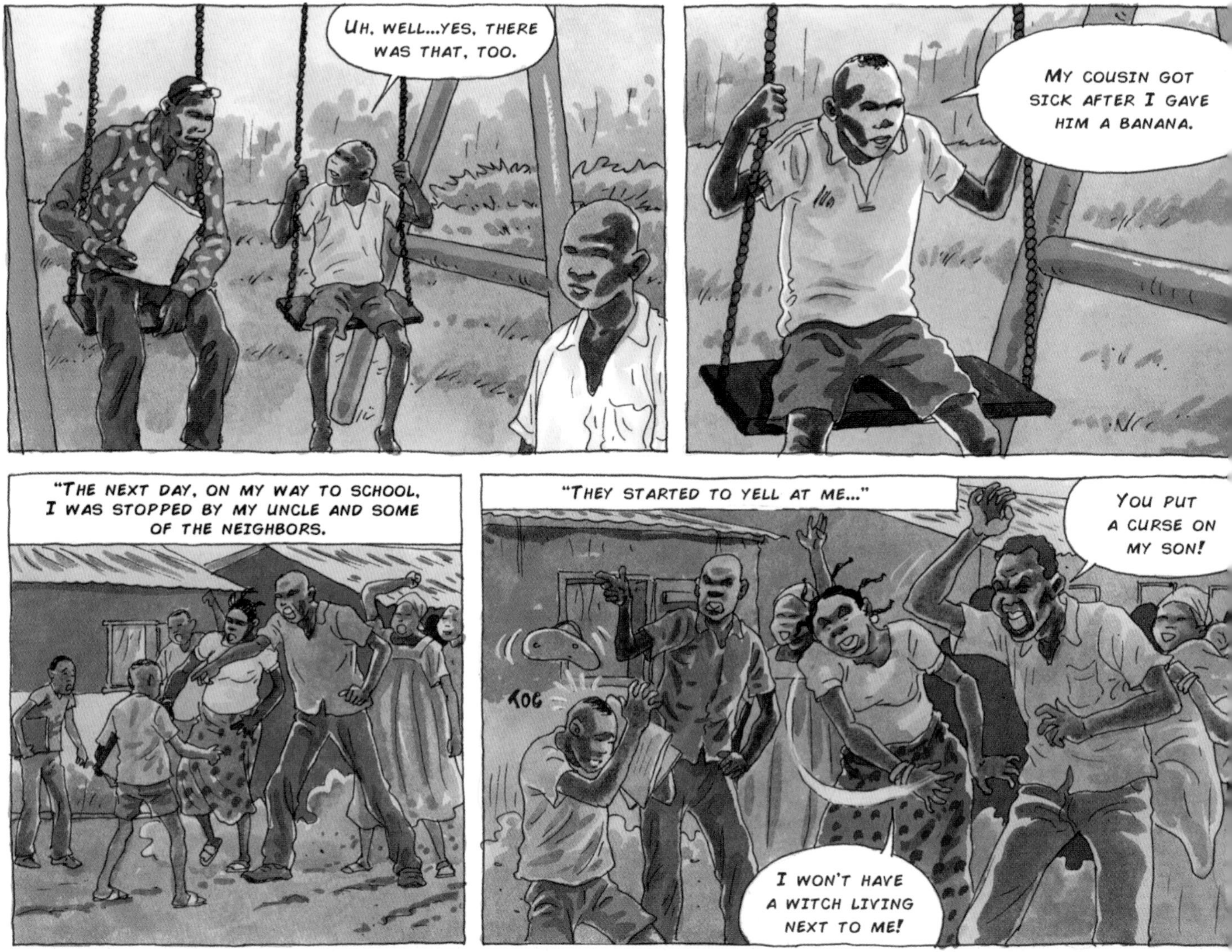
UH, WELL...YES, THERE WAS THAT, TOO.
MY COUSIN GOT SICK AFTER I GAVE HIM A BANANA.
"THE NEXT DAY, ON MY WAY TO SCHOOL, I WAS STOPPED BY MY UNCLE AND SOME OF THE NEIGHBORS.
"THEY STARTED TO YELL AT ME..."
YOU PUT A CURSE ON MY SON!
TOG
I WON'T HAVE A WITCH LIVING NEXT TO ME!

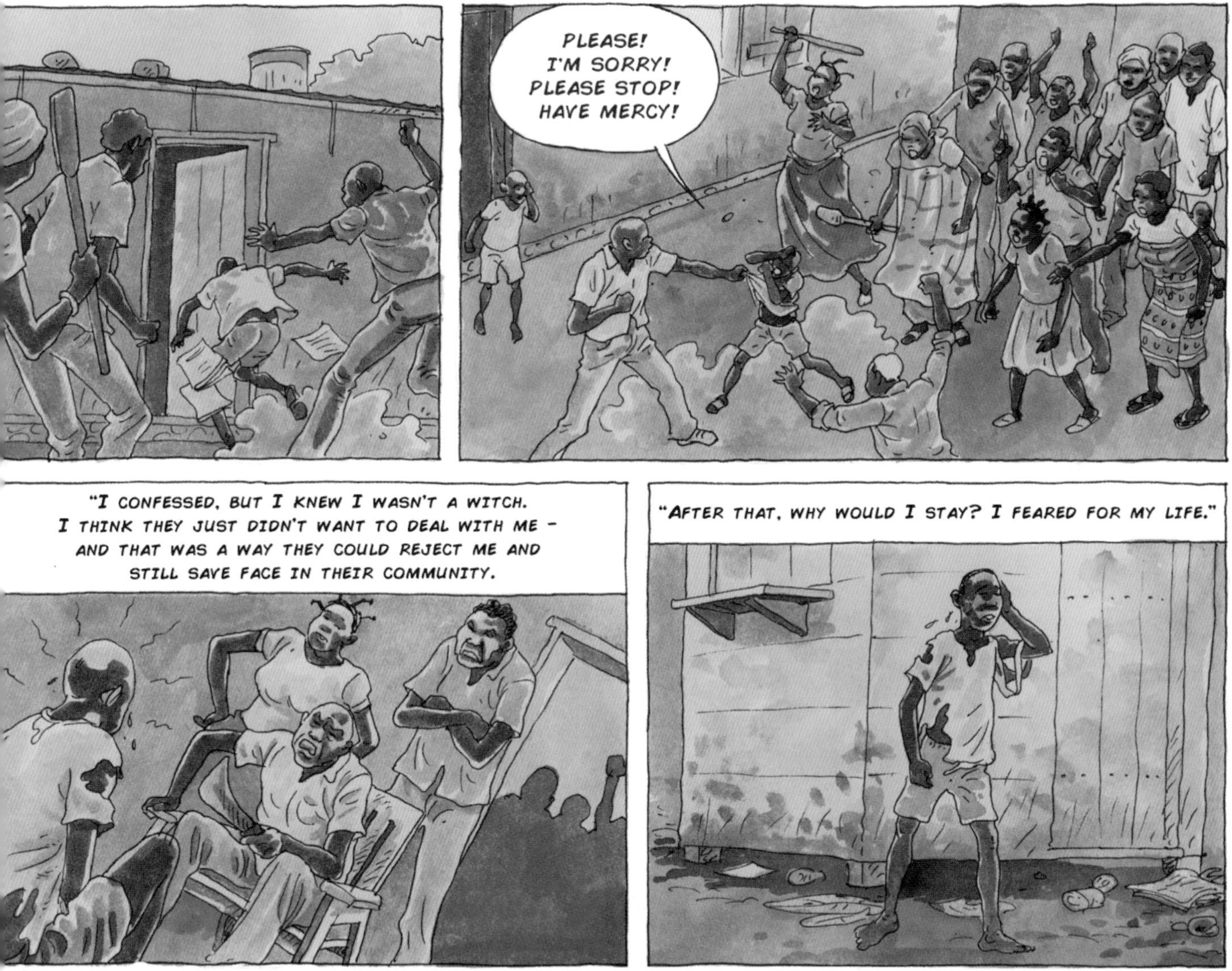
PLEASE! I'M SORRY! PLEASE STOP! HAVE MERCY!
"I CONFESSED, BUT I KNEW I WASN'T A WITCH. I THINK THEY JUST DIDN'T WANT TO DEAL WITH ME – AND THAT WAS A WAY THEY COULD REJECT ME AND STILL SAVE FACE IN THEIR COMMUNITY.
"AFTER THAT, WHY WOULD I STAY? I FEARED FOR MY LIFE."

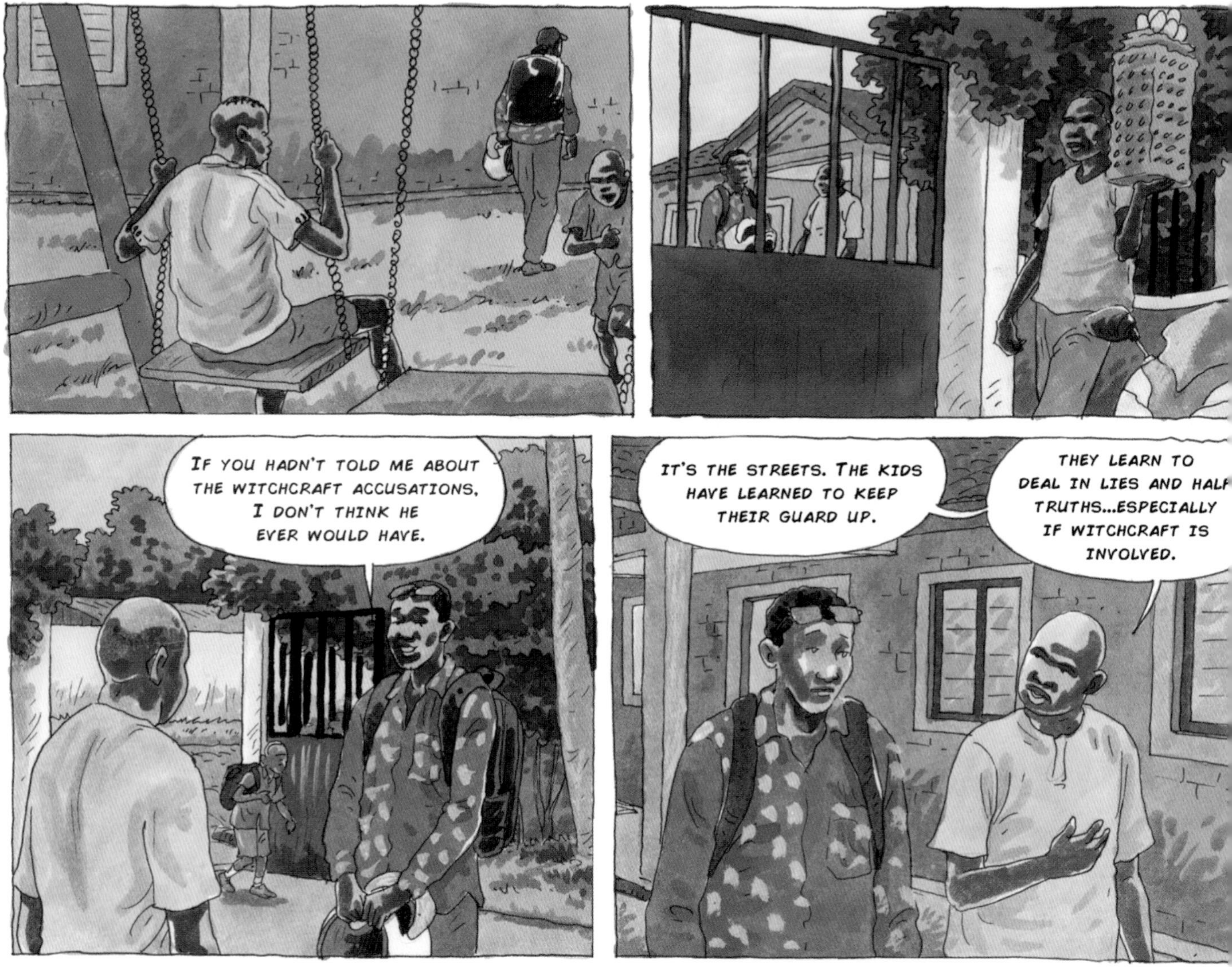
IF YOU HADN'T TOLD ME ABOUT THE WITCHCRAFT ACCUSATIONS, I DON'T THINK HE EVER WOULD HAVE.
IT'S THE STREETS. THE KIDS HAVE LEARNED TO KEEP THEIR GUARD UP.
THEY LEARN TO DEAL IN LIES AND HALF TRUTHS...ESPECIALLY IF WITCHCRAFT IS INVOLVED.

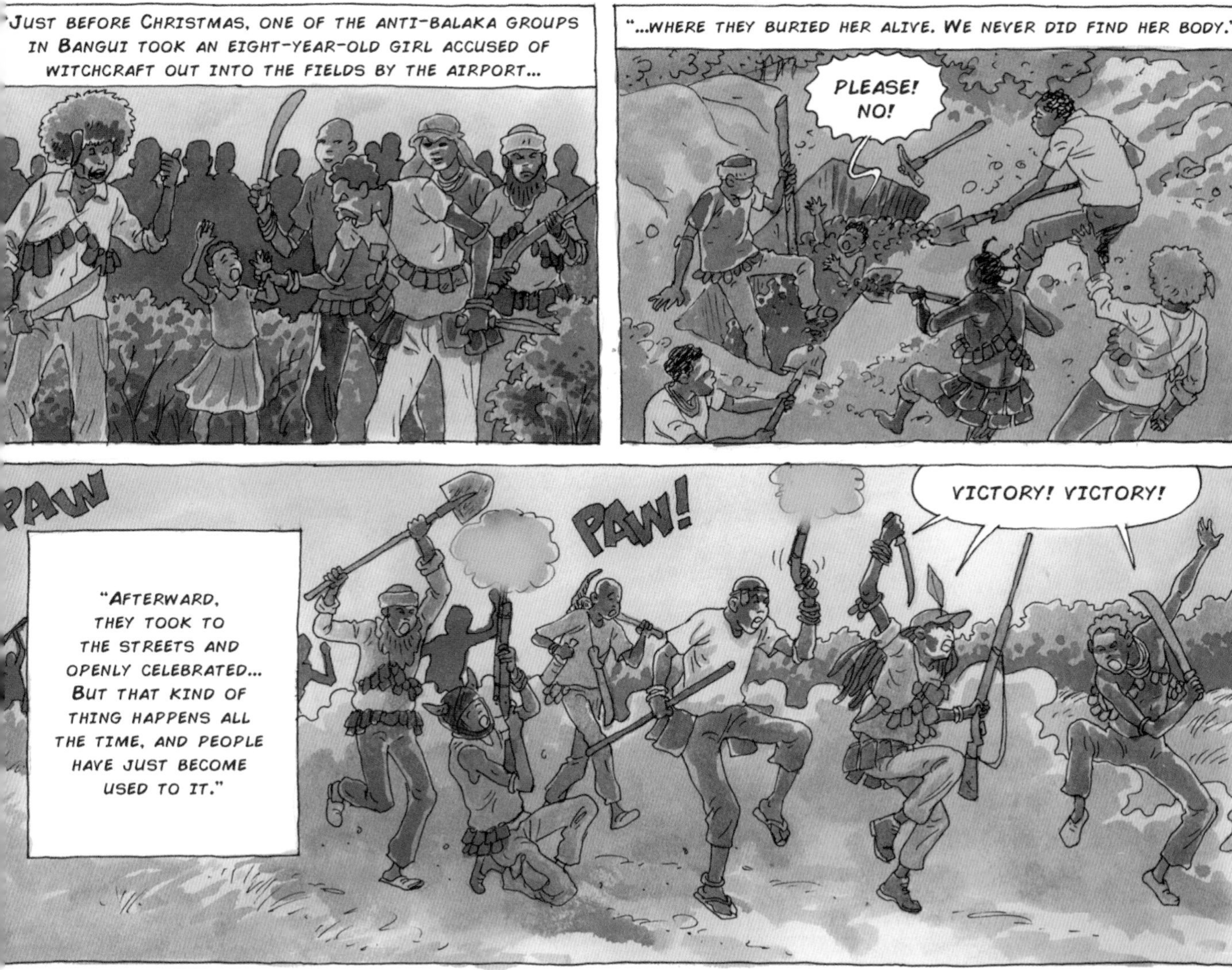
"JUST BEFORE CHRISTMAS, ONE OF THE ANTI-BALAKA GROUPS IN BANGUI TOOK AN EIGHT-YEAR-OLD GIRL ACCUSED OF WITCHCRAFT OUT INTO THE FIELDS BY THE AIRPORT...
"...WHERE THEY BURIED HER ALIVE. WE NEVER DID FIND HER BODY."
PLEASE! NO!
PAW
"AFTERWARD, THEY TOOK TO THE STREETS AND OPENLY CELEBRATED... BUT THAT KIND OF THING HAPPENS ALL THE TIME, AND PEOPLE HAVE JUST BECOME USED TO IT."
PAW!
VICTORY! VICTORY!

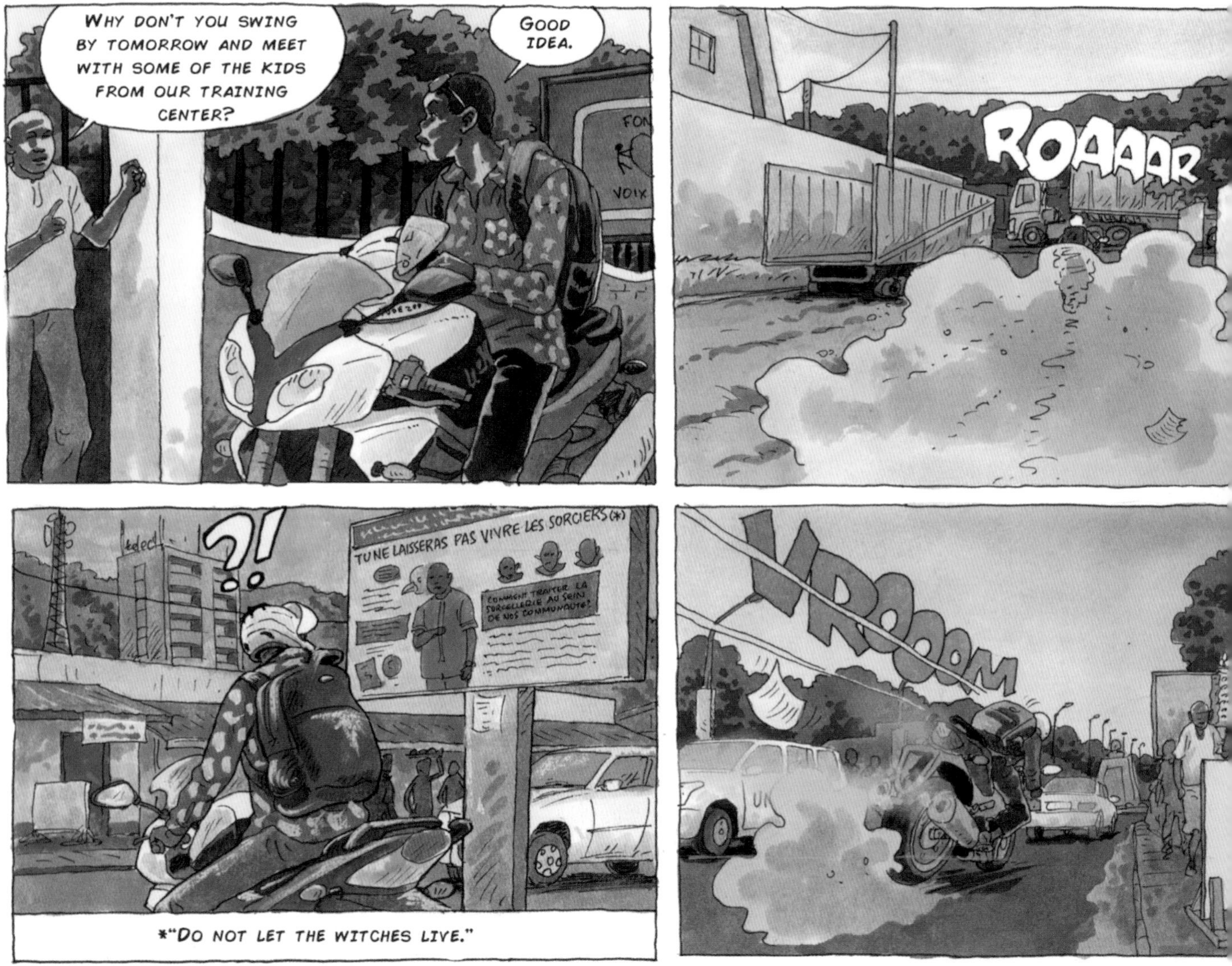

WHY DON'T YOU SWING BY TOMORROW AND MEET WITH SOME OF THE KIDS FROM OUR TRAINING CENTER?
GOOD IDEA.
ROAAAR
TU NE LAISSERAS PAS VIVRE LES SORCIERS(*)
COMMENT TRAITER LA SORCELLERIE AU SEIN DE NOS COMMUNAUTÉS?
?!
*"DO NOT LET THE WITCHES LIVE."
VROOOOM

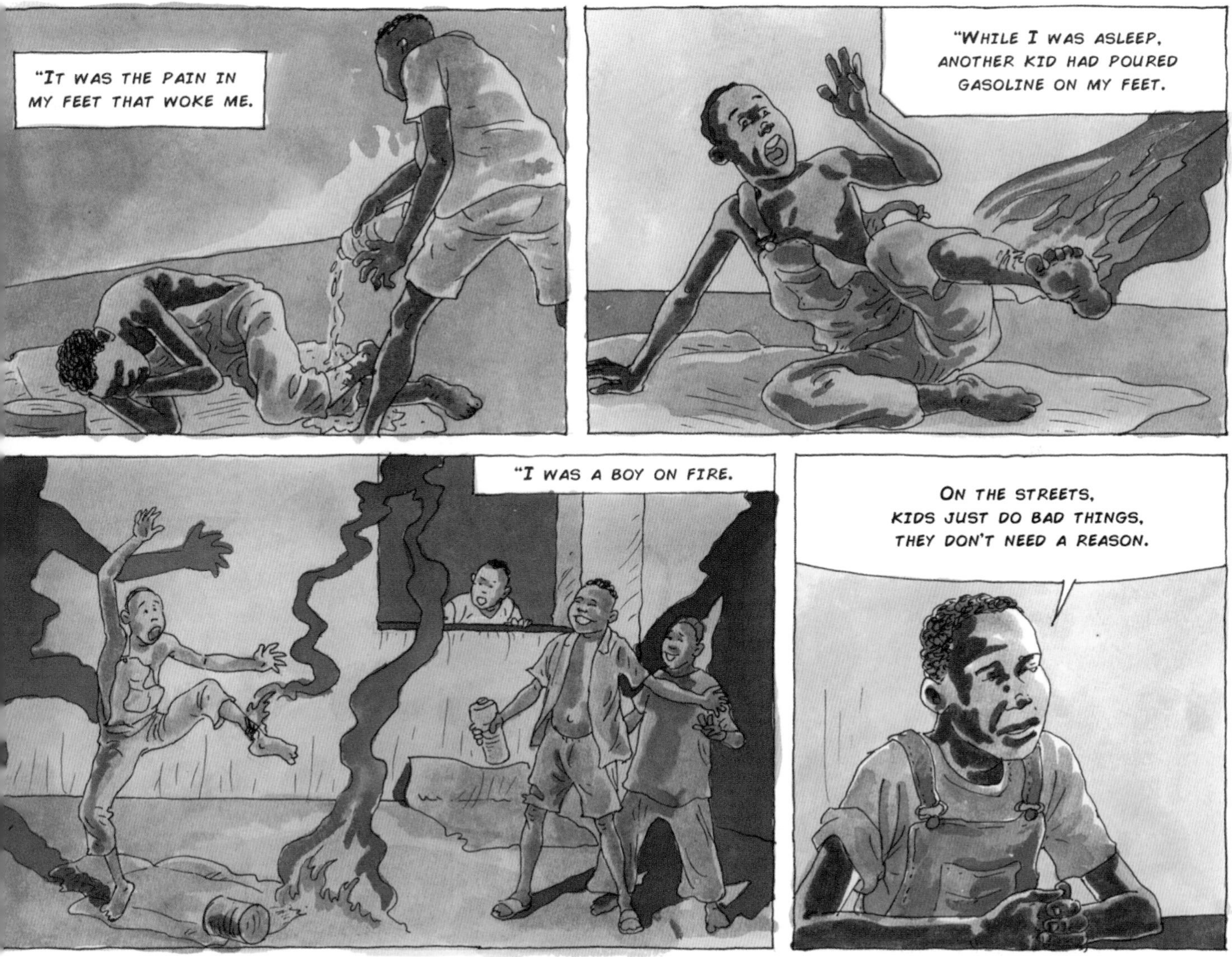
"It was the pain in my feet that woke me.
"While I was asleep, another kid had poured gasoline on my feet.
"I was a boy on fire.
On the streets, kids just do bad things, they don't need a reason.

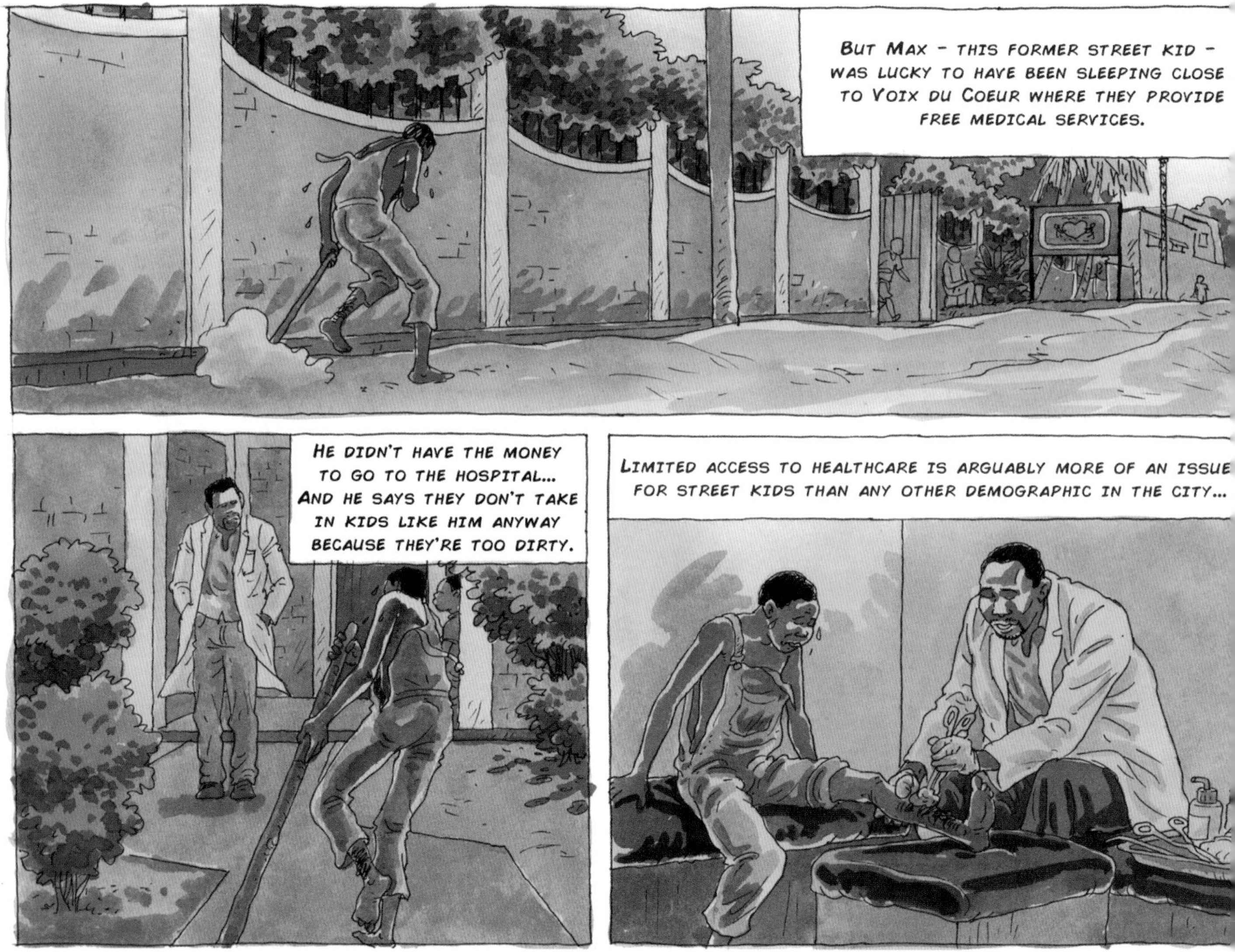
BUT MAX - THIS FORMER STREET KID - WAS LUCKY TO HAVE BEEN SLEEPING CLOSE TO VOIX DU COEUR WHERE THEY PROVIDE FREE MEDICAL SERVICES.
HE DIDN'T HAVE THE MONEY TO GO TO THE HOSPITAL... AND HE SAYS THEY DON'T TAKE IN KIDS LIKE HIM ANYWAY BECAUSE THEY'RE TOO DIRTY.
LIMITED ACCESS TO HEALTHCARE IS ARGUABLY MORE OF AN ISSUE FOR STREET KIDS THAN ANY OTHER DEMOGRAPHIC IN THE CITY...

SLEEPING OUTDOORS INCREASES THEIR CHANCES OF CONTRACTING MALARIA OR RESPIRATORY INFECTIONS...

UNCIRCUMCISED BOYS CAN GET INFECTIONS AFTER BEING FORCIBLY CUT BY ONE OF THEIR GANG MEMBERS...

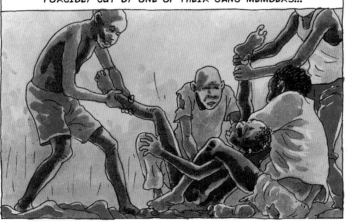

POOR GENERAL HYGIENE CAN LEAD TO TYPHOID, AND A POOR DIET TO MALNUTRITION...

SOME EVEN BECOME INFECTED WITH HIV AS A RESULT OF SEXUAL ABUSE BY ADULTS OR OTHER STREET KIDS.

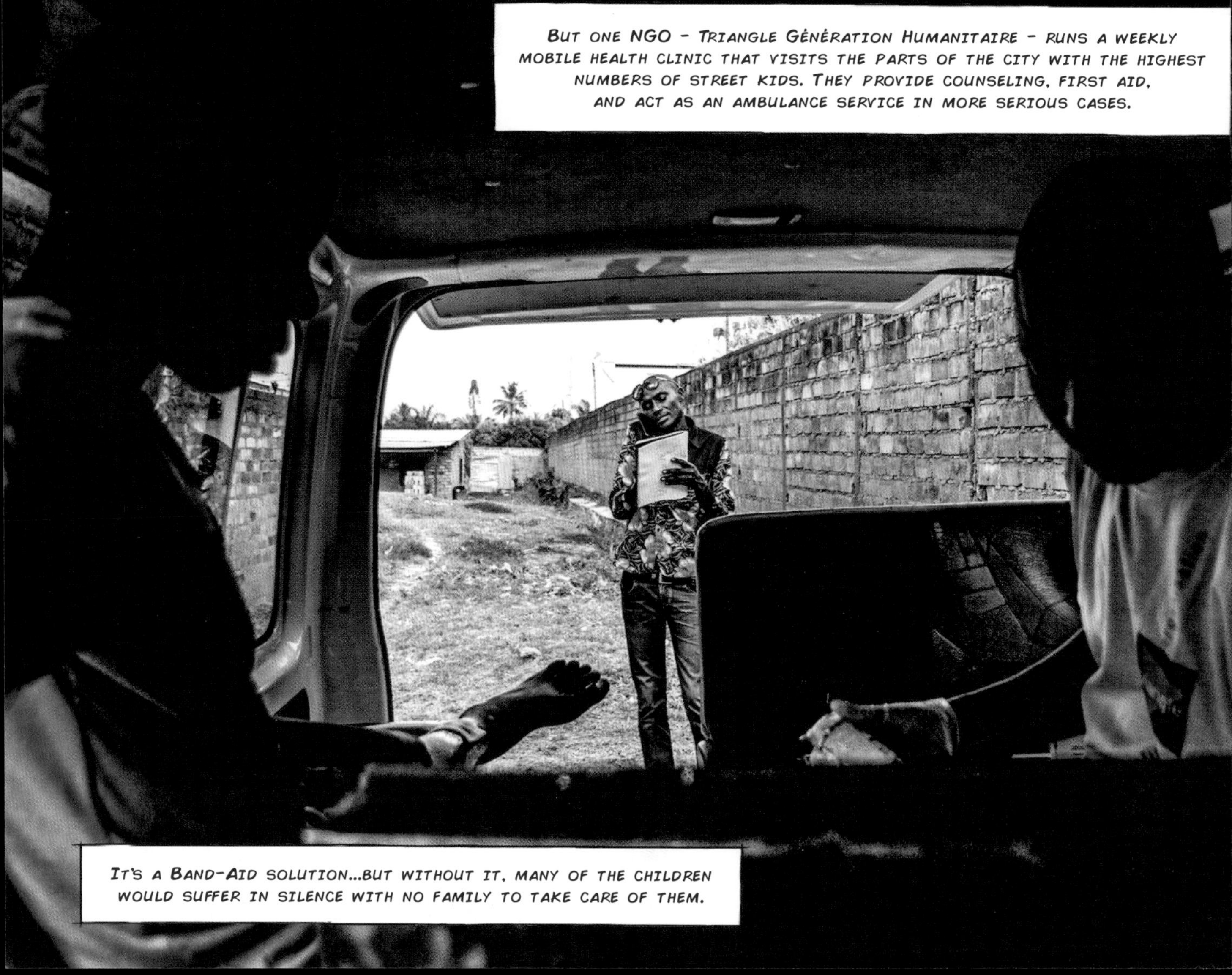
BUT ONE NGO - TRIANGLE GÉNÉRATION HUMANITAIRE - RUNS A WEEKLY MOBILE HEALTH CLINIC THAT VISITS THE PARTS OF THE CITY WITH THE HIGHEST NUMBERS OF STREET KIDS. THEY PROVIDE COUNSELING, FIRST AID, AND ACT AS AN AMBULANCE SERVICE IN MORE SERIOUS CASES.
IT'S A BAND-AID SOLUTION...BUT WITHOUT IT, MANY OF THE CHILDREN WOULD SUFFER IN SILENCE WITH NO FAMILY TO TAKE CARE OF THEM.

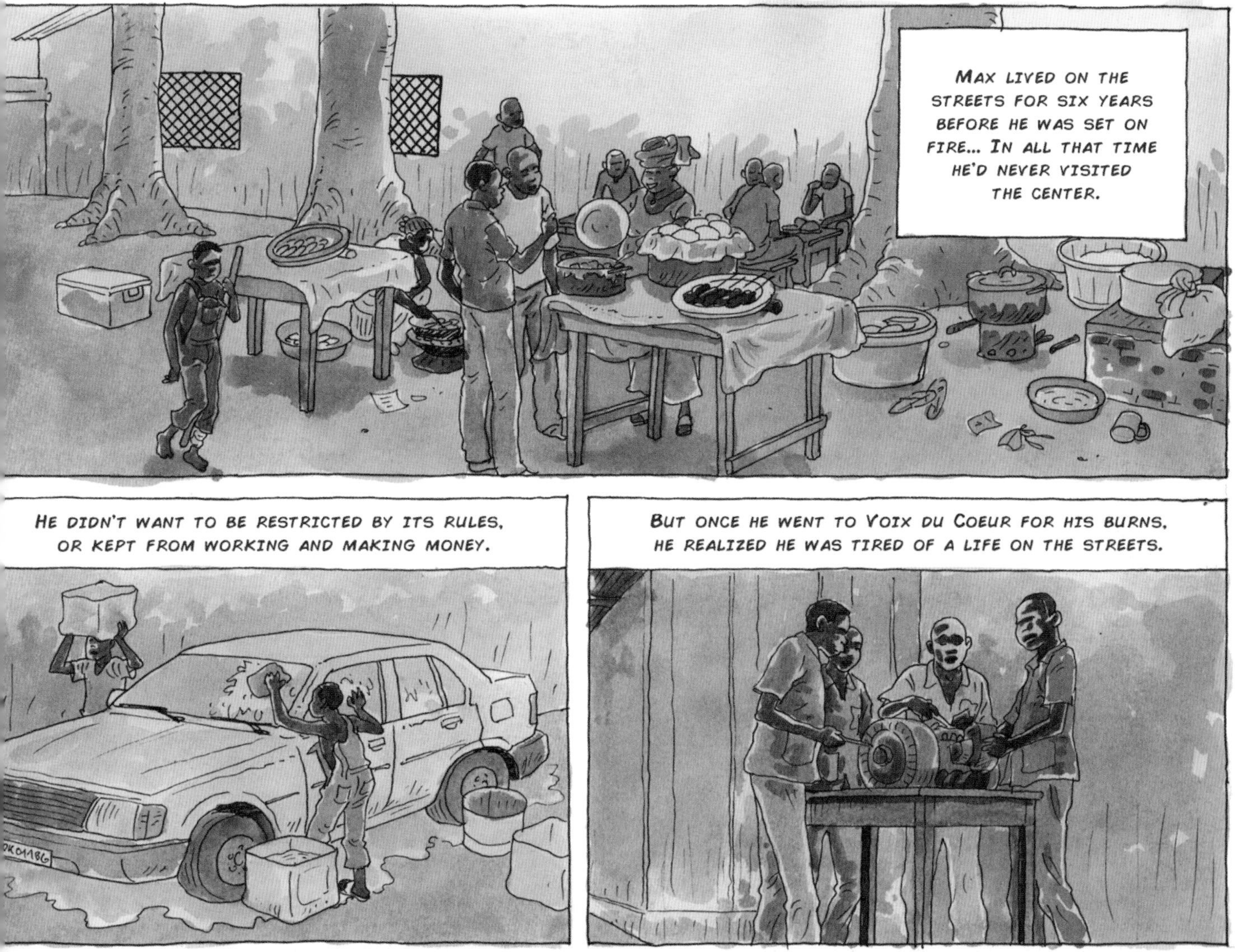
MAX LIVED ON THE STREETS FOR SIX YEARS BEFORE HE WAS SET ON FIRE... IN ALL THAT TIME HE'D NEVER VISITED THE CENTER.
HE DIDN'T WANT TO BE RESTRICTED BY ITS RULES, OR KEPT FROM WORKING AND MAKING MONEY.
DK01186
BUT ONCE HE WENT TO VOIX DU COEUR FOR HIS BURNS, HE REALIZED HE WAS TIRED OF A LIFE ON THE STREETS.

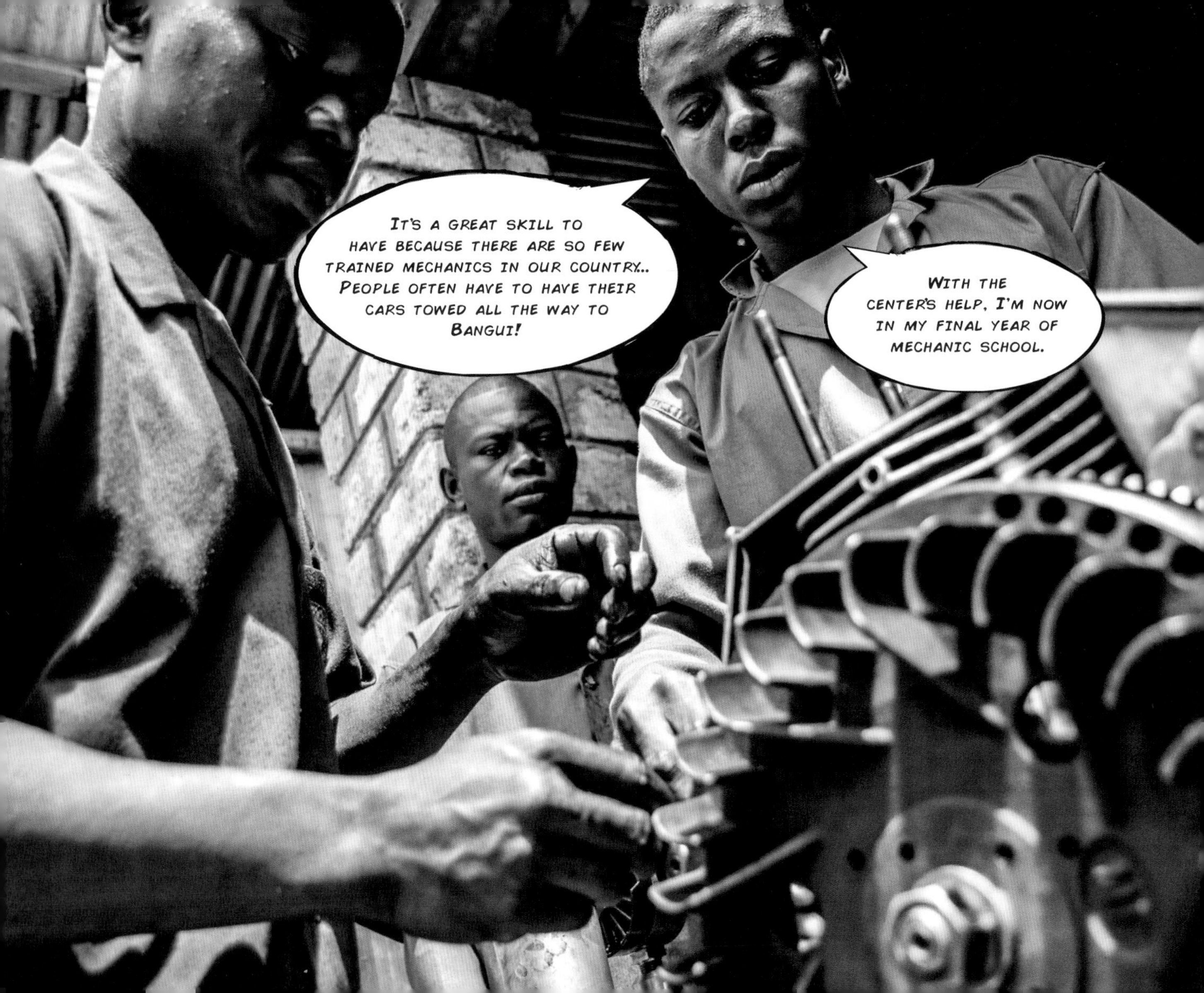
It's a great skill to have because there are so few trained mechanics in our country.. People often have to have their cars towed all the way to Bangui!
With the center's help, I'm now in my final year of mechanic school.

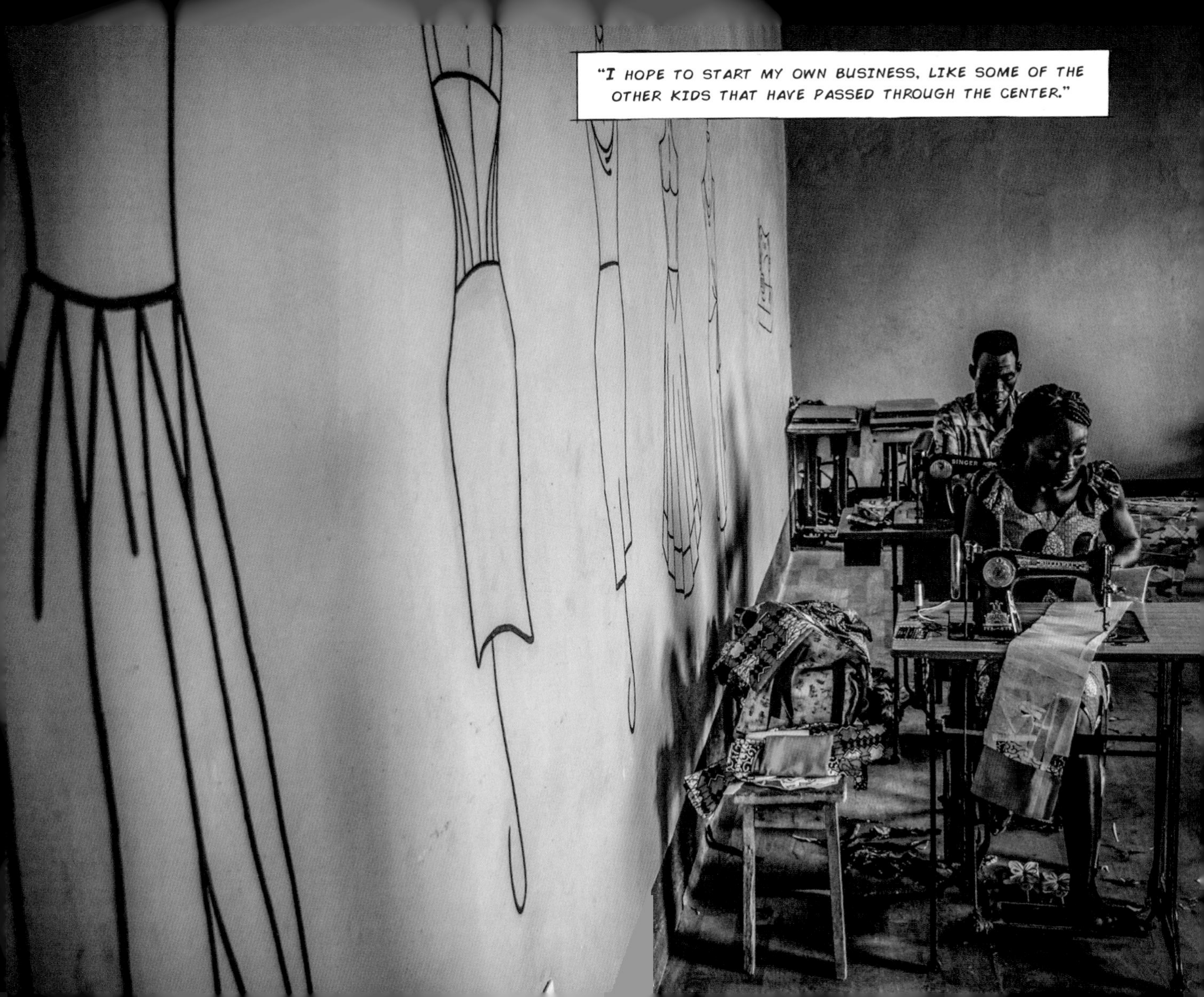
"I HOPE TO START MY OWN BUSINESS, LIKE SOME OF THE OTHER KIDS THAT HAVE PASSED THROUGH THE CENTER."

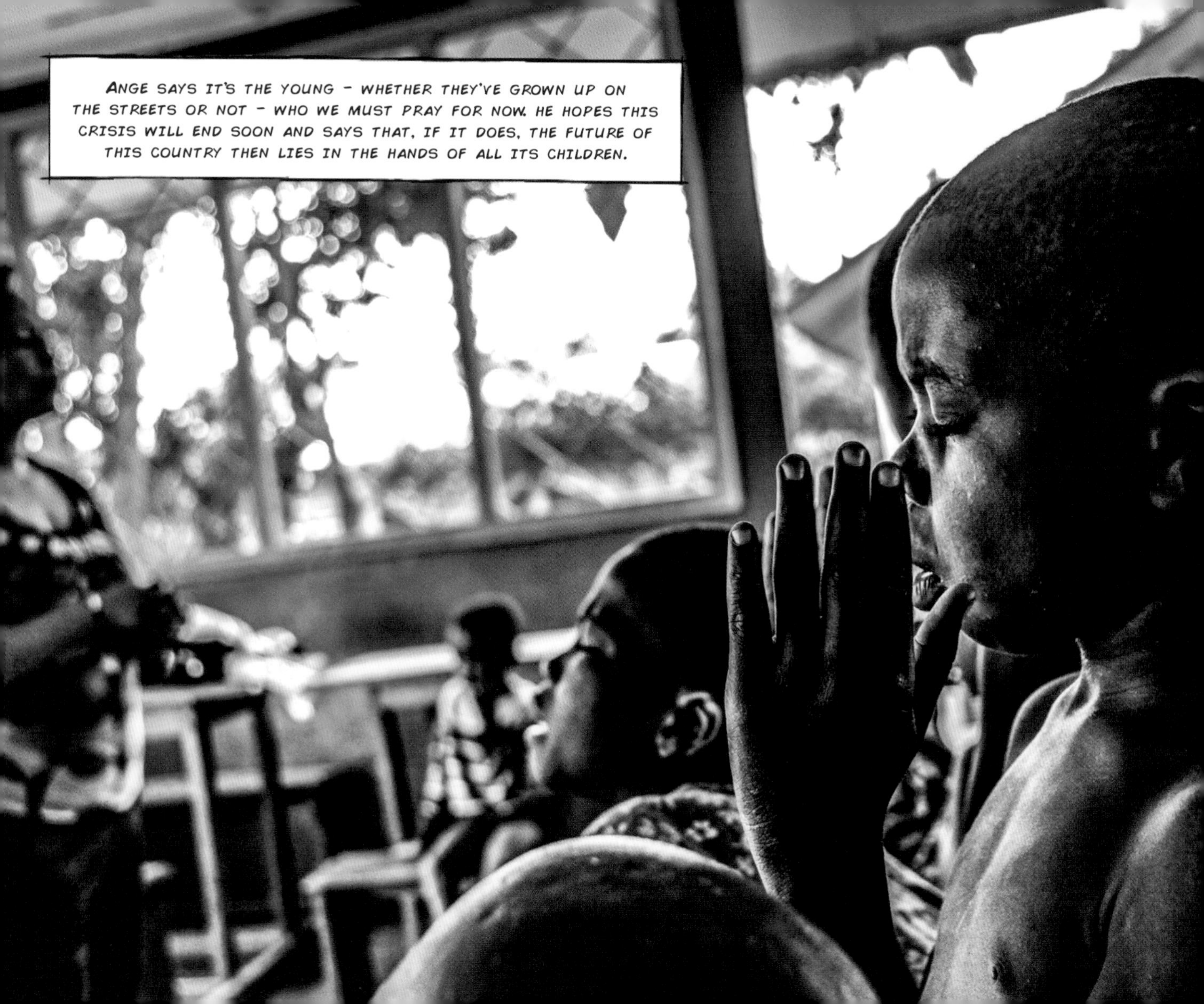
ANGE SAYS IT'S THE YOUNG - WHETHER THEY'VE GROWN UP ON THE STREETS OR NOT - WHO WE MUST PRAY FOR NOW. HE HOPES THIS CRISIS WILL END SOON AND SAYS THAT, IF IT DOES, THE FUTURE OF THIS COUNTRY THEN LIES IN THE HANDS OF ALL ITS CHILDREN.

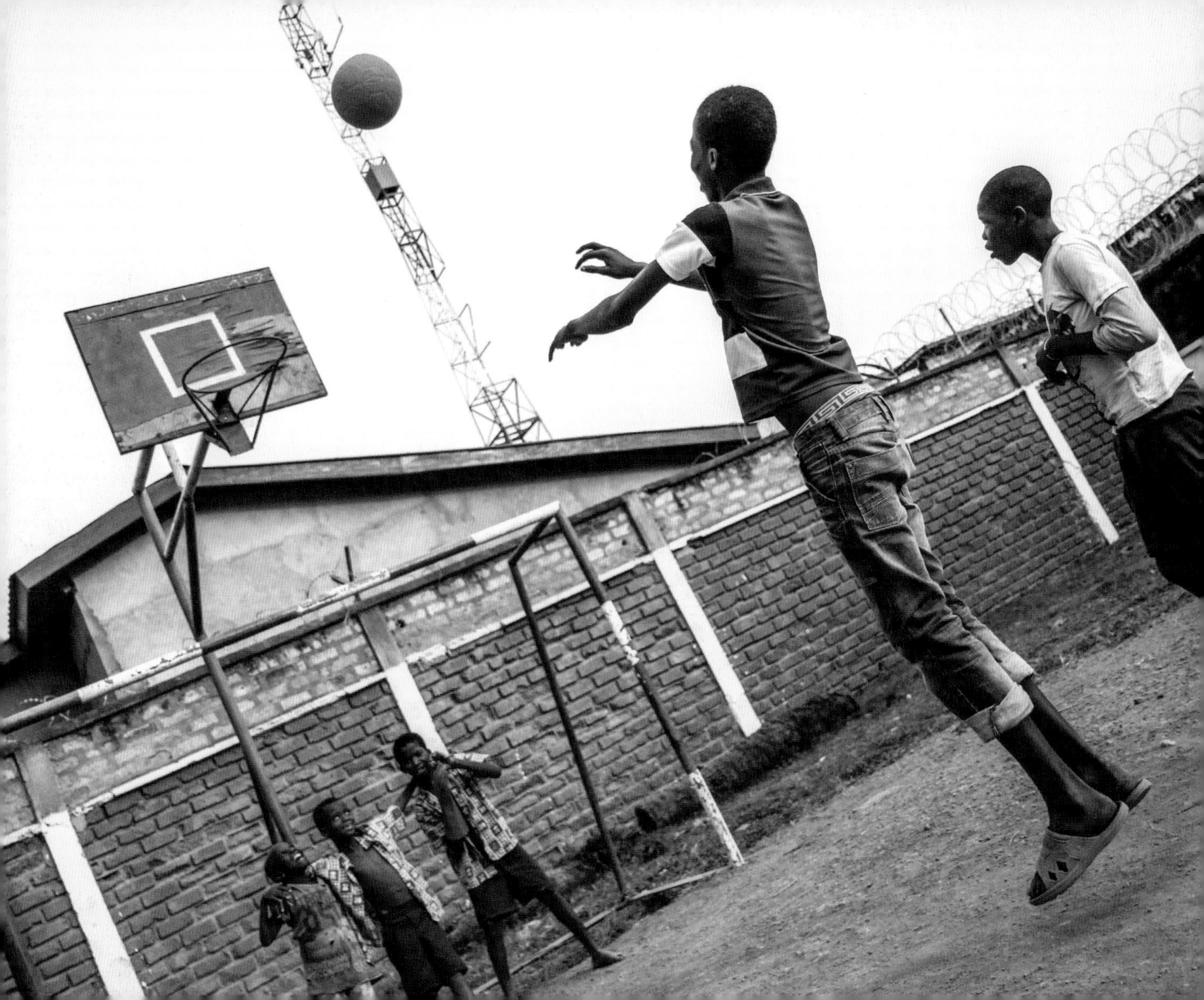

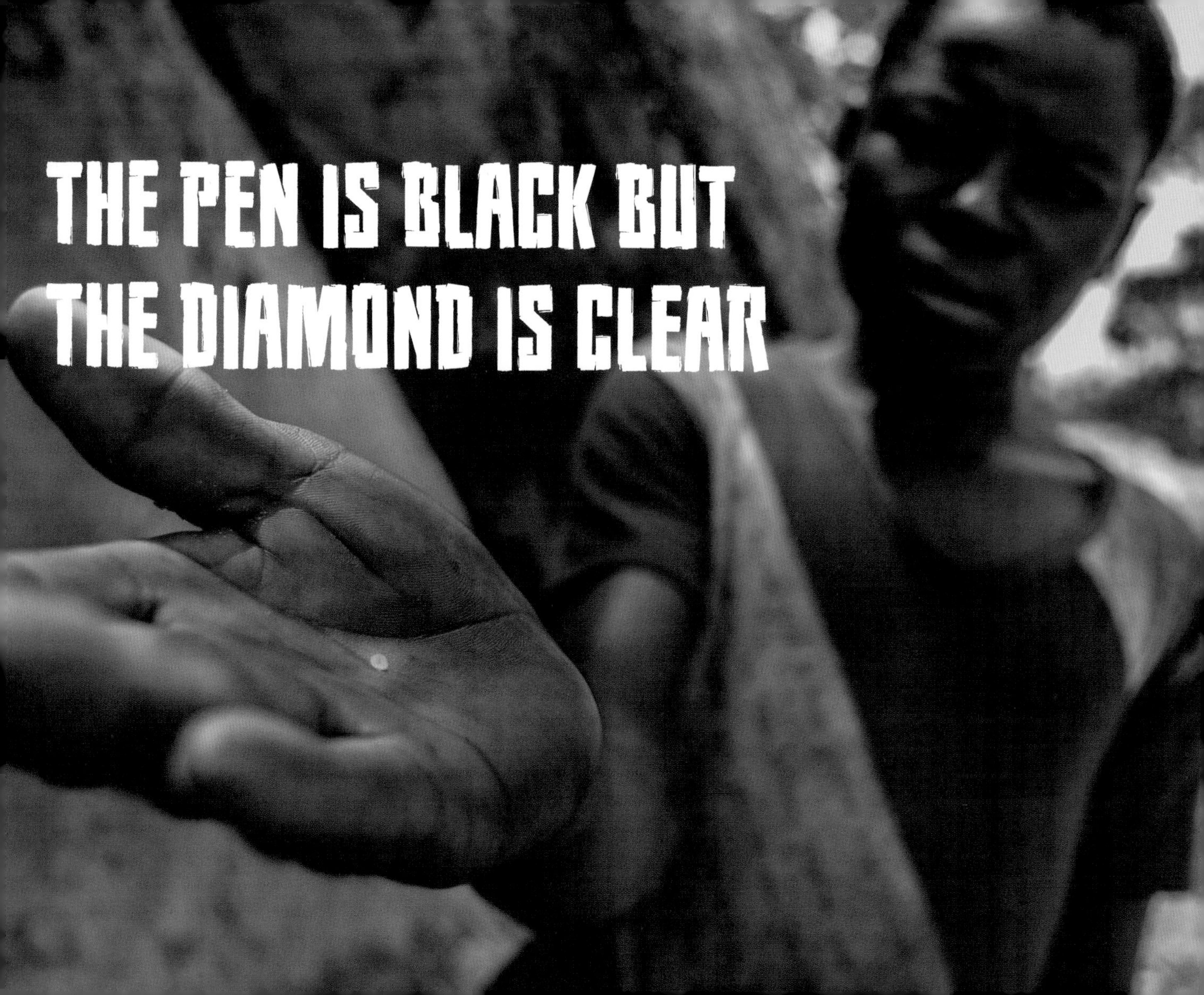

THE PEN IS BLACK BUT THE DIAMOND IS CLEAR

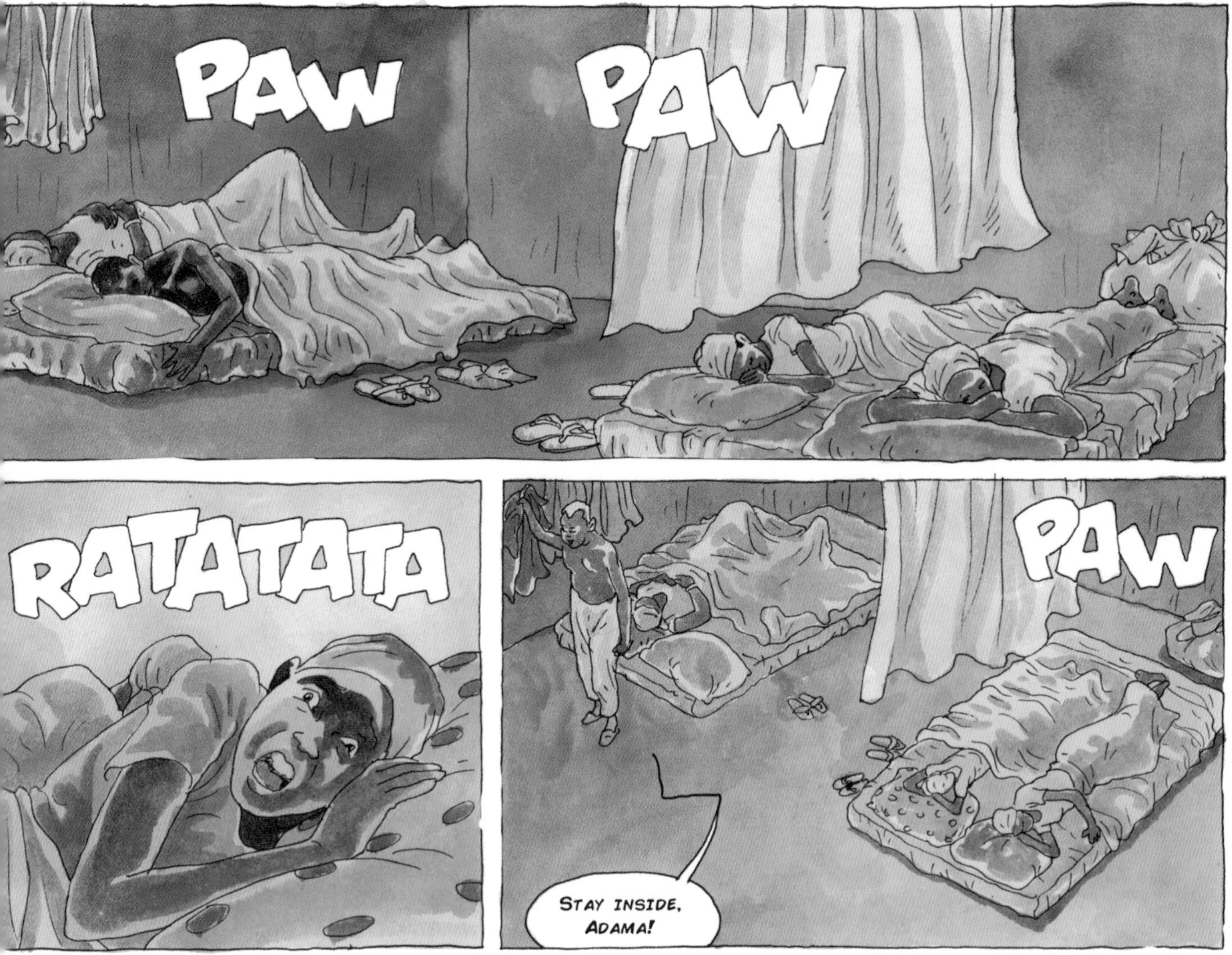
PAW
PAW
RATATATA
PAW
STAY INSIDE, ADAMA!

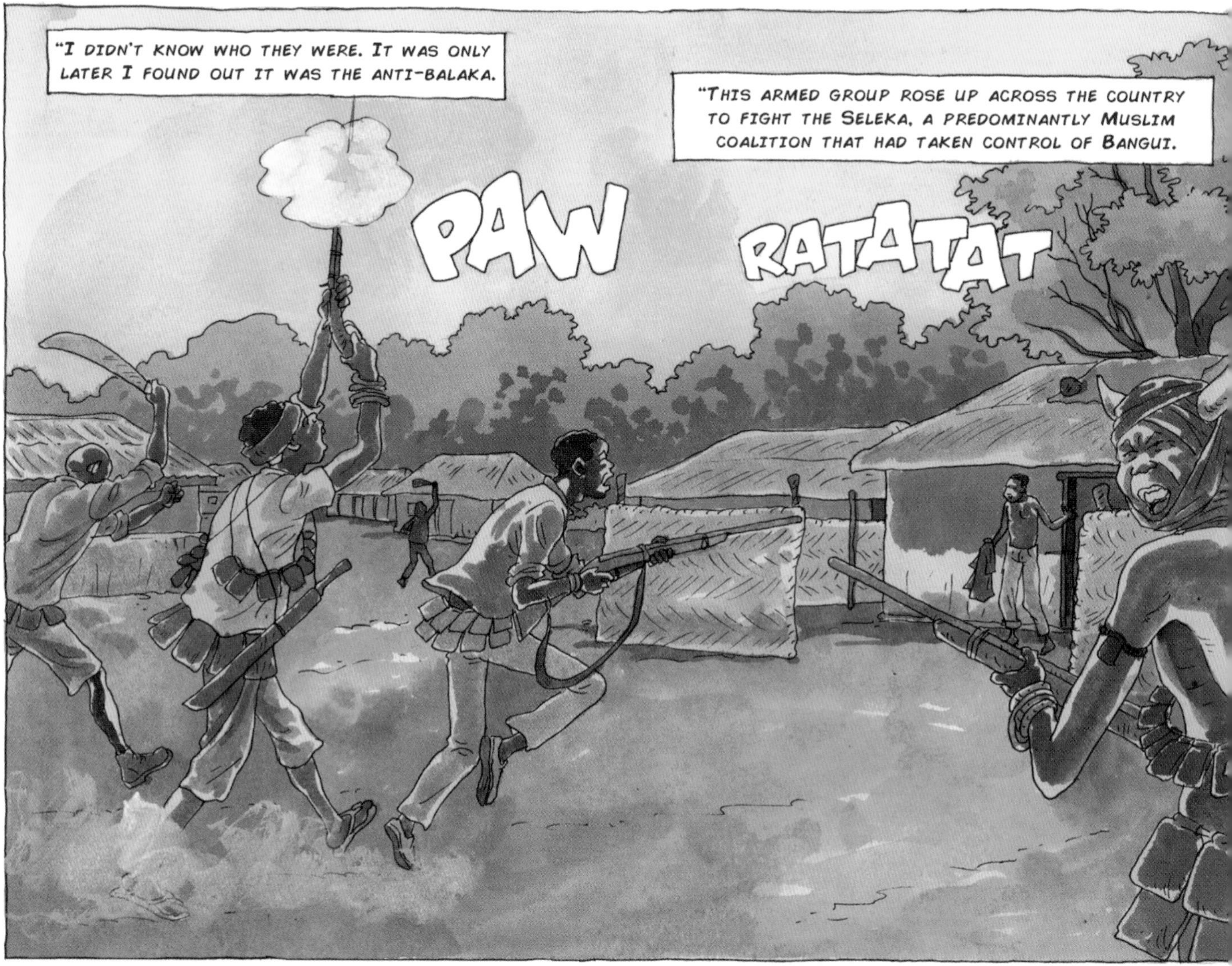
"I DIDN'T KNOW WHO THEY WERE. IT WAS ONLY LATER I FOUND OUT IT WAS THE ANTI-BALAKA.
"THIS ARMED GROUP ROSE UP ACROSS THE COUNTRY TO FIGHT THE SELEKA, A PREDOMINANTLY MUSLIM COALITION THAT HAD TAKEN CONTROL OF BANGUI.
PAW
RATATAT

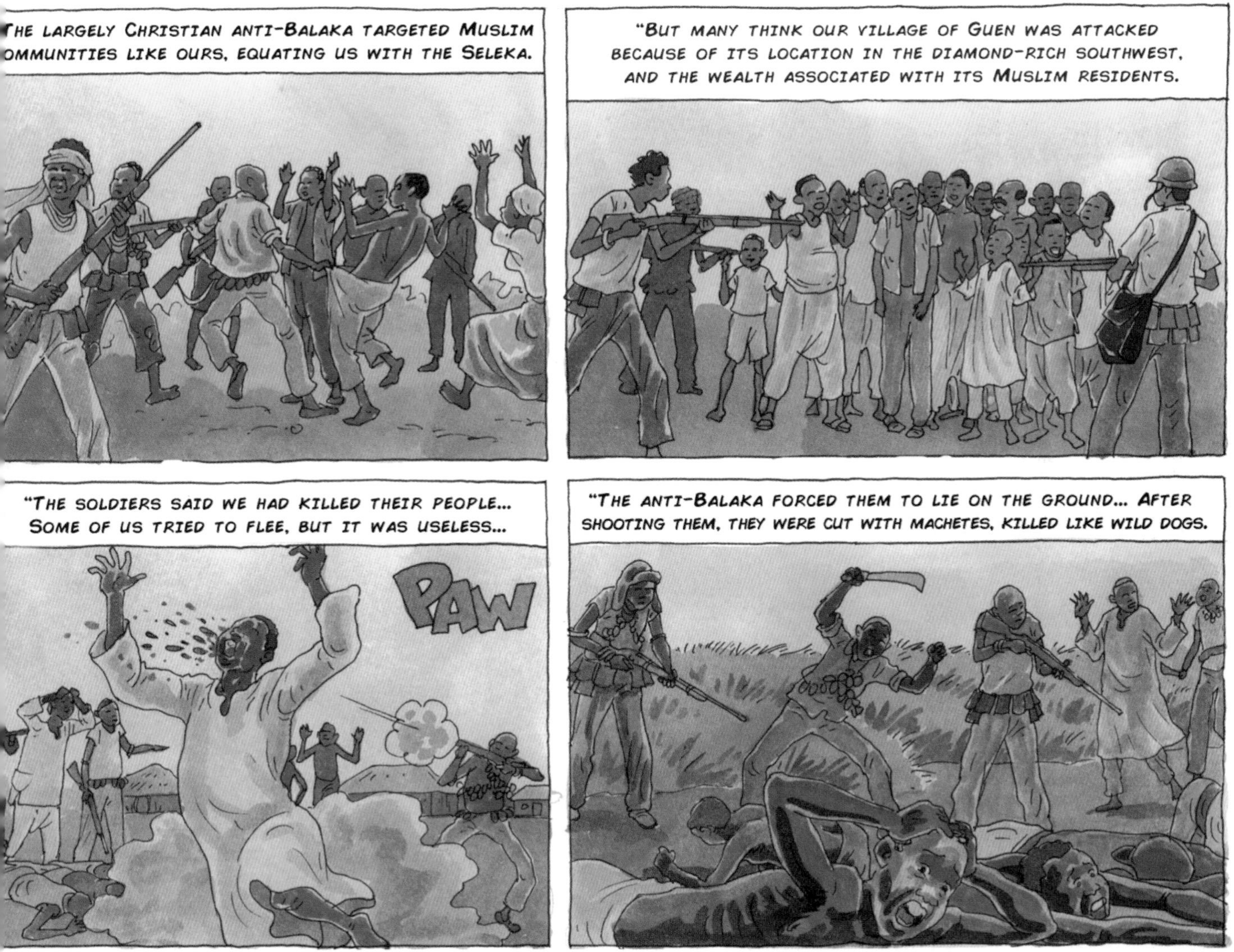
THE LARGELY CHRISTIAN ANTI-BALAKA TARGETED MUSLIM
OMMUNITIES LIKE OURS, EQUATING US WITH THE SELEKA.
"BUT MANY THINK OUR VILLAGE OF GUEN WAS ATTACKED BECAUSE OF ITS LOCATION IN THE DIAMOND-RICH SOUTHWEST, AND THE WEALTH ASSOCIATED WITH ITS MUSLIM RESIDENTS.
"THE SOLDIERS SAID WE HAD KILLED THEIR PEOPLE... SOME OF US TRIED TO FLEE, BUT IT WAS USELESS...
PAW
"THE ANTI-BALAKA FORCED THEM TO LIE ON THE GROUND... AFTER SHOOTING THEM, THEY WERE CUT WITH MACHETES, KILLED LIKE WILD DOGS.

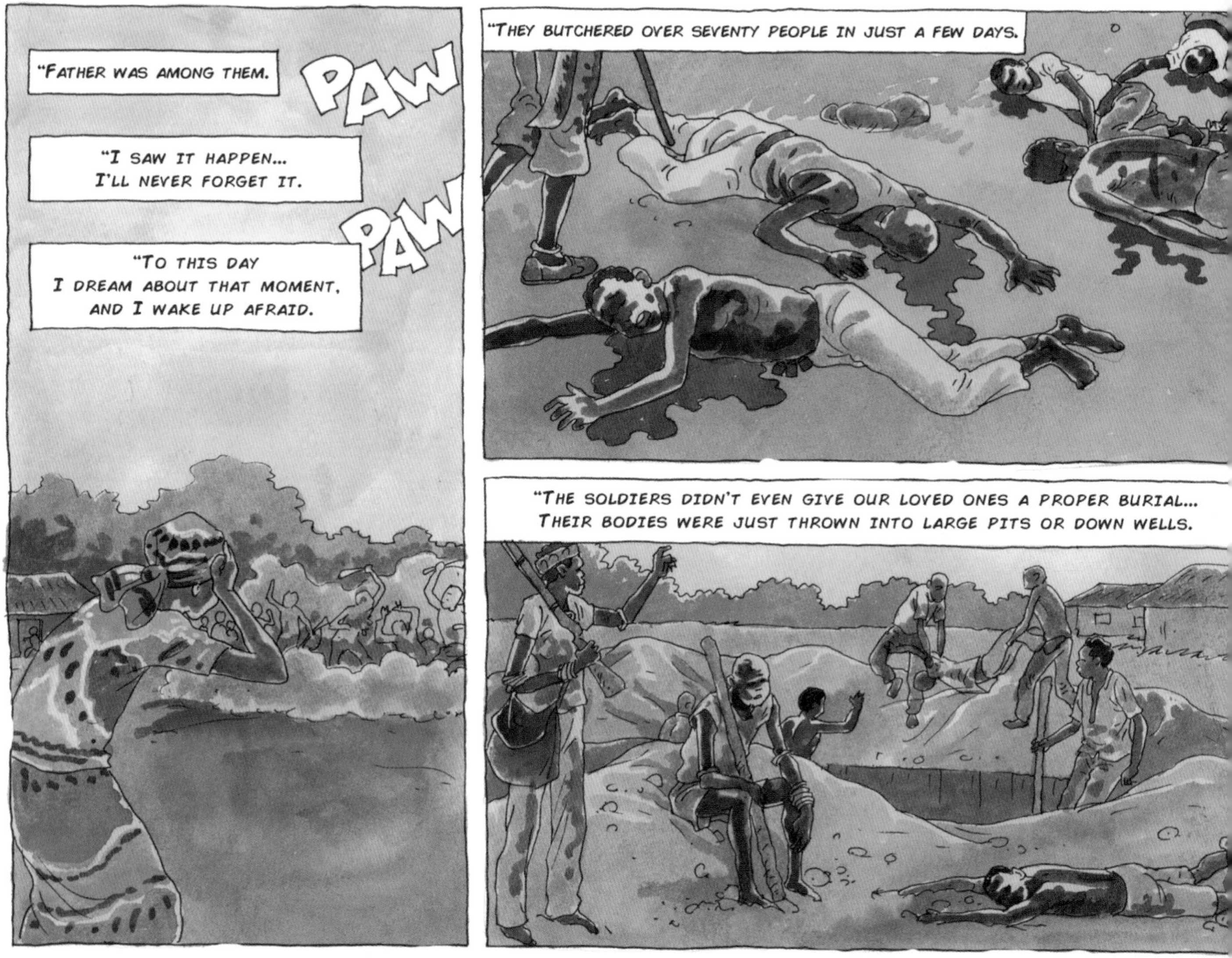
"FATHER WAS AMONG THEM.
PAW
"I SAW IT HAPPEN... I'LL NEVER FORGET IT.
PAW
"TO THIS DAY I DREAM ABOUT THAT MOMENT, AND I WAKE UP AFRAID.
"THEY BUTCHERED OVER SEVENTY PEOPLE IN JUST A FEW DAYS.
"THE SOLDIERS DIDN'T EVEN GIVE OUR LOVED ONES A PROPER BURIAL... THEIR BODIES WERE JUST THROWN INTO LARGE PITS OR DOWN WELLS.

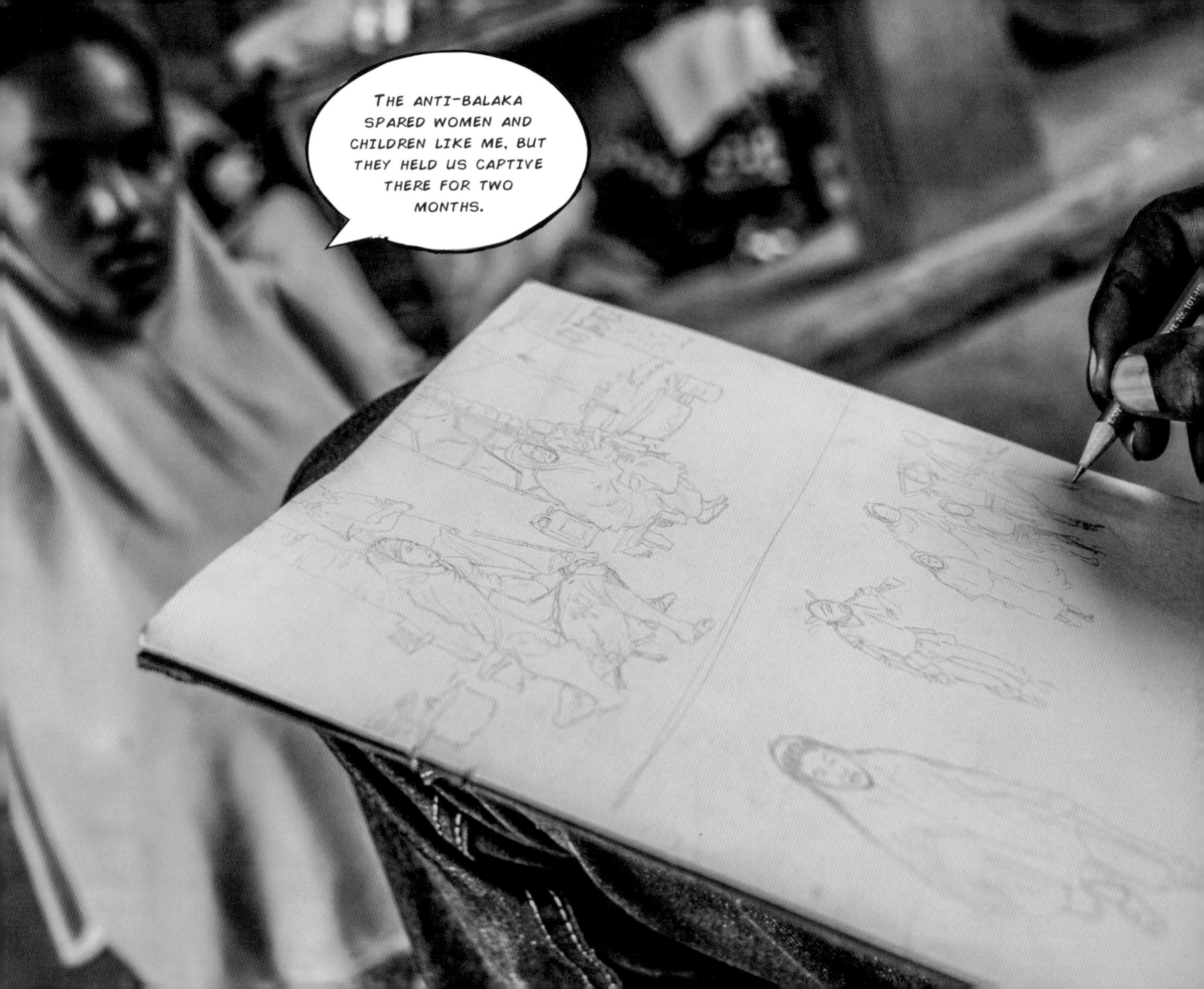
THE ANTI-BALAKA SPARED WOMEN AND CHILDREN LIKE ME, BUT THEY HELD US CAPTIVE THERE FOR TWO MONTHS.

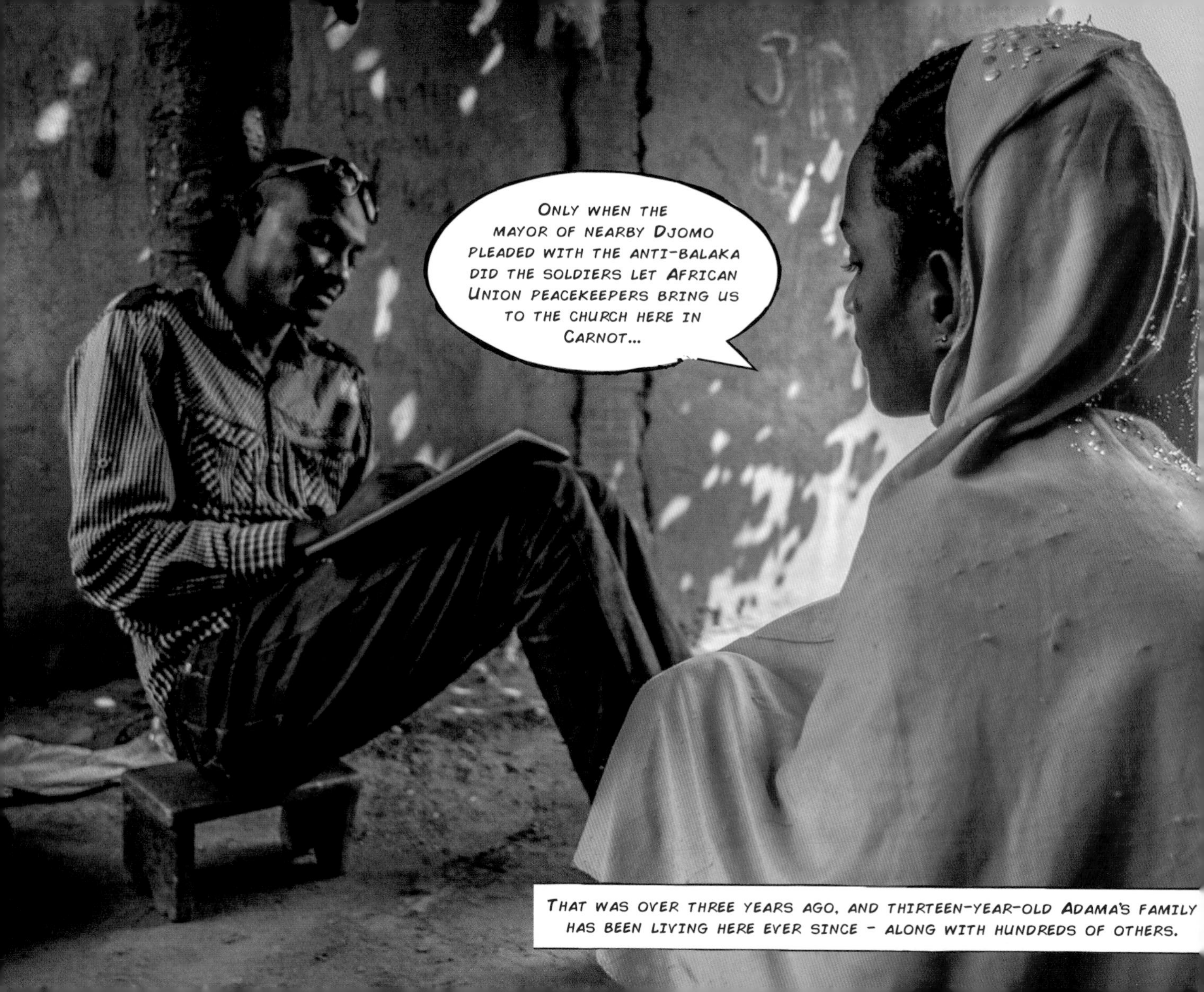
ONLY WHEN THE MAYOR OF NEARBY DJOMO PLEADED WITH THE ANTI-BALAKA DID THE SOLDIERS LET AFRICAN UNION PEACEKEEPERS BRING US TO THE CHURCH HERE IN CARNOT...
THAT WAS OVER THREE YEARS AGO, AND THIRTEEN-YEAR-OLD ADAMA'S FAMILY HAS BEEN LIVING HERE EVER SINCE - ALONG WITH HUNDREDS OF OTHERS.

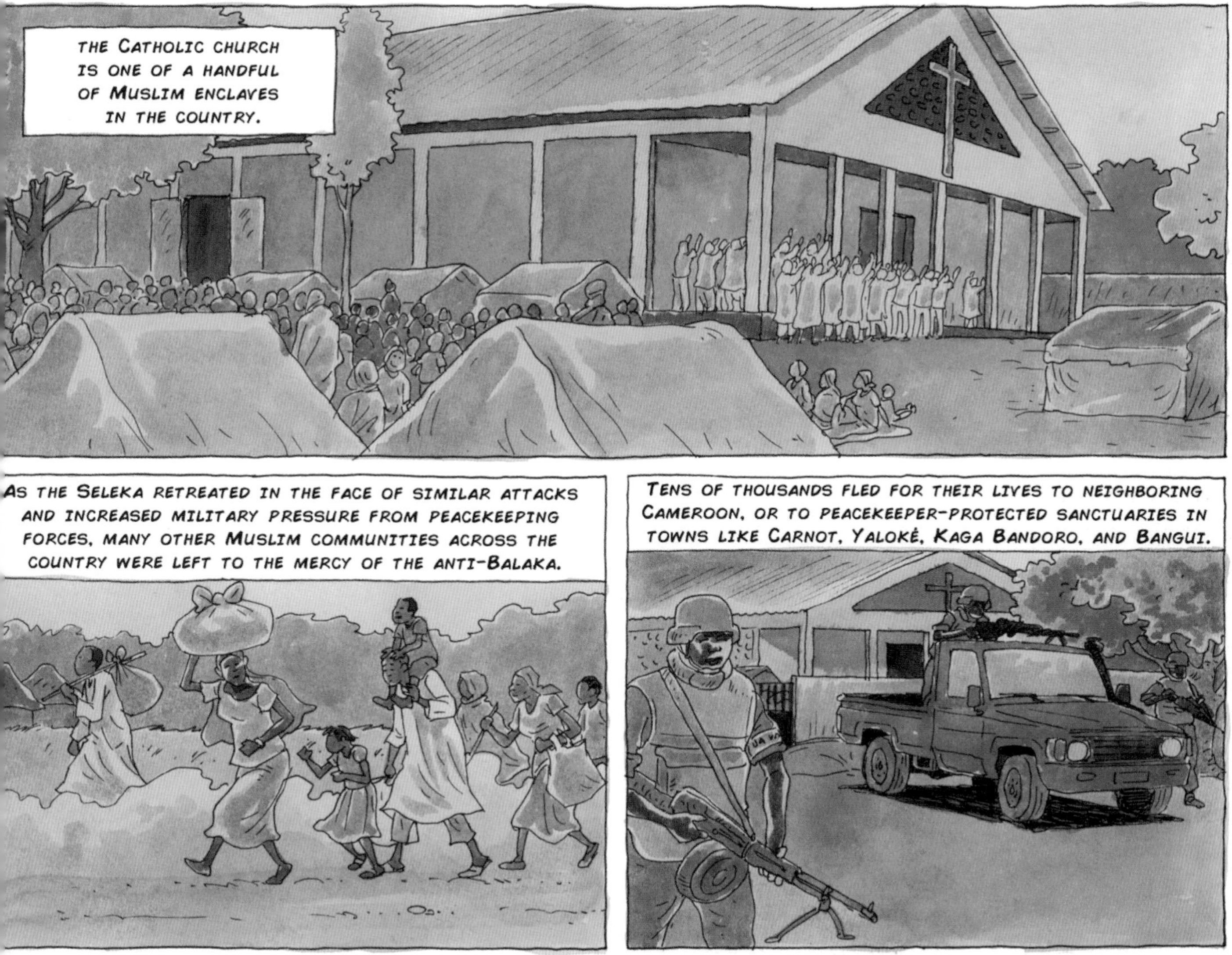
THE CATHOLIC CHURCH IS ONE OF A HANDFUL OF MUSLIM ENCLAVES IN THE COUNTRY.
AS THE SELEKA RETREATED IN THE FACE OF SIMILAR ATTACKS AND INCREASED MILITARY PRESSURE FROM PEACEKEEPING FORCES, MANY OTHER MUSLIM COMMUNITIES ACROSS THE COUNTRY WERE LEFT TO THE MERCY OF THE ANTI-BALAKA.
TENS OF THOUSANDS FLED FOR THEIR LIVES TO NEIGHBORING CAMEROON, OR TO PEACEKEEPER-PROTECTED SANCTUARIES IN TOWNS LIKE CARNOT, YALOKÉ, KAGA BANDORO, AND BANGUI.

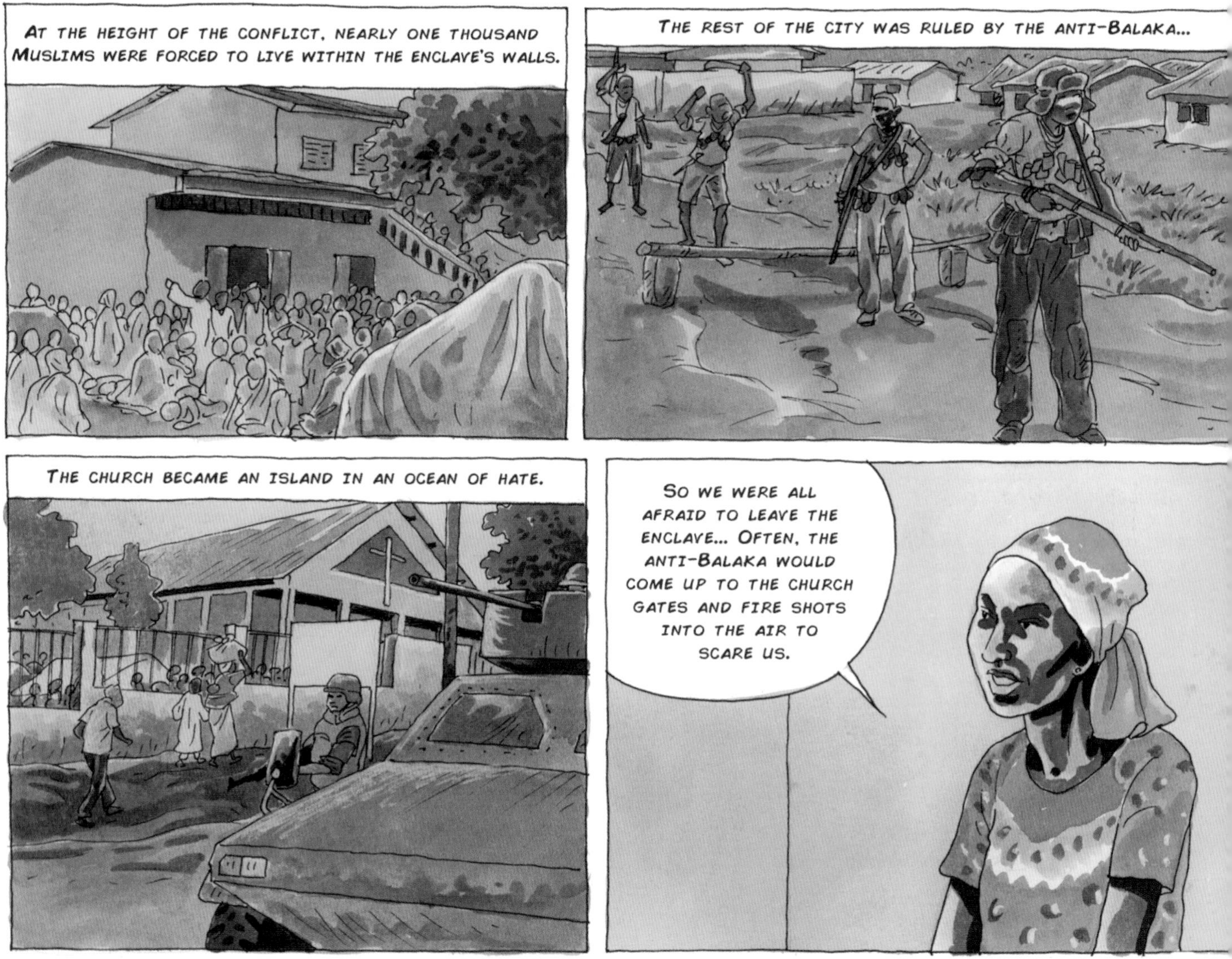
AT THE HEIGHT OF THE CONFLICT, NEARLY ONE THOUSAND MUSLIMS WERE FORCED TO LIVE WITHIN THE ENCLAVE'S WALLS.
THE REST OF THE CITY WAS RULED BY THE ANTI-BALAKA...
THE CHURCH BECAME AN ISLAND IN AN OCEAN OF HATE.
SO WE WERE ALL AFRAID TO LEAVE THE ENCLAVE... OFTEN, THE ANTI-BALAKA WOULD COME UP TO THE CHURCH GATES AND FIRE SHOTS INTO THE AIR TO SCARE US.

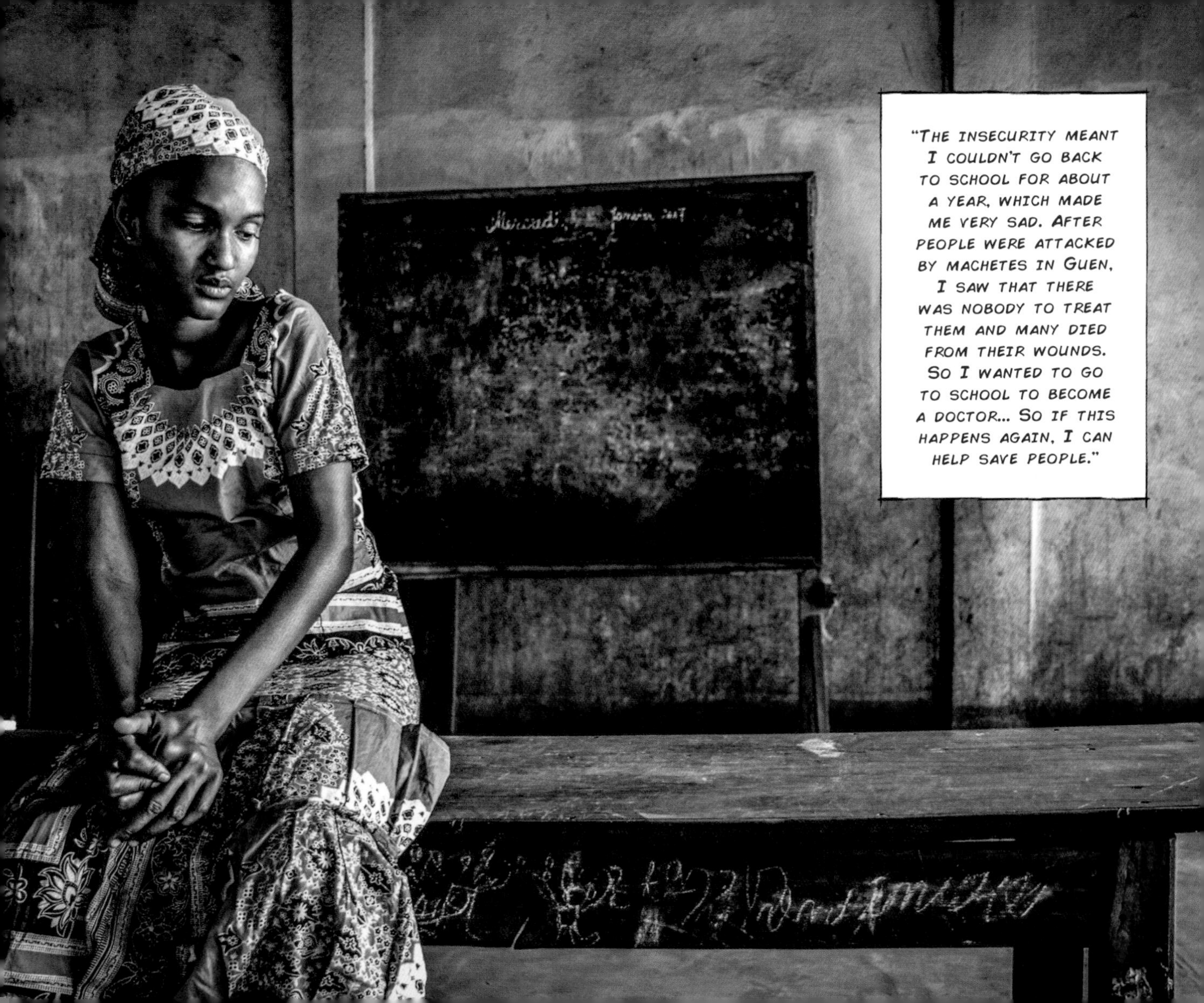
"THE INSECURITY MEANT I COULDN'T GO BACK TO SCHOOL FOR ABOUT A YEAR, WHICH MADE ME VERY SAD. AFTER PEOPLE WERE ATTACKED BY MACHETES IN GUEN, I SAW THAT THERE WAS NOBODY TO TREAT THEM AND MANY DIED FROM THEIR WOUNDS. SO I WANTED TO GO TO SCHOOL TO BECOME A DOCTOR... SO IF THIS HAPPENS AGAIN, I CAN HELP SAVE PEOPLE."

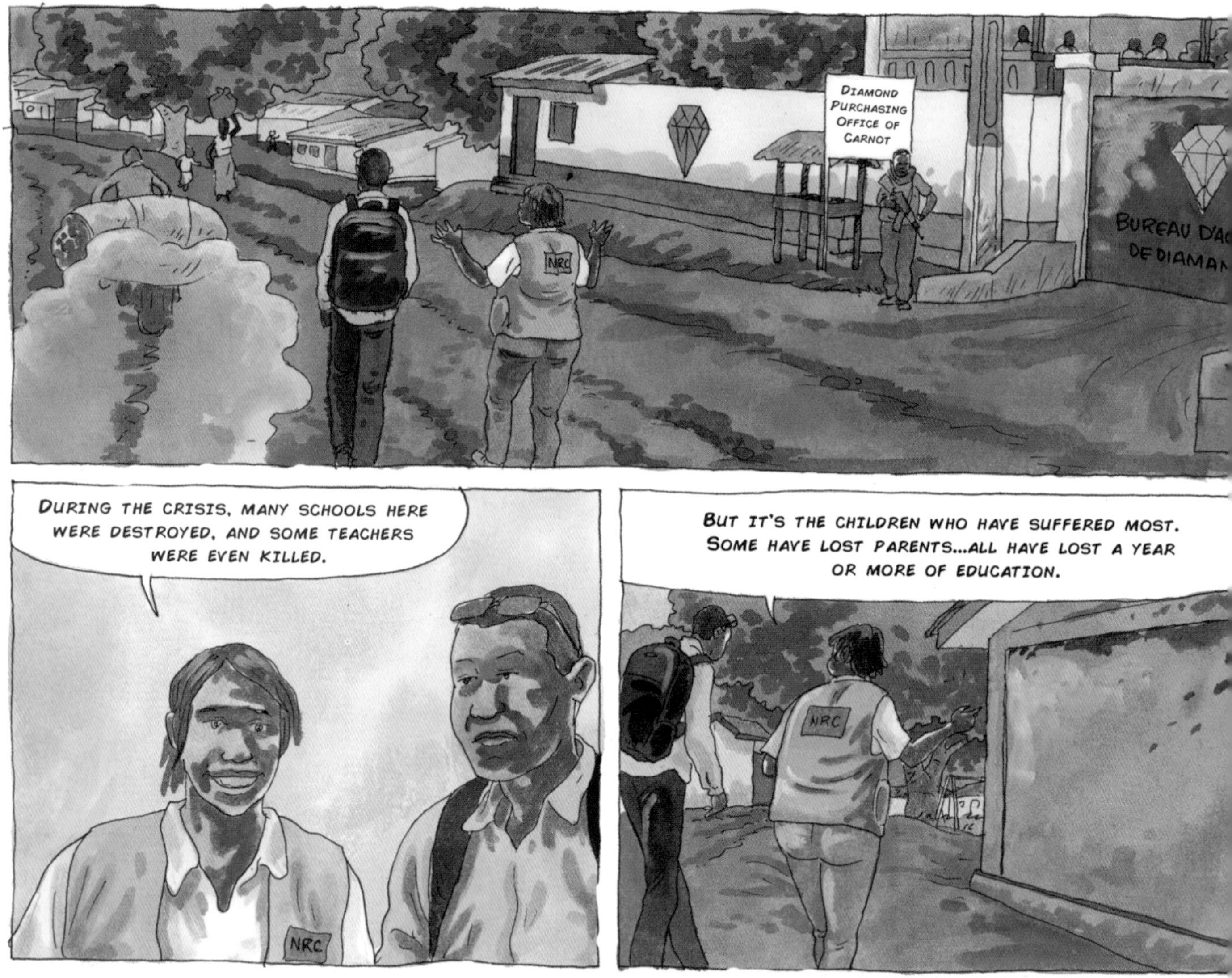
DIAMOND PURCHASING OFFICE OF CARNOT
DURING THE CRISIS, MANY SCHOOLS HERE WERE DESTROYED, AND SOME TEACHERS WERE EVEN KILLED.
BUT IT'S THE CHILDREN WHO HAVE SUFFERED MOST. SOME HAVE LOST PARENTS...ALL HAVE LOST A YEAR OR MORE OF EDUCATION.

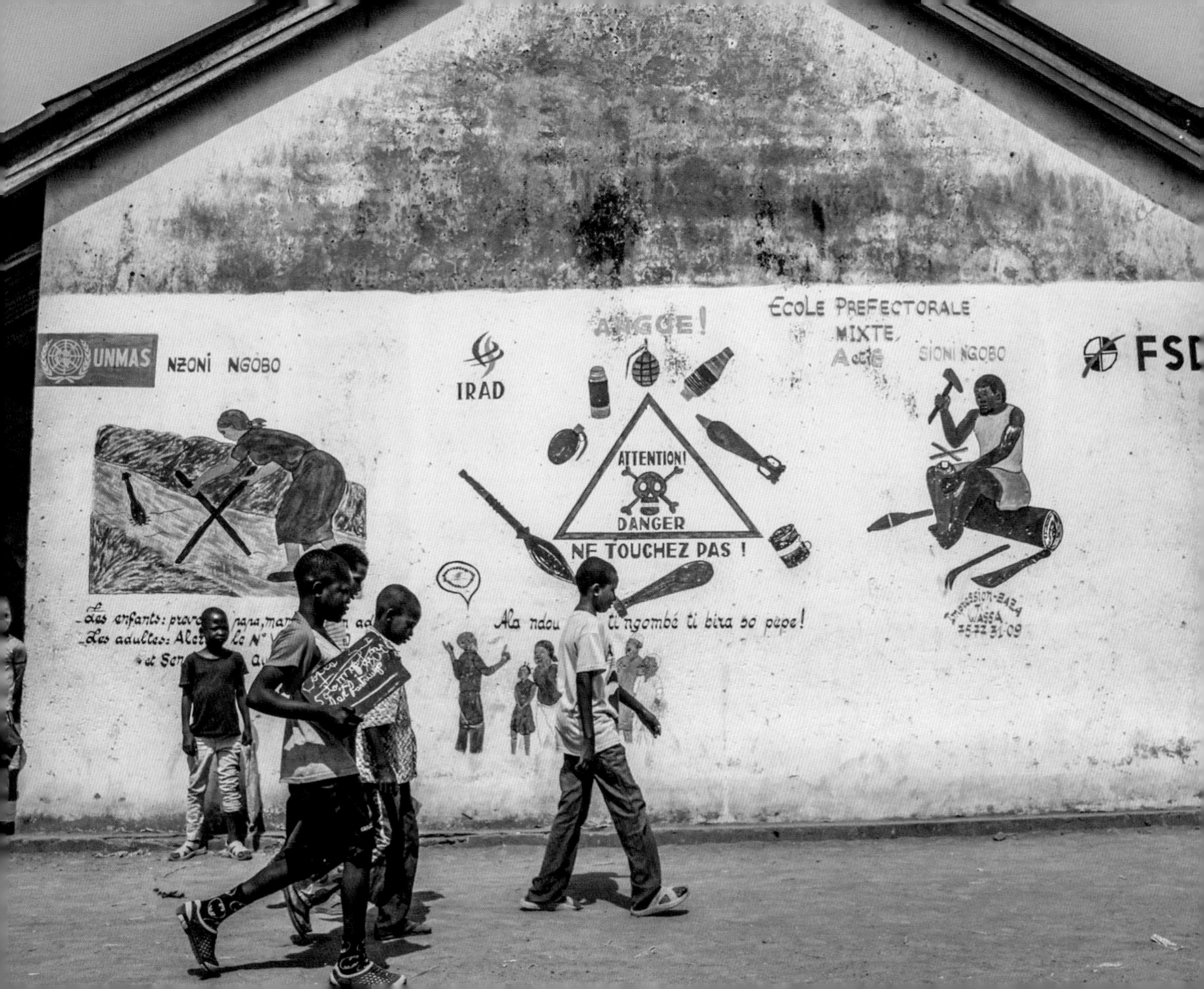
UNMAS
NZONI NGOBO
IRAD
ECOLE PREFECTORALE
MIXTE
SIONI NGOBO
FSD
ATTENTION!
DANGER
NE TOUCHEZ PAS !

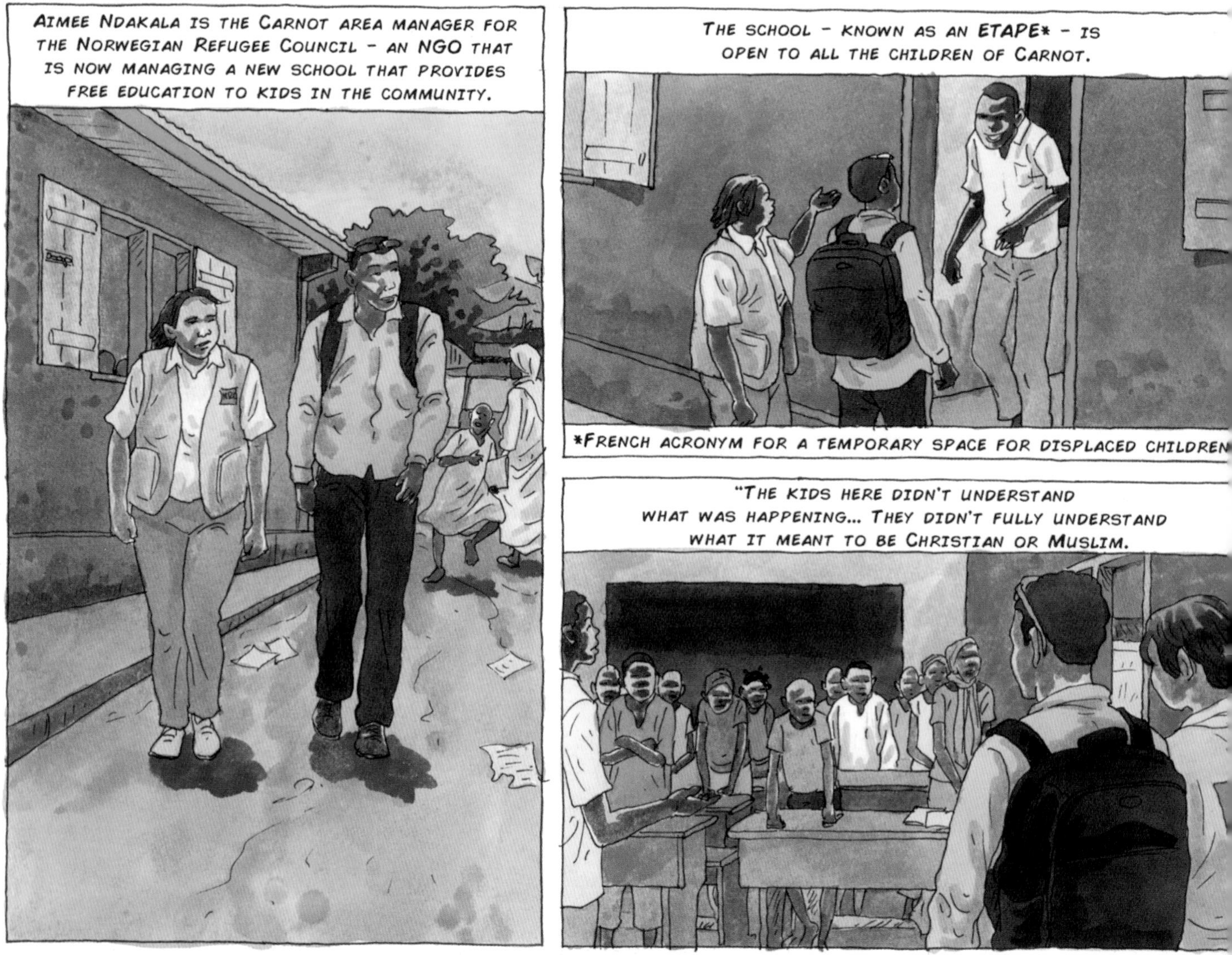
AIMEE NDAKALA IS THE CARNOT AREA MANAGER FOR THE NORWEGIAN REFUGEE COUNCIL - AN NGO THAT IS NOW MANAGING A NEW SCHOOL THAT PROVIDES FREE EDUCATION TO KIDS IN THE COMMUNITY.
THE SCHOOL - KNOWN AS AN ETAPE* - IS OPEN TO ALL THE CHILDREN OF CARNOT.
*FRENCH ACRONYM FOR A TEMPORARY SPACE FOR DISPLACED CHILDREN
“THE KIDS HERE DIDN'T UNDERSTAND WHAT WAS HAPPENING... THEY DIDN'T FULLY UNDERSTAND WHAT IT MEANT TO BE CHRISTIAN OR MUSLIM.

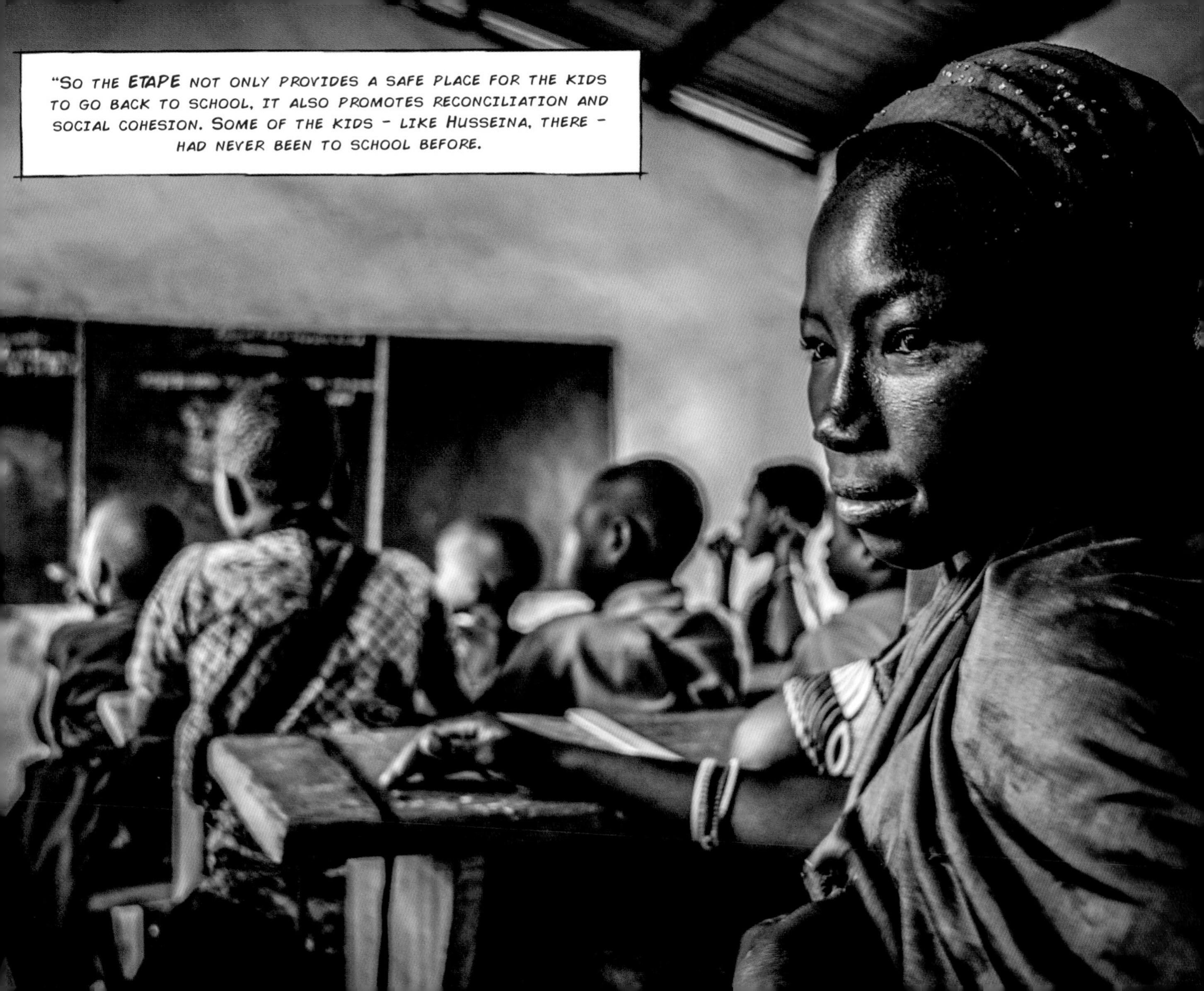
"SO THE ETAPE NOT ONLY PROVIDES A SAFE PLACE FOR THE KIDS TO GO BACK TO SCHOOL, IT ALSO PROMOTES RECONCILIATION AND SOCIAL COHESION. SOME OF THE KIDS - LIKE HUSSEINA, THERE - HAD NEVER BEEN TO SCHOOL BEFORE.

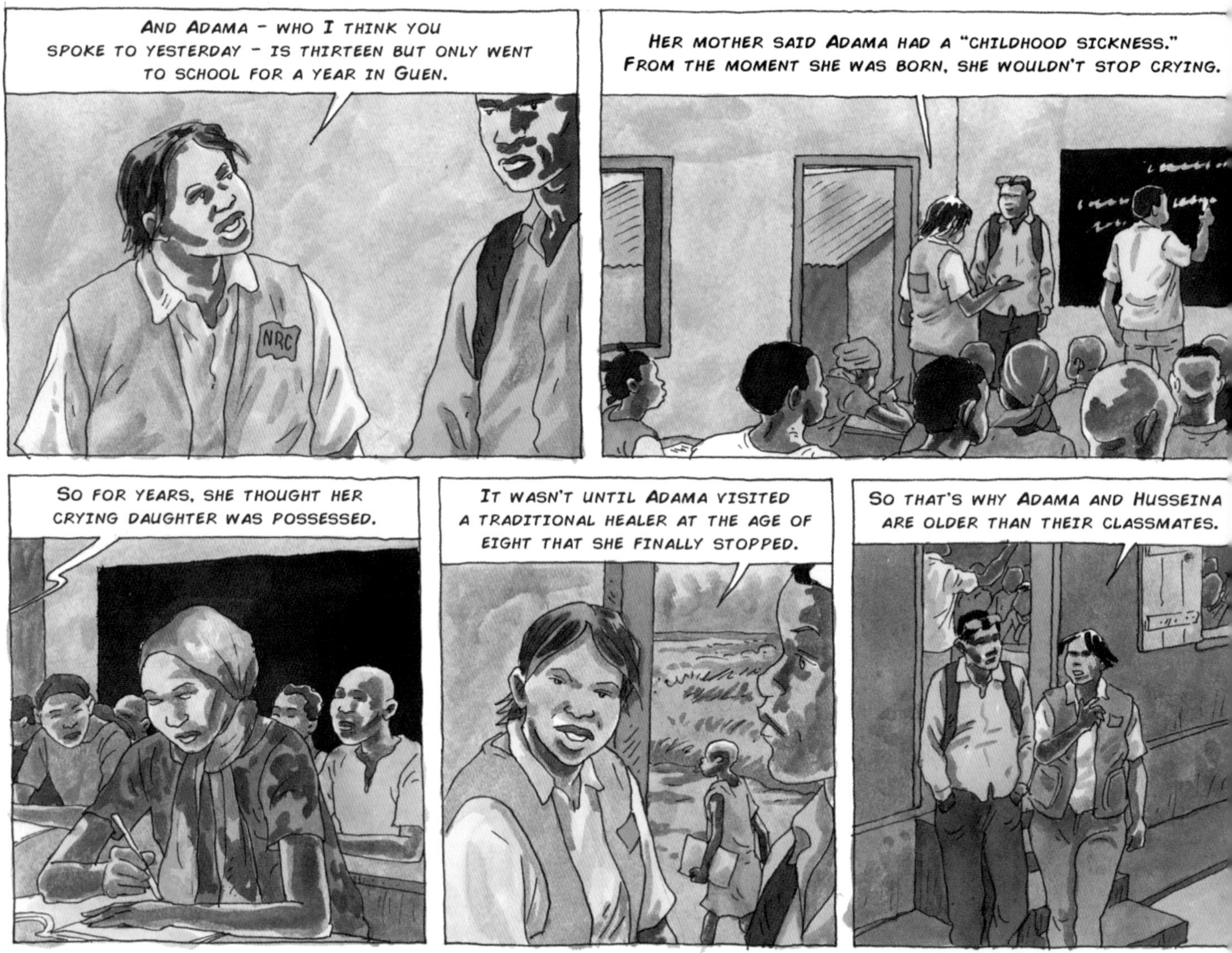

AND ADAMA - WHO I THINK YOU SPOKE TO YESTERDAY - IS THIRTEEN BUT ONLY WENT TO SCHOOL FOR A YEAR IN GUEN.
HER MOTHER SAID ADAMA HAD A "CHILDHOOD SICKNESS." FROM THE MOMENT SHE WAS BORN, SHE WOULDN'T STOP CRYING.
SO FOR YEARS, SHE THOUGHT HER CRYING DAUGHTER WAS POSSESSED.
IT WASN'T UNTIL ADAMA VISITED A TRADITIONAL HEALER AT THE AGE OF EIGHT THAT SHE FINALLY STOPPED.
SO THAT'S WHY ADAMA AND HUSSEINA ARE OLDER THAN THEIR CLASSMATES.
NRC

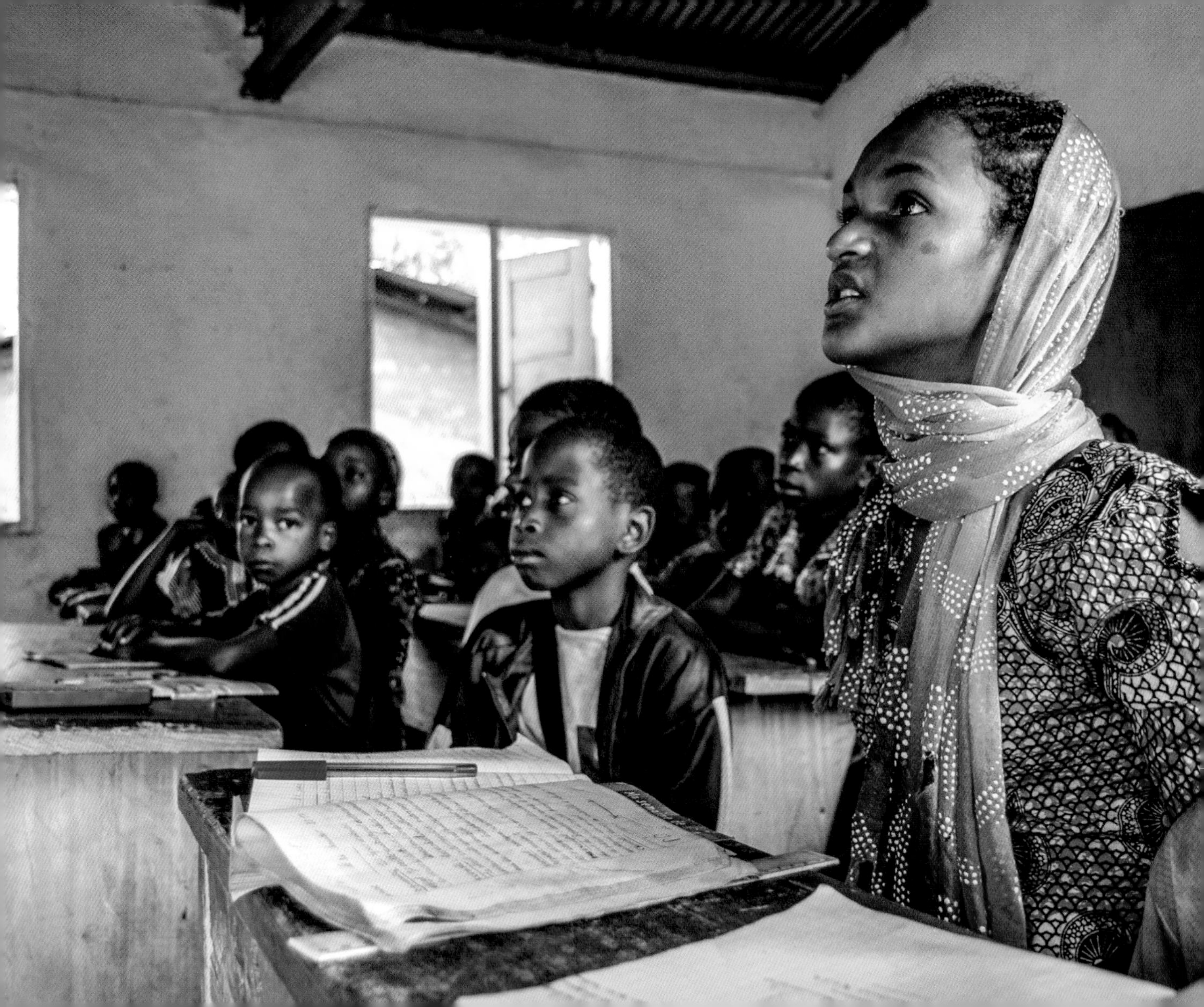

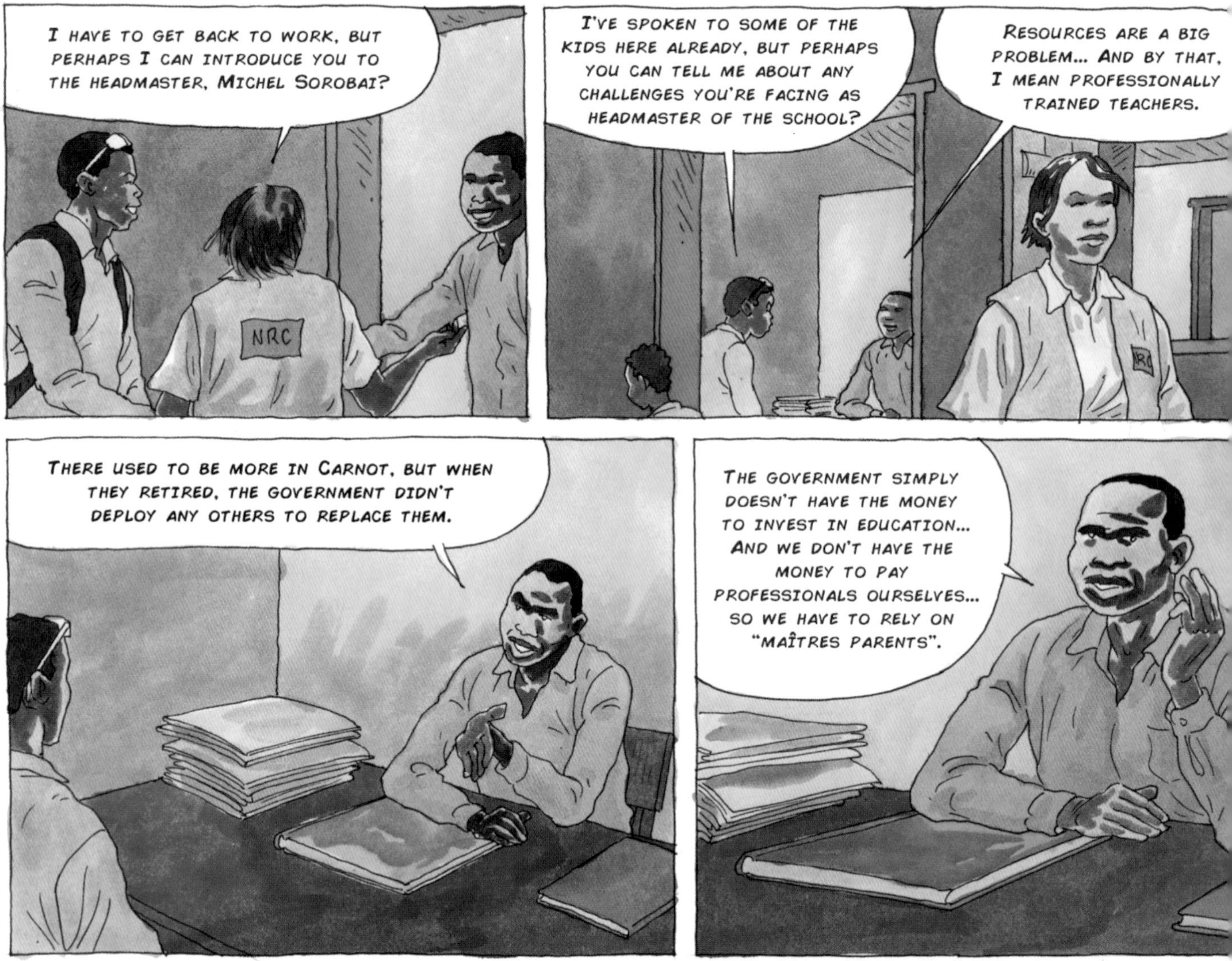
I HAVE TO GET BACK TO WORK, BUT PERHAPS I CAN INTRODUCE YOU TO THE HEADMASTER, MICHEL SOROBAI?
I'VE SPOKEN TO SOME OF THE KIDS HERE ALREADY, BUT PERHAPS YOU CAN TELL ME ABOUT ANY CHALLENGES YOU'RE FACING AS HEADMASTER OF THE SCHOOL?
RESOURCES ARE A BIG PROBLEM... AND BY THAT, I MEAN PROFESSIONALLY TRAINED TEACHERS.
THERE USED TO BE MORE IN CARNOT, BUT WHEN THEY RETIRED, THE GOVERNMENT DIDN'T DEPLOY ANY OTHERS TO REPLACE THEM.
THE GOVERNMENT SIMPLY DOESN'T HAVE THE MONEY TO INVEST IN EDUCATION... AND WE DON'T HAVE THE MONEY TO PAY PROFESSIONALS OURSELVES... SO WE HAVE TO RELY ON "MAÎTRES PARENTS".

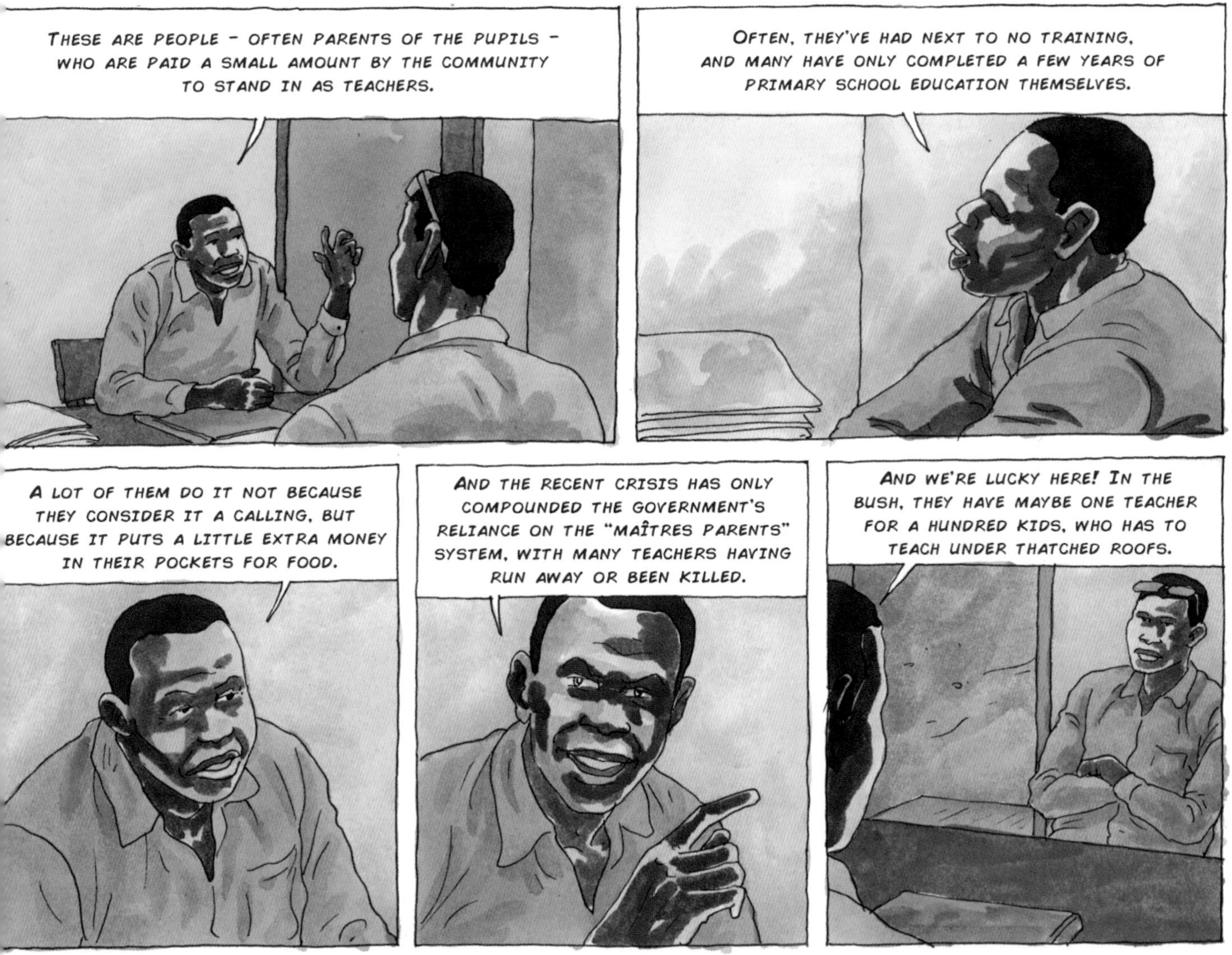

THESE ARE PEOPLE - OFTEN PARENTS OF THE PUPILS - WHO ARE PAID A SMALL AMOUNT BY THE COMMUNITY TO STAND IN AS TEACHERS.
OFTEN, THEY'VE HAD NEXT TO NO TRAINING, AND MANY HAVE ONLY COMPLETED A FEW YEARS OF PRIMARY SCHOOL EDUCATION THEMSELVES.
A LOT OF THEM DO IT NOT BECAUSE THEY CONSIDER IT A CALLING, BUT BECAUSE IT PUTS A LITTLE EXTRA MONEY IN THEIR POCKETS FOR FOOD.
AND THE RECENT CRISIS HAS ONLY COMPOUNDED THE GOVERNMENT'S RELIANCE ON THE "MAÎTRES PARENTS" SYSTEM, WITH MANY TEACHERS HAVING RUN AWAY OR BEEN KILLED.
AND WE'RE LUCKY HERE! IN THE BUSH, THEY HAVE MAYBE ONE TEACHER FOR A HUNDRED KIDS, WHO HAS TO TEACH UNDER THATCHED ROOFS.

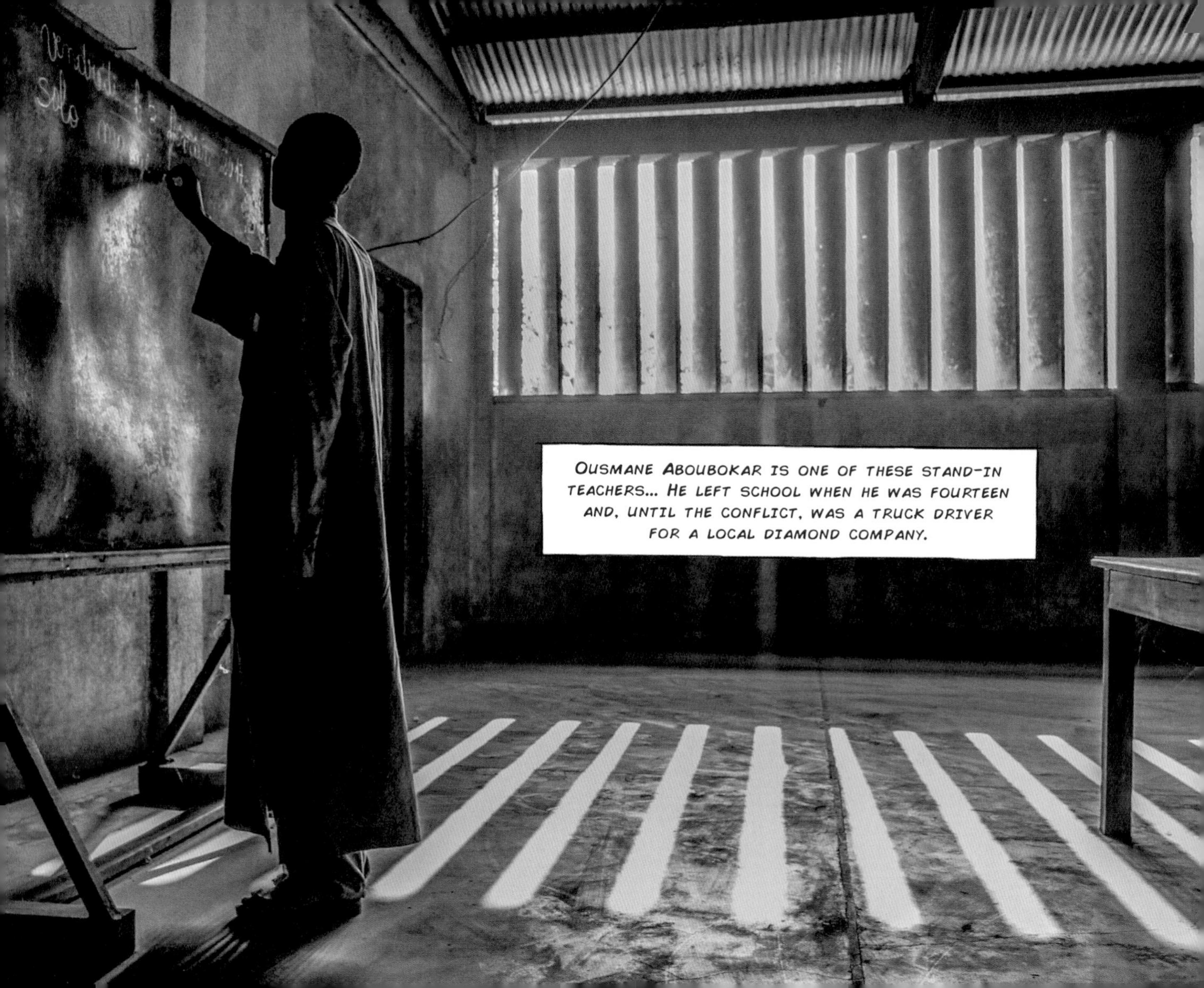
OUSMANE ABOUBOKAR IS ONE OF THESE STAND-IN TEACHERS... HE LEFT SCHOOL WHEN HE WAS FOURTEEN AND, UNTIL THE CONFLICT, WAS A TRUCK DRIVER FOR A LOCAL DIAMOND COMPANY.

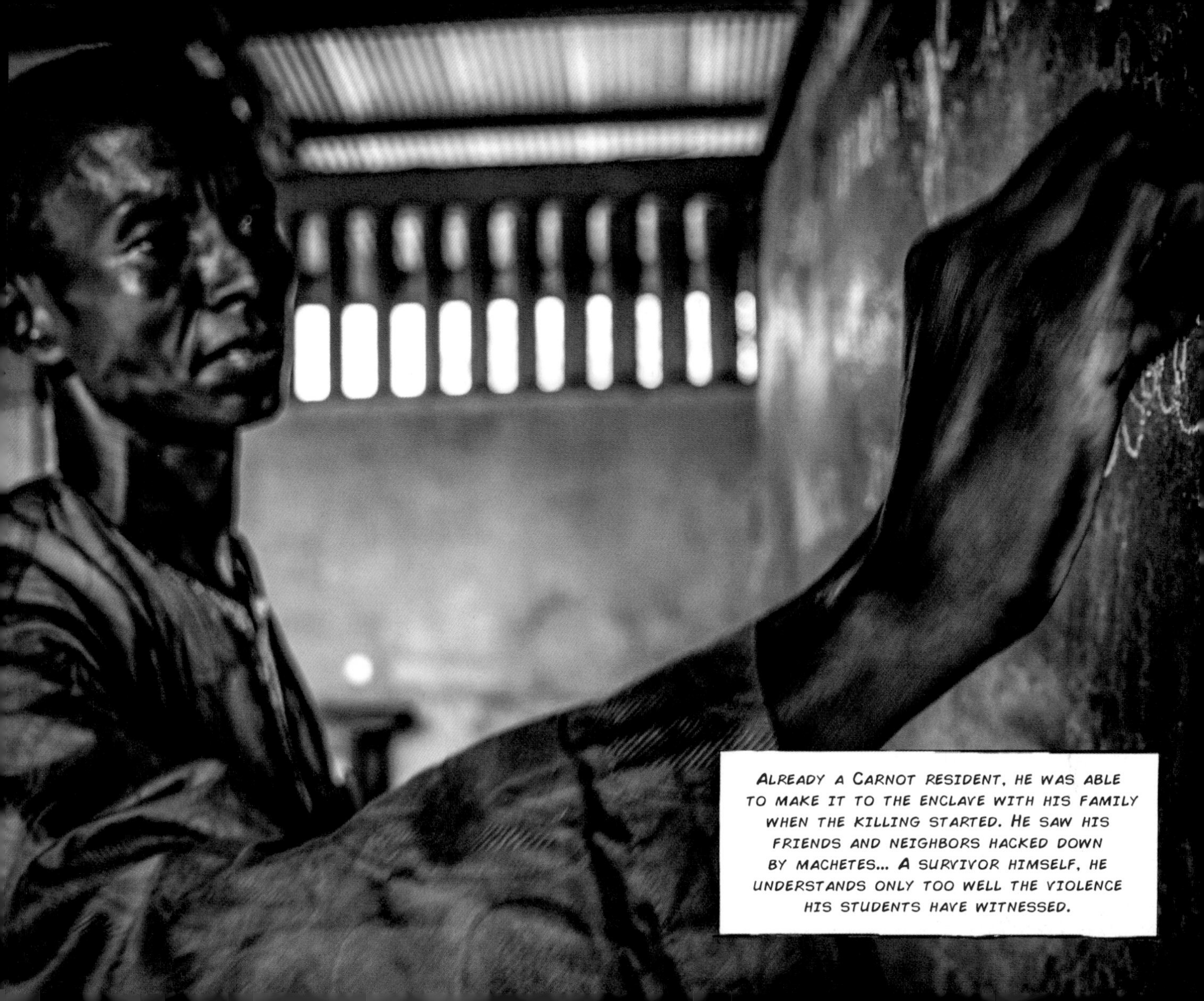
ALREADY A CARNOT RESIDENT, HE WAS ABLE TO MAKE IT TO THE ENCLAVE WITH HIS FAMILY WHEN THE KILLING STARTED. HE SAW HIS FRIENDS AND NEIGHBORS HACKED DOWN BY MACHETES... A SURVIVOR HIMSELF, HE UNDERSTANDS ONLY TOO WELL THE VIOLENCE HIS STUDENTS HAVE WITNESSED.

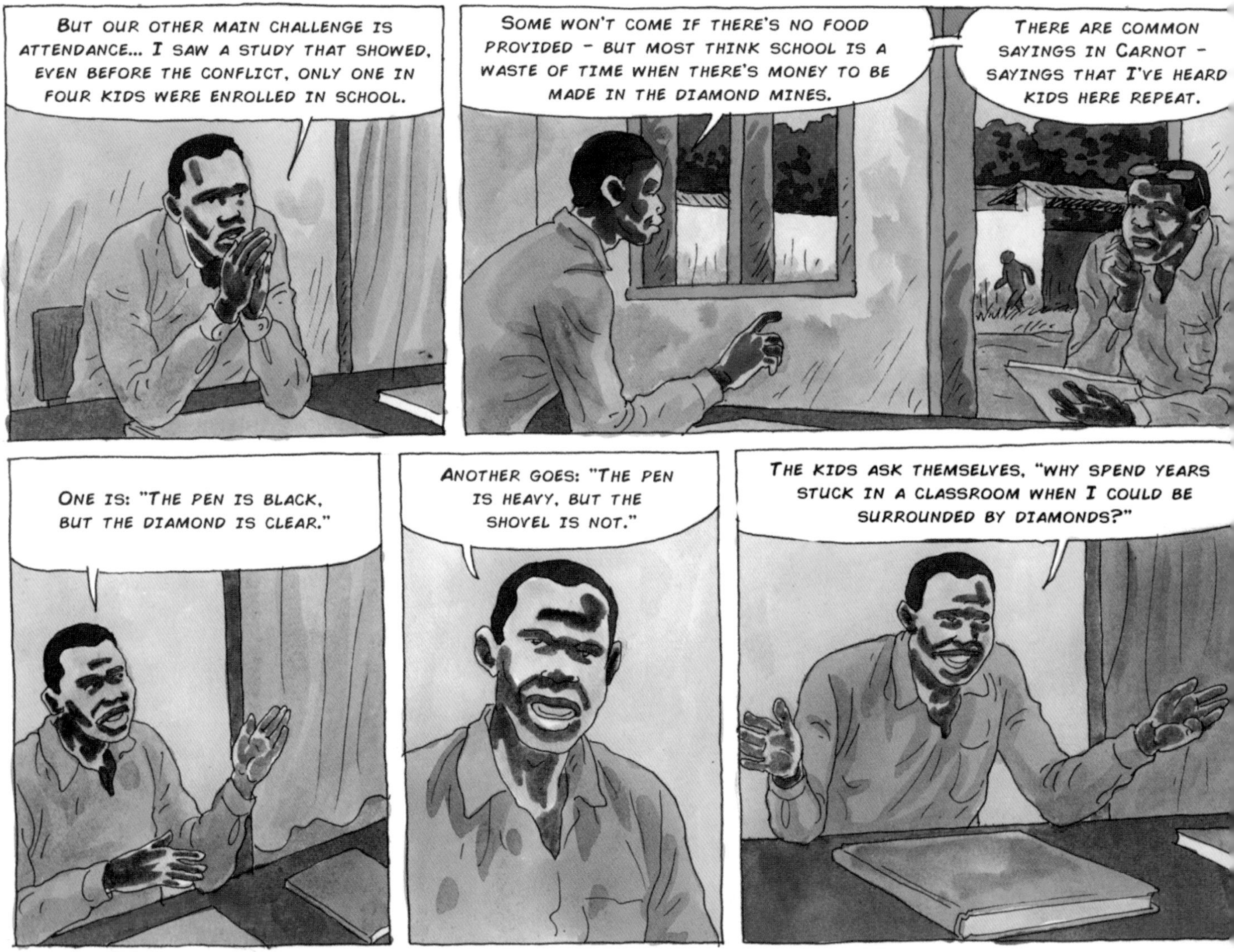
BUT OUR OTHER MAIN CHALLENGE IS ATTENDANCE... I SAW A STUDY THAT SHOWED, EVEN BEFORE THE CONFLICT, ONLY ONE IN FOUR KIDS WERE ENROLLED IN SCHOOL.
SOME WON'T COME IF THERE'S NO FOOD PROVIDED - BUT MOST THINK SCHOOL IS A WASTE OF TIME WHEN THERE'S MONEY TO BE MADE IN THE DIAMOND MINES.
THERE ARE COMMON SAYINGS IN CARNOT - SAYINGS THAT I'VE HEARD KIDS HERE REPEAT.
ONE IS: "THE PEN IS BLACK, BUT THE DIAMOND IS CLEAR."
ANOTHER GOES: "THE PEN IS HEAVY, BUT THE SHOVEL IS NOT."
THE KIDS ASK THEMSELVES, "WHY SPEND YEARS STUCK IN A CLASSROOM WHEN I COULD BE SURROUNDED BY DIAMONDS?"

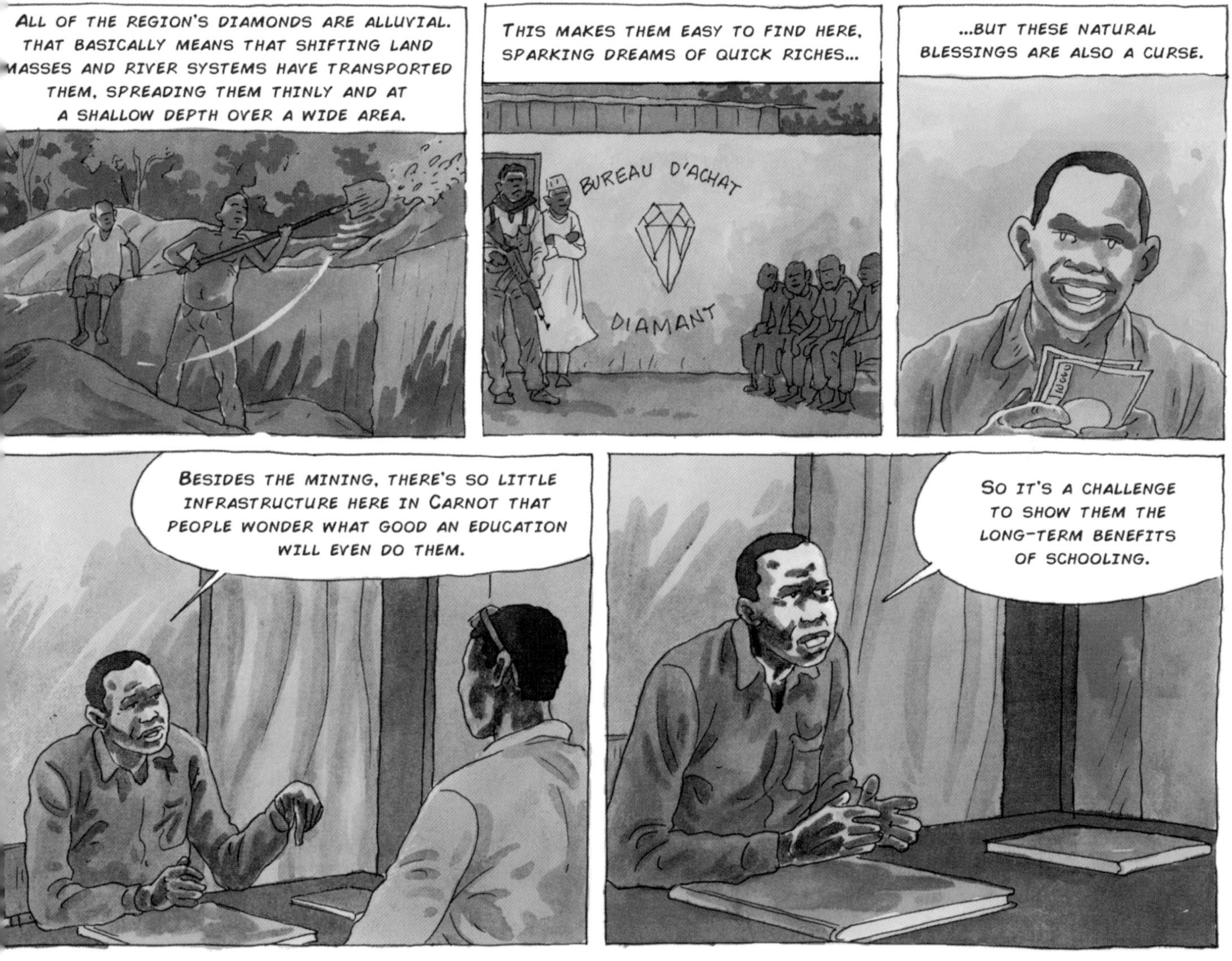
ALL OF THE REGION'S DIAMONDS ARE ALLUVIAL. THAT BASICALLY MEANS THAT SHIFTING LAND MASSES AND RIVER SYSTEMS HAVE TRANSPORTED THEM, SPREADING THEM THINLY AND AT A SHALLOW DEPTH OVER A WIDE AREA.
THIS MAKES THEM EASY TO FIND HERE, SPARKING DREAMS OF QUICK RICHES...
BUREAU D'ACHAT
DIAMANT
...BUT THESE NATURAL BLESSINGS ARE ALSO A CURSE.
BESIDES THE MINING, THERE'S SO LITTLE INFRASTRUCTURE HERE IN CARNOT THAT PEOPLE WONDER WHAT GOOD AN EDUCATION WILL EVEN DO THEM.
SO IT'S A CHALLENGE TO SHOW THEM THE LONG-TERM BENEFITS OF SCHOOLING.

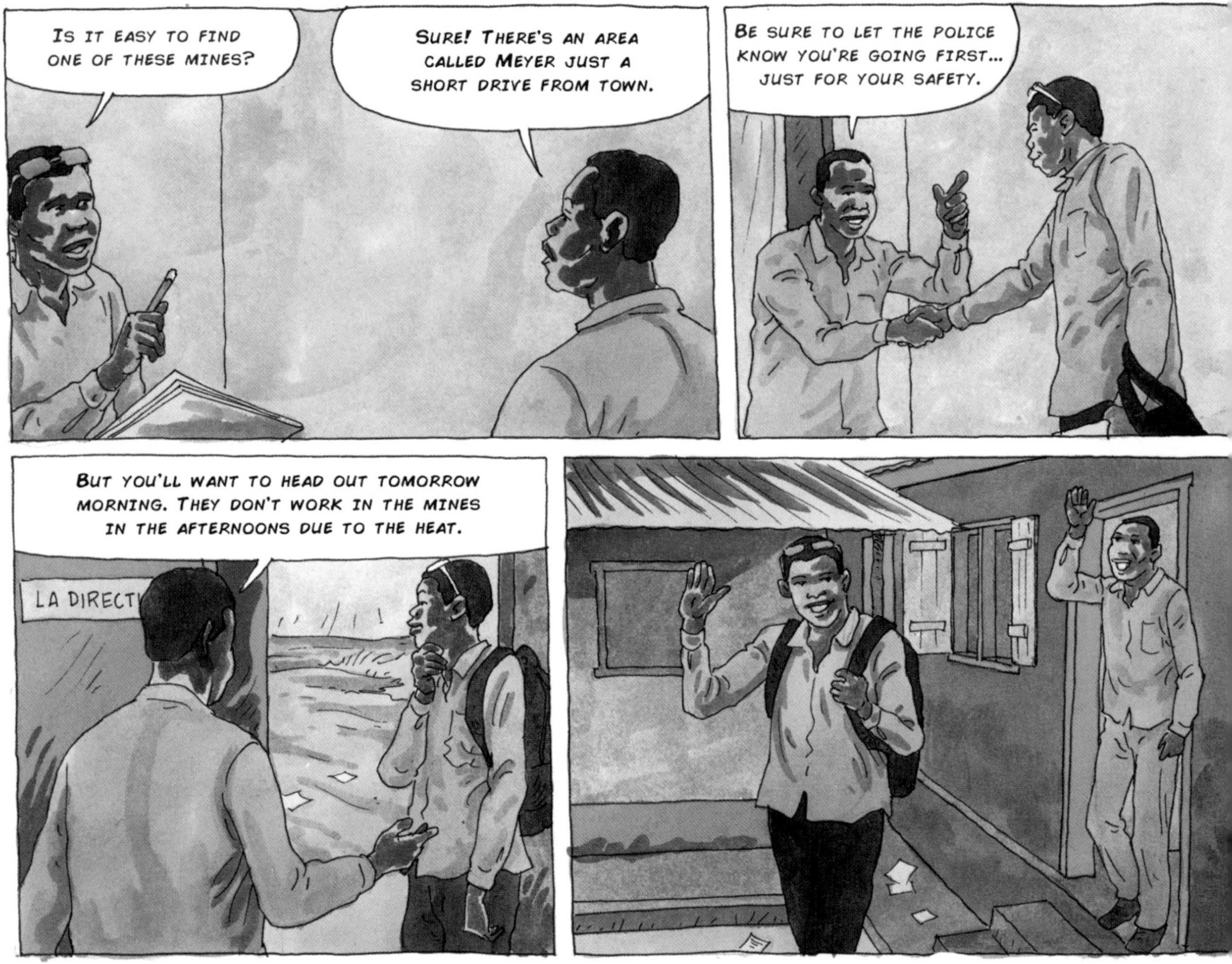
IS IT EASY TO FIND ONE OF THESE MINES?
SURE! THERE'S AN AREA CALLED MEYER JUST A SHORT DRIVE FROM TOWN.
BE SURE TO LET THE POLICE KNOW YOU'RE GOING FIRST... JUST FOR YOUR SAFETY.
BUT YOU'LL WANT TO HEAD OUT TOMORROW MORNING. THEY DON'T WORK IN THE MINES IN THE AFTERNOONS DUE TO THE HEAT.
LA DIRECT

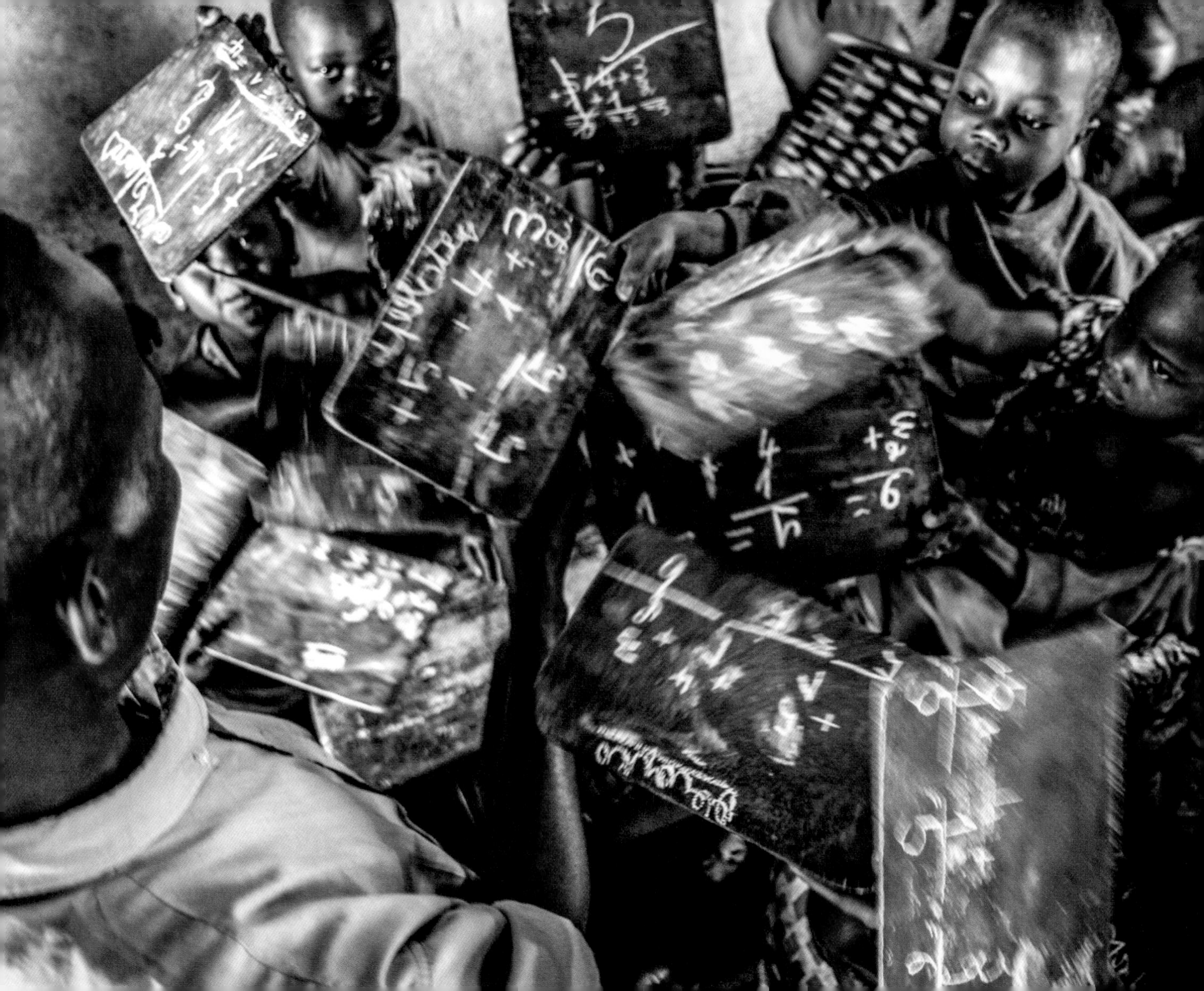

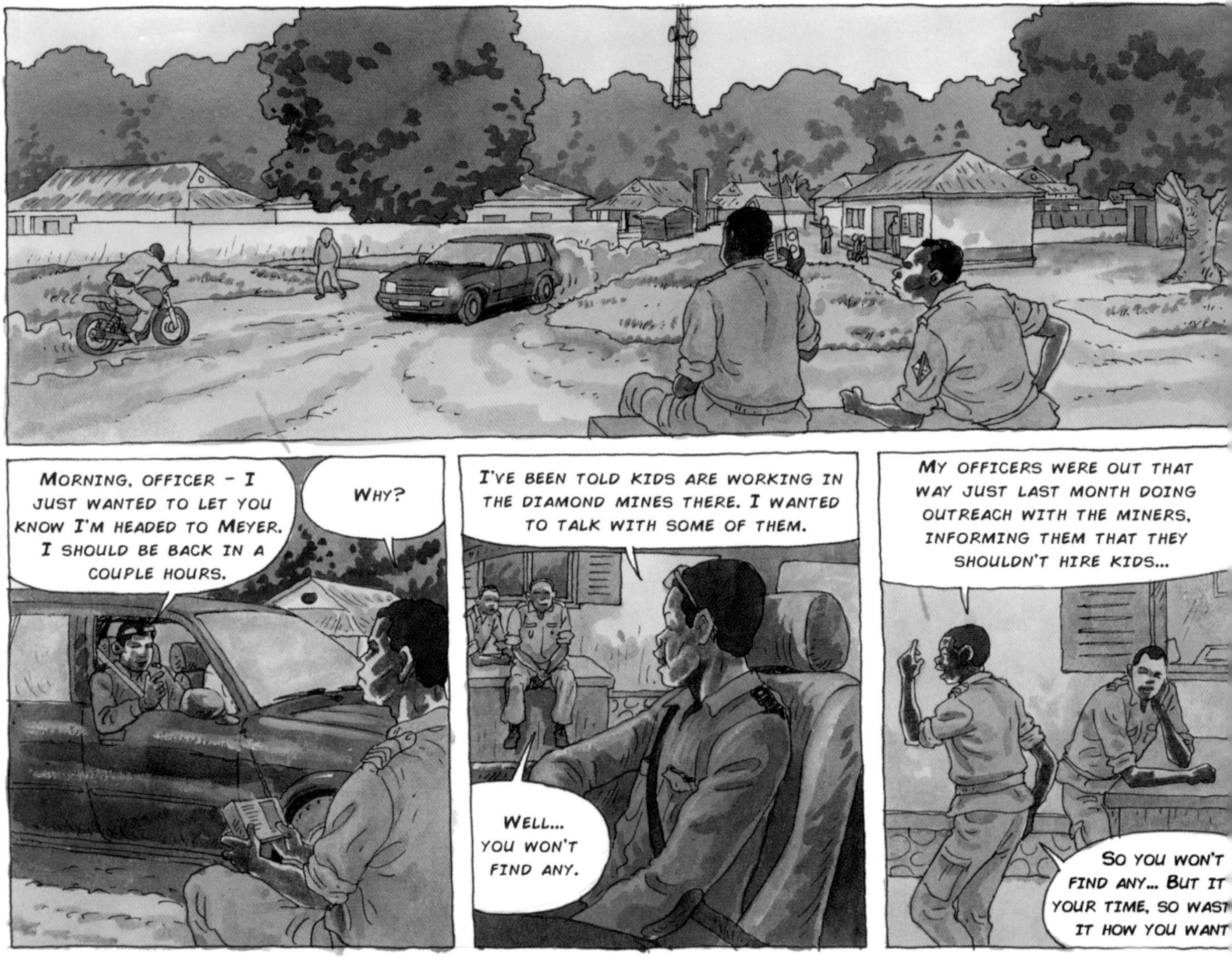
MORNING, OFFICER - I JUST WANTED TO LET YOU KNOW I'M HEADED TO MEYER. I SHOULD BE BACK IN A COUPLE HOURS.
WHY?
I'VE BEEN TOLD KIDS ARE WORKING IN THE DIAMOND MINES THERE. I WANTED TO TALK WITH SOME OF THEM.
WELL... YOU WON'T FIND ANY.
MY OFFICERS WERE OUT THAT WAY JUST LAST MONTH DOING OUTREACH WITH THE MINERS, INFORMING THEM THAT THEY SHOULDN'T HIRE KIDS...
SO YOU WON'T FIND ANY... BUT IT YOUR TIME, SO WAST IT HOW YOU WANT

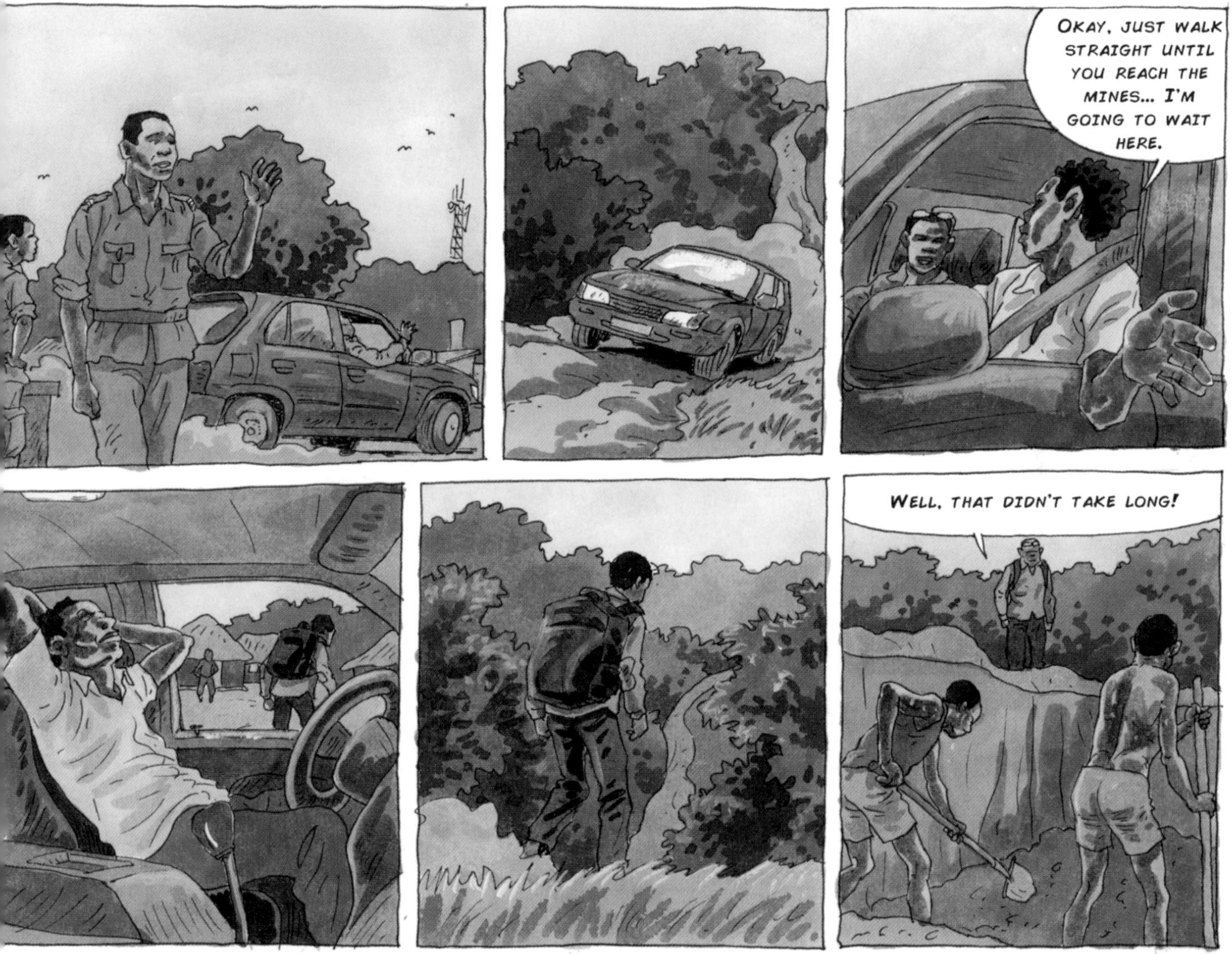

OKAY, JUST WALK STRAIGHT UNTIL YOU REACH THE MINES... I'M GOING TO WAIT HERE.
WELL, THAT DIDN'T TAKE LONG!

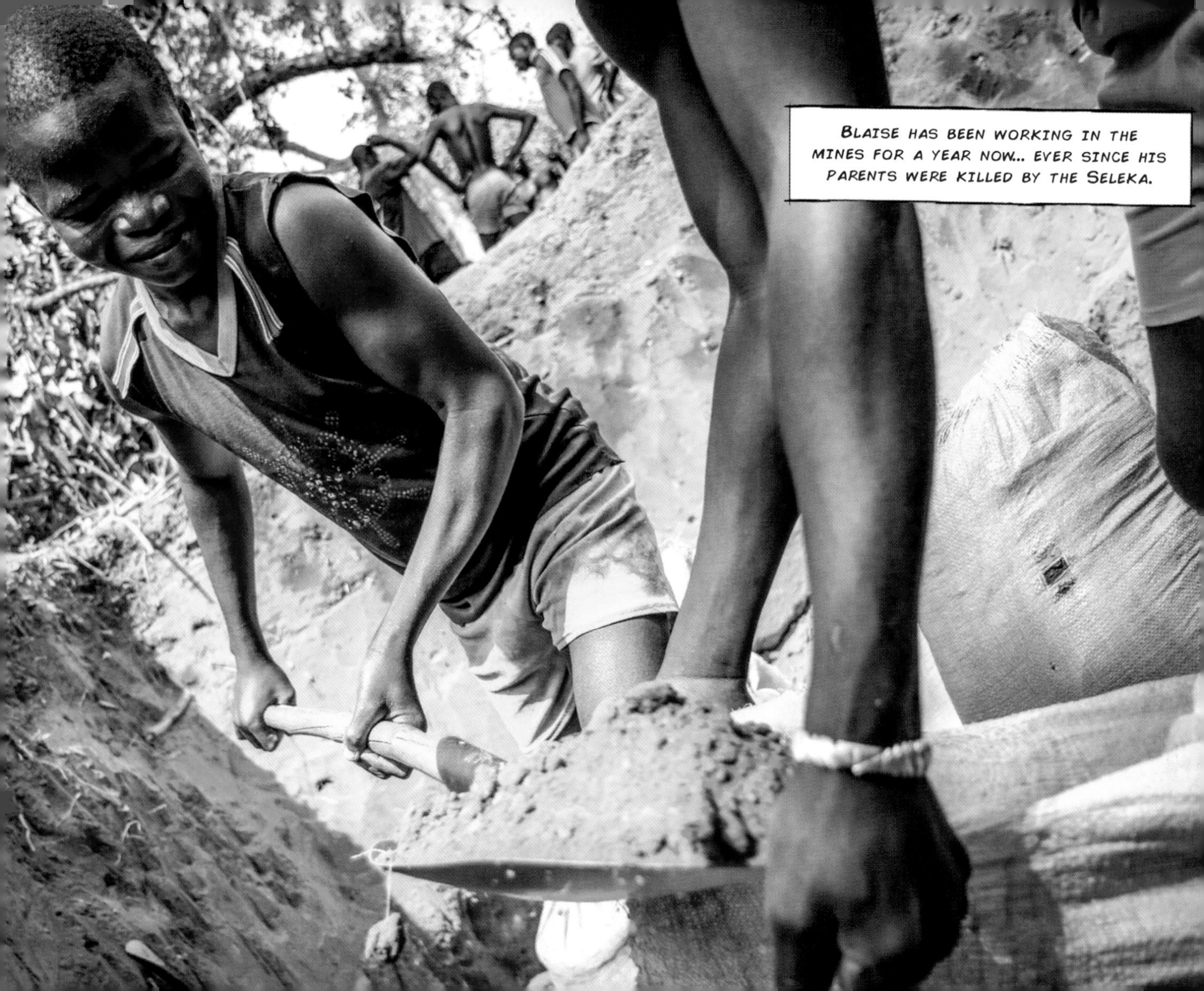
BLAISE HAS BEEN WORKING IN THE MINES FOR A YEAR NOW... EVER SINCE HIS PARENTS WERE KILLED BY THE SELEKA.

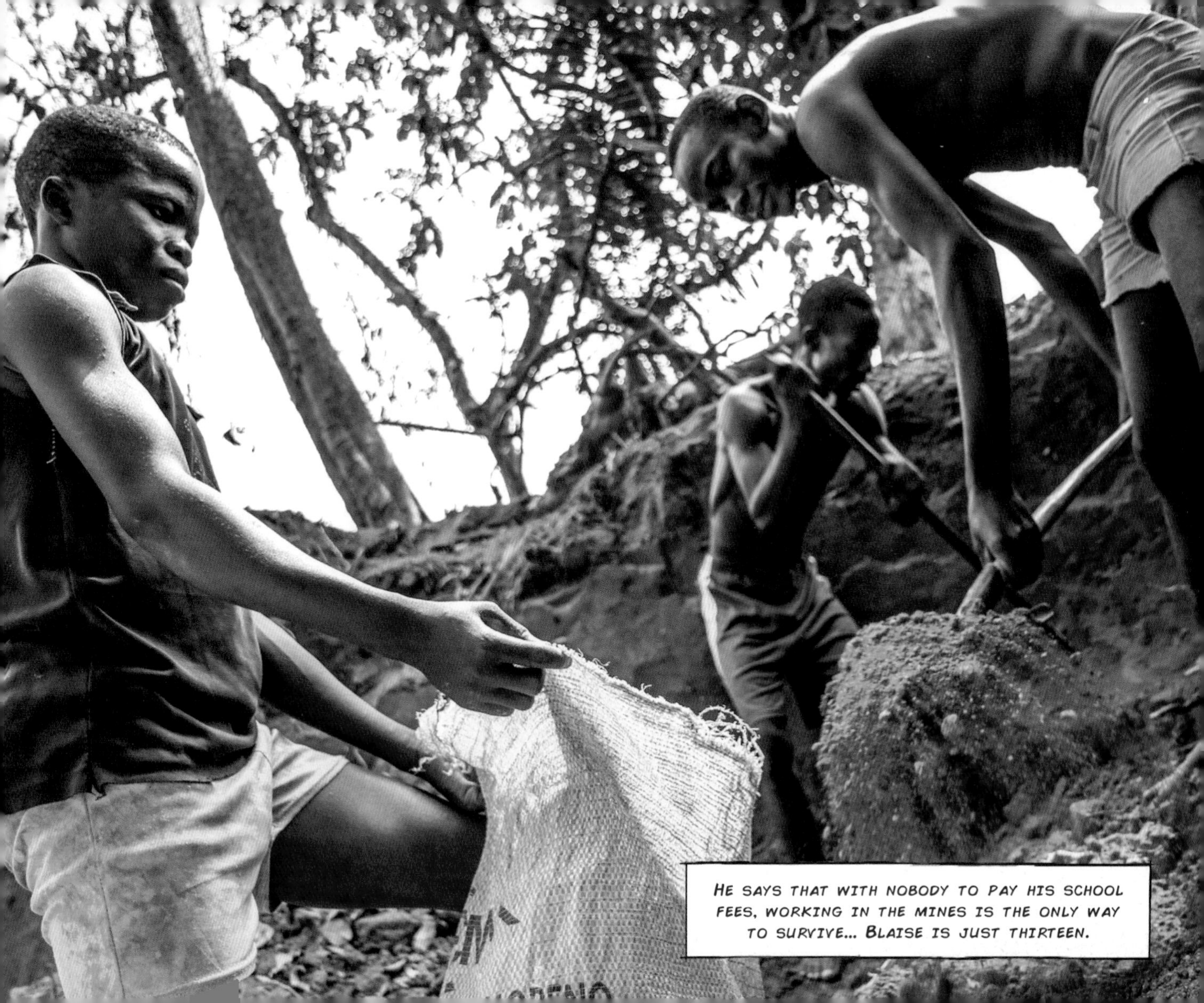
HE SAYS THAT WITH NOBODY TO PAY HIS SCHOOL FEES, WORKING IN THE MINES IS THE ONLY WAY TO SURVIVE... BLAISE IS JUST THIRTEEN.

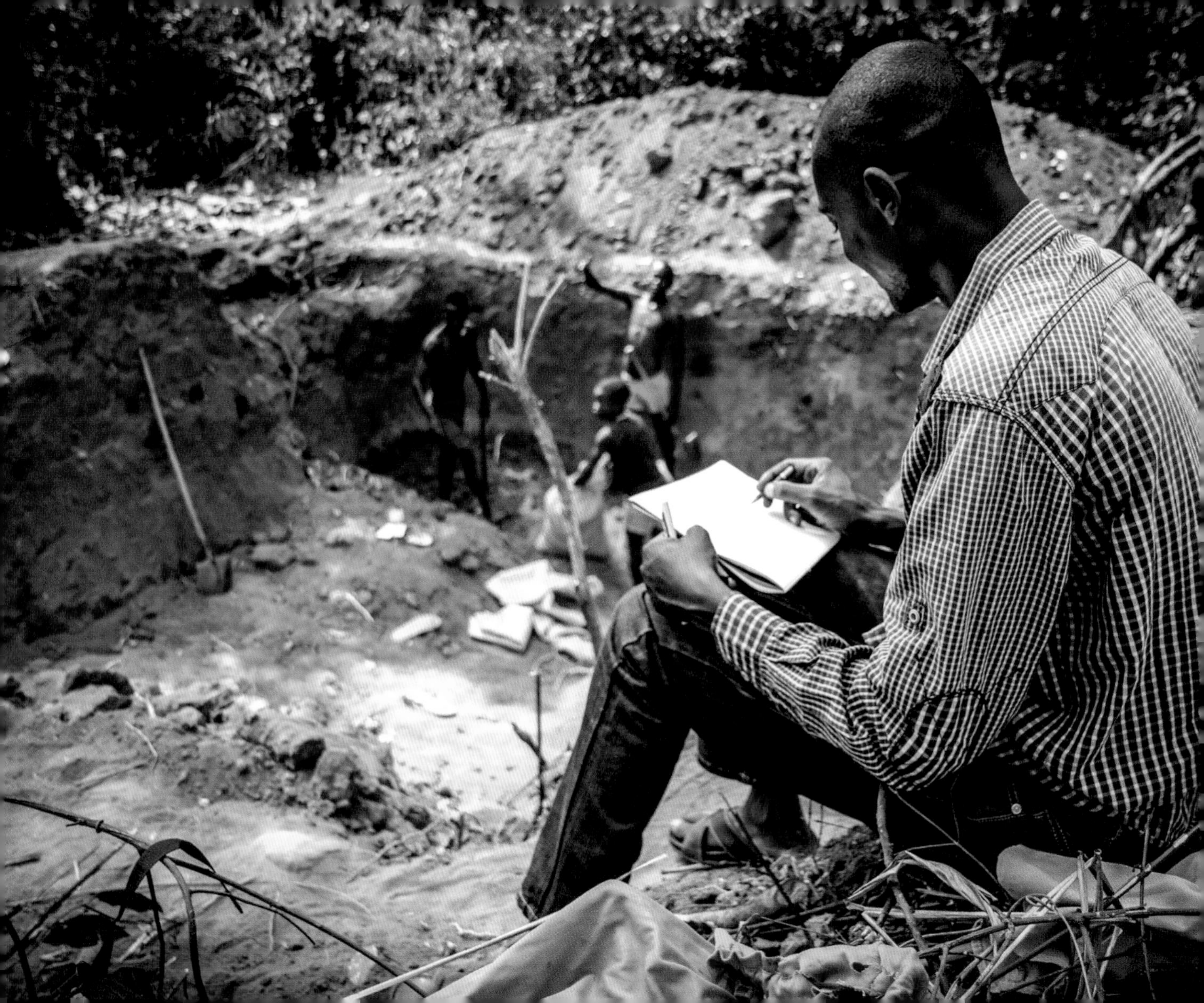

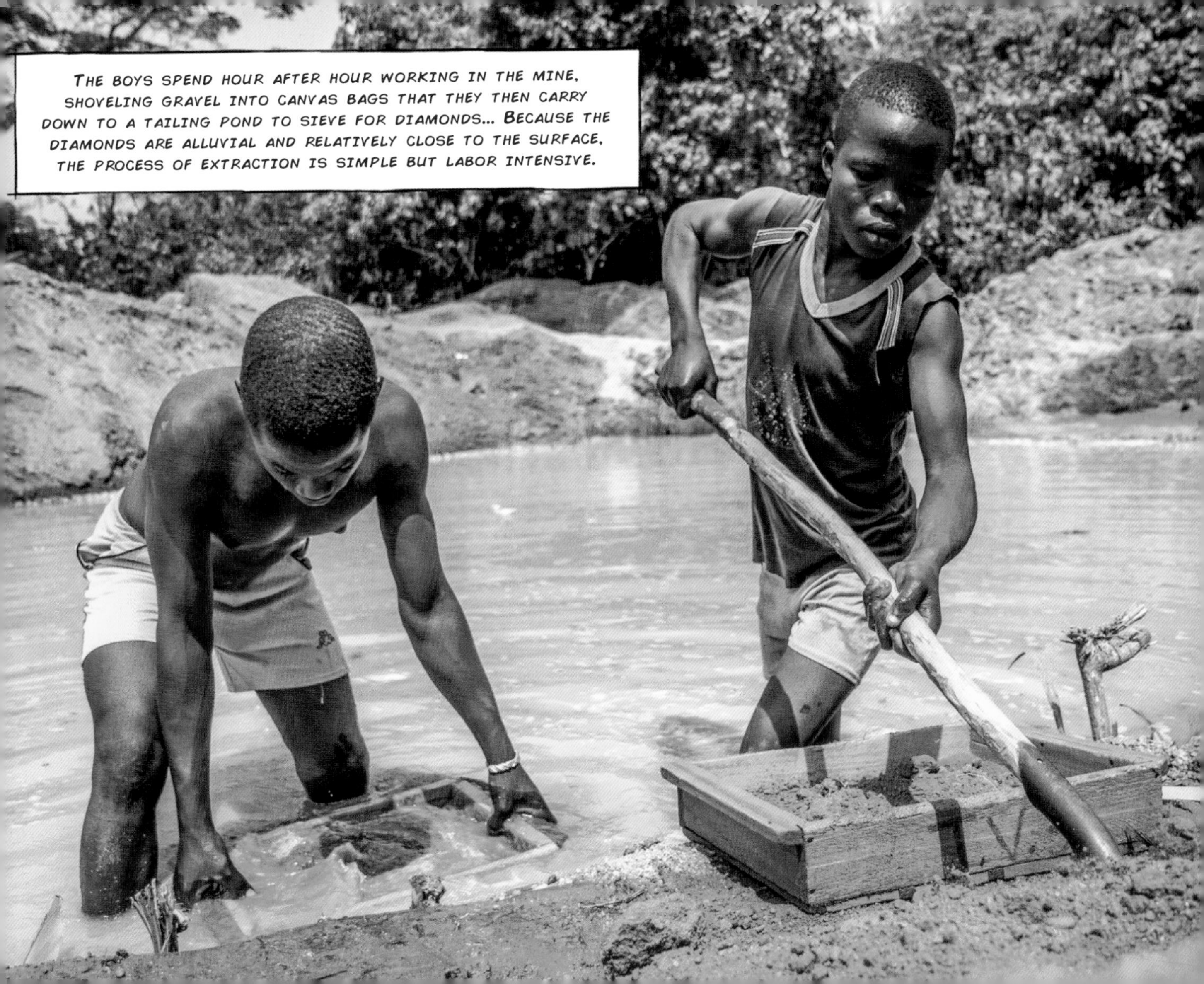
THE BOYS SPEND HOUR AFTER HOUR WORKING IN THE MINE, SHOVELING GRAVEL INTO CANVAS BAGS THAT THEY THEN CARRY DOWN TO A TAILING POND TO SIEVE FOR DIAMONDS... BECAUSE THE DIAMONDS ARE ALLUVIAL AND RELATIVELY CLOSE TO THE SURFACE, THE PROCESS OF EXTRACTION IS SIMPLE BUT LABOR INTENSIVE.

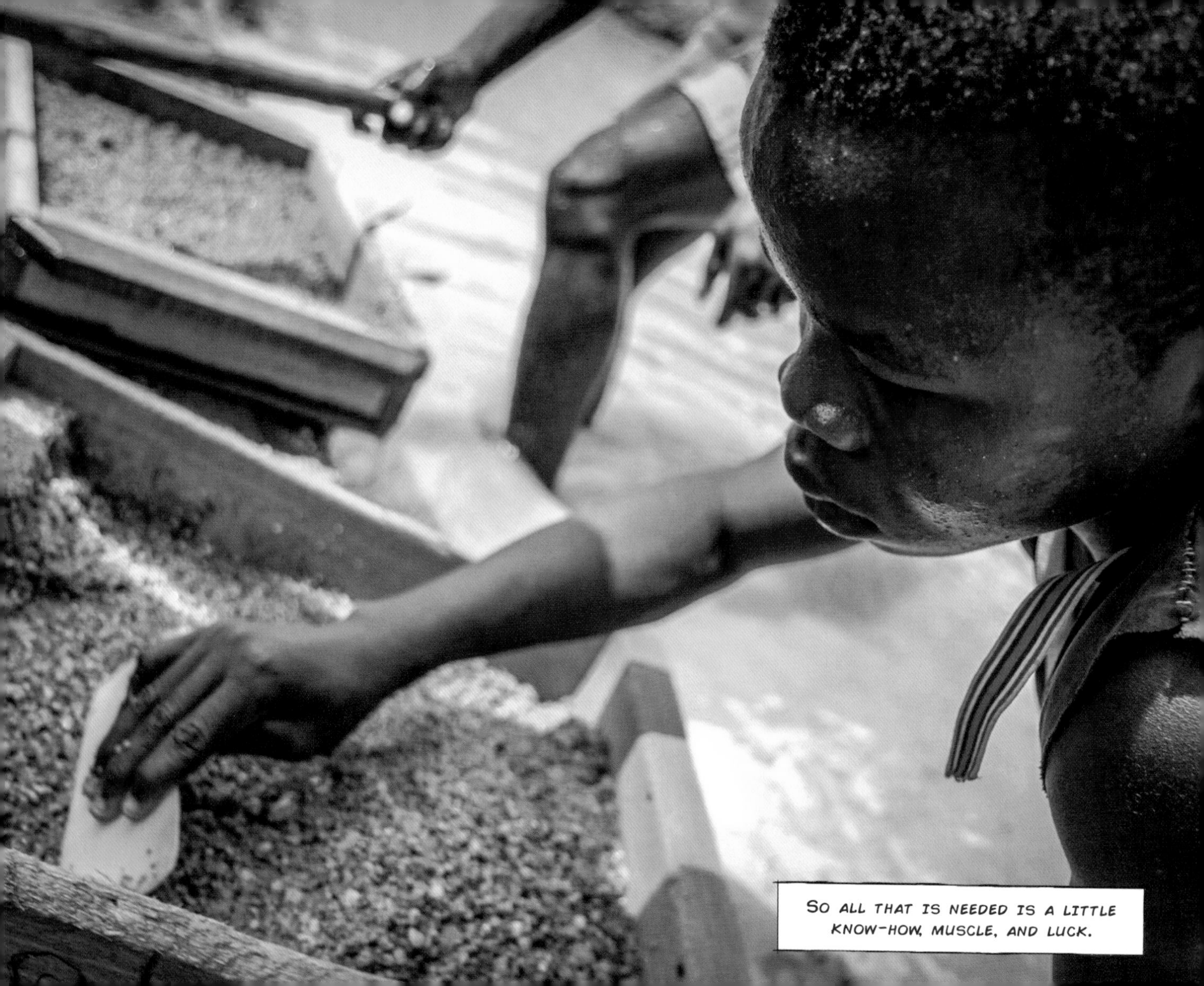
SO ALL THAT IS NEEDED IS A LITTLE
KNOW-HOW, MUSCLE, AND LUCK.

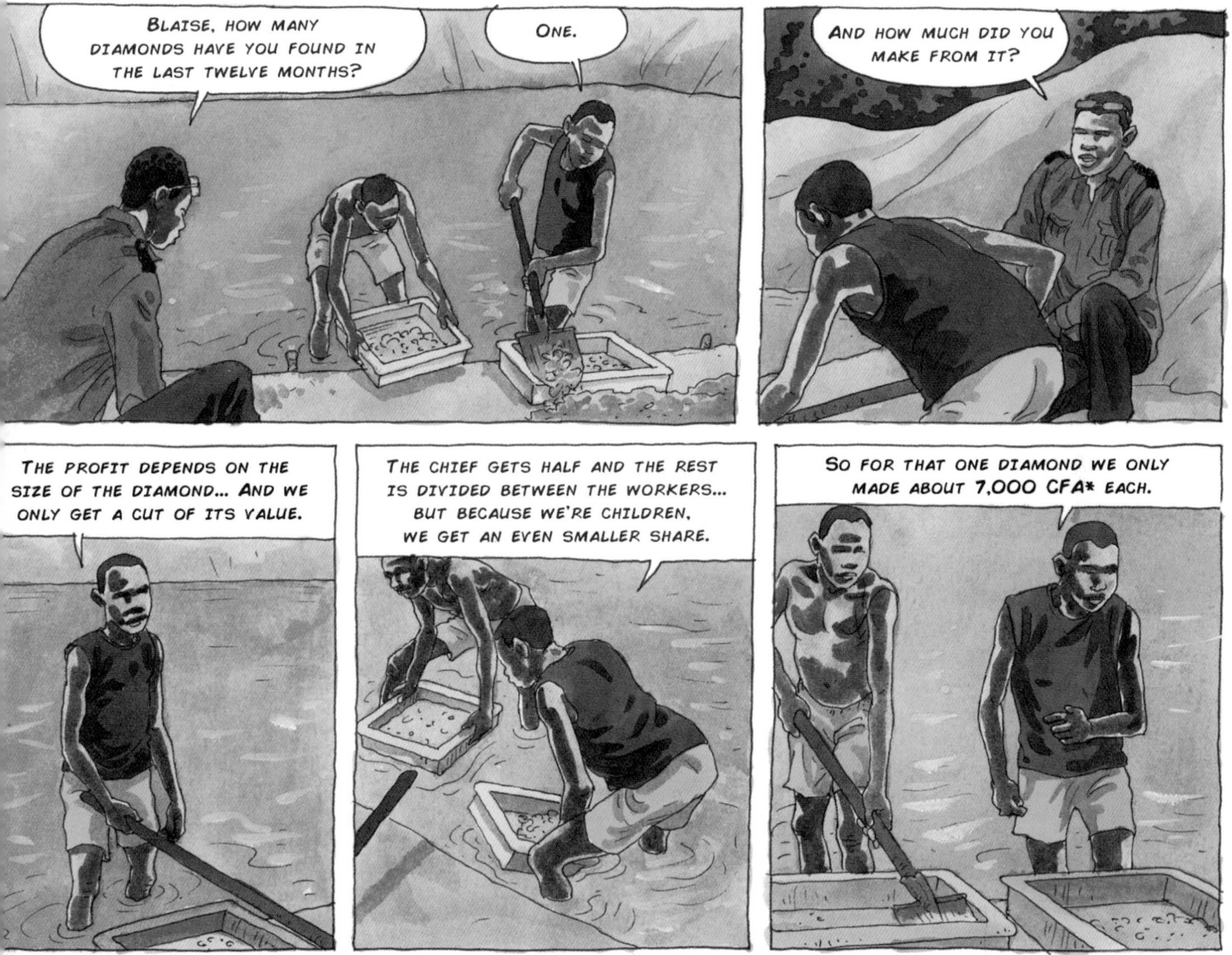
BLAISE, HOW MANY DIAMONDS HAVE YOU FOUND IN THE LAST TWELVE MONTHS?
ONE.
AND HOW MUCH DID YOU MAKE FROM IT?
THE PROFIT DEPENDS ON THE SIZE OF THE DIAMOND... AND WE ONLY GET A CUT OF ITS VALUE.
THE CHIEF GETS HALF AND THE REST IS DIVIDED BETWEEN THE WORKERS... BUT BECAUSE WE'RE CHILDREN, WE GET AN EVEN SMALLER SHARE.
SO FOR THAT ONE DIAMOND WE ONLY MADE ABOUT 7,000 CFA* EACH.

ENTRAL AFRICAN FRANC (I.E. ABOUT TWELVE US DOLLARS).

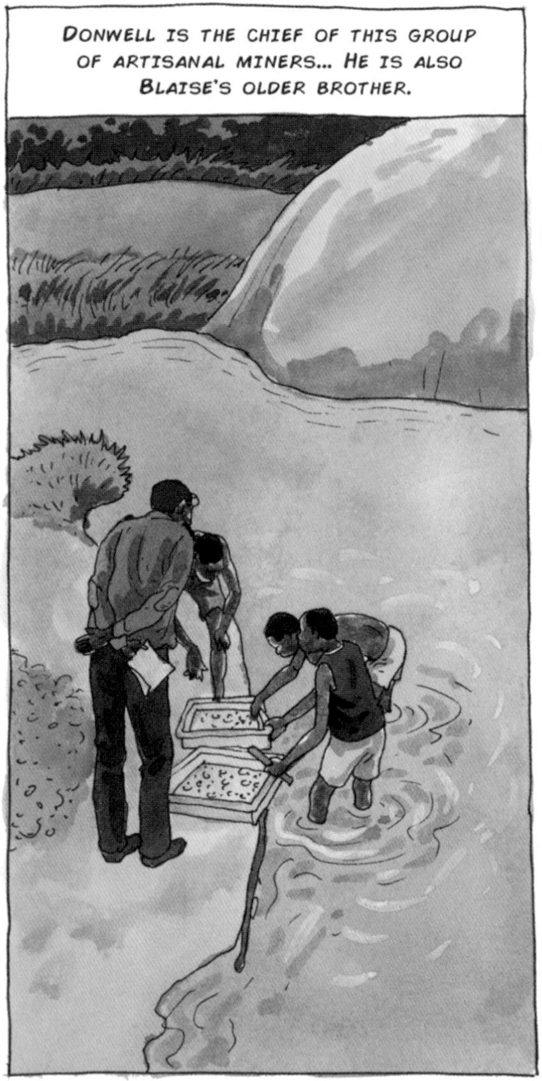
DONWELL IS THE CHIEF OF THIS GROUP OF ARTISANAL MINERS... HE IS ALSO BLAISE'S OLDER BROTHER.

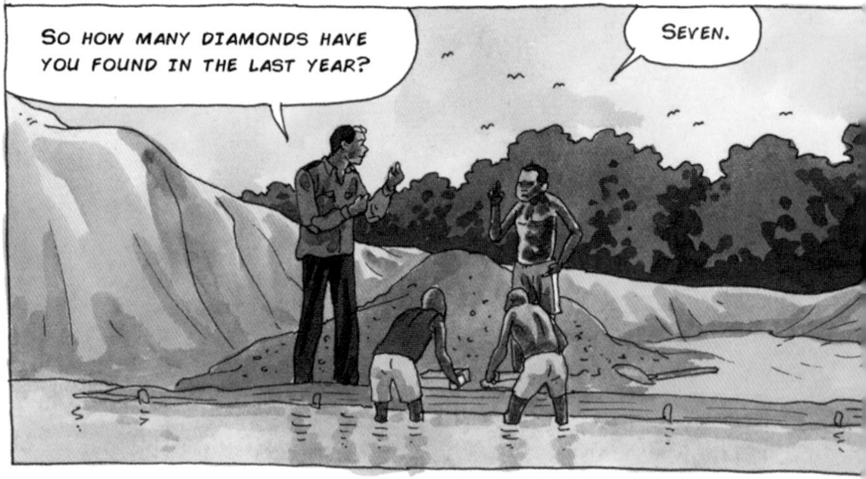
SO HOW MANY DIAMONDS HAVE YOU FOUND IN THE LAST YEAR?
SEVEN.

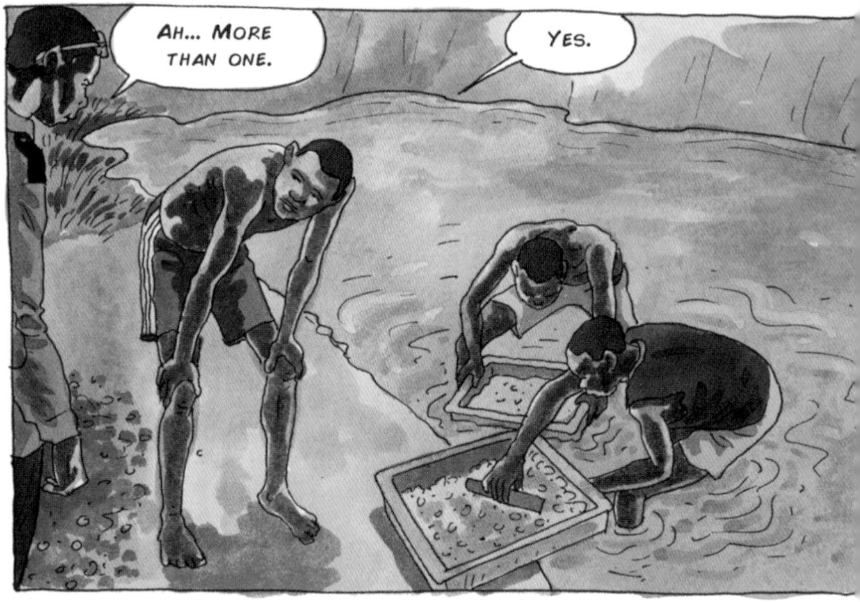
AH... MORE THAN ONE.
YES.

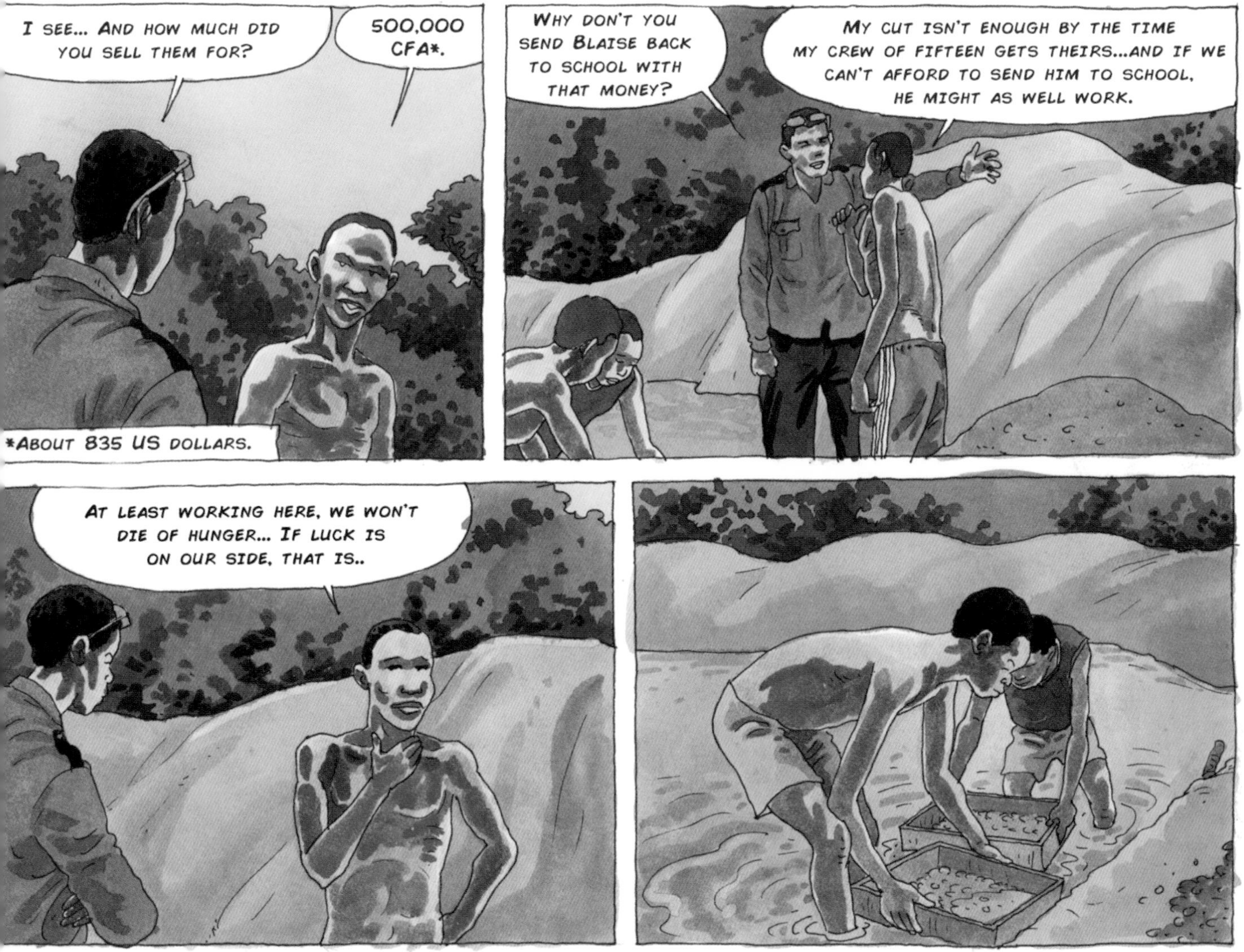

I SEE... AND HOW MUCH DID YOU SELL THEM FOR?
500,000 CFA*.
*ABOUT 835 US DOLLARS.
WHY DON'T YOU SEND BLAISE BACK TO SCHOOL WITH THAT MONEY?
MY CUT ISN'T ENOUGH BY THE TIME MY CREW OF FIFTEEN GETS THEIRS...AND IF WE CAN'T AFFORD TO SEND HIM TO SCHOOL, HE MIGHT AS WELL WORK.
AT LEAST WORKING HERE, WE WON'T DIE OF HUNGER... IF LUCK IS ON OUR SIDE, THAT IS..

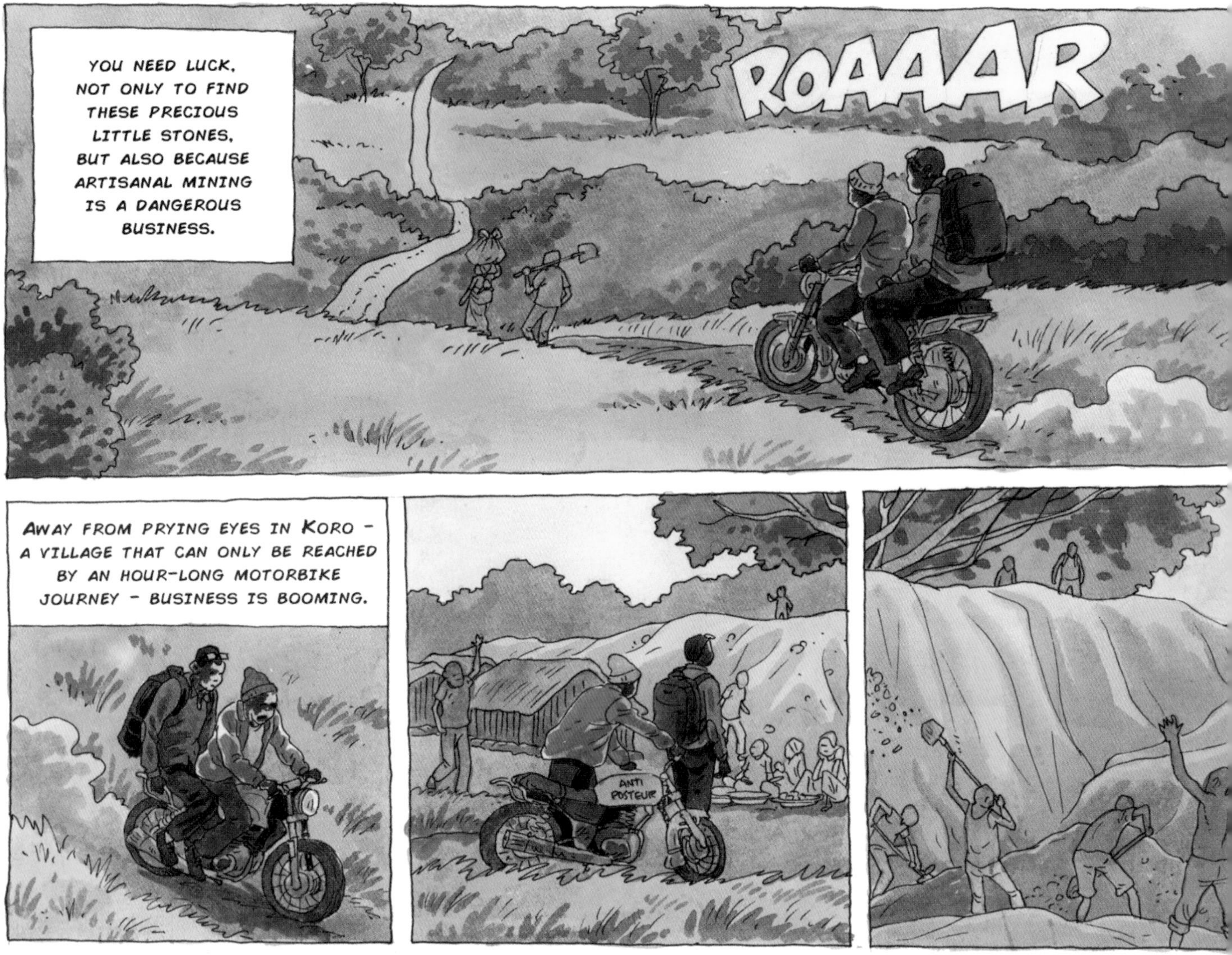
YOU NEED LUCK, NOT ONLY TO FIND THESE PRECIOUS LITTLE STONES, BUT ALSO BECAUSE ARTISANAL MINING IS A DANGEROUS BUSINESS.
ROAAAR
AWAY FROM PRYING EYES IN KORO - A VILLAGE THAT CAN ONLY BE REACHED BY AN HOUR-LONG MOTORBIKE JOURNEY - BUSINESS IS BOOMING.
ANTI POSTEUR

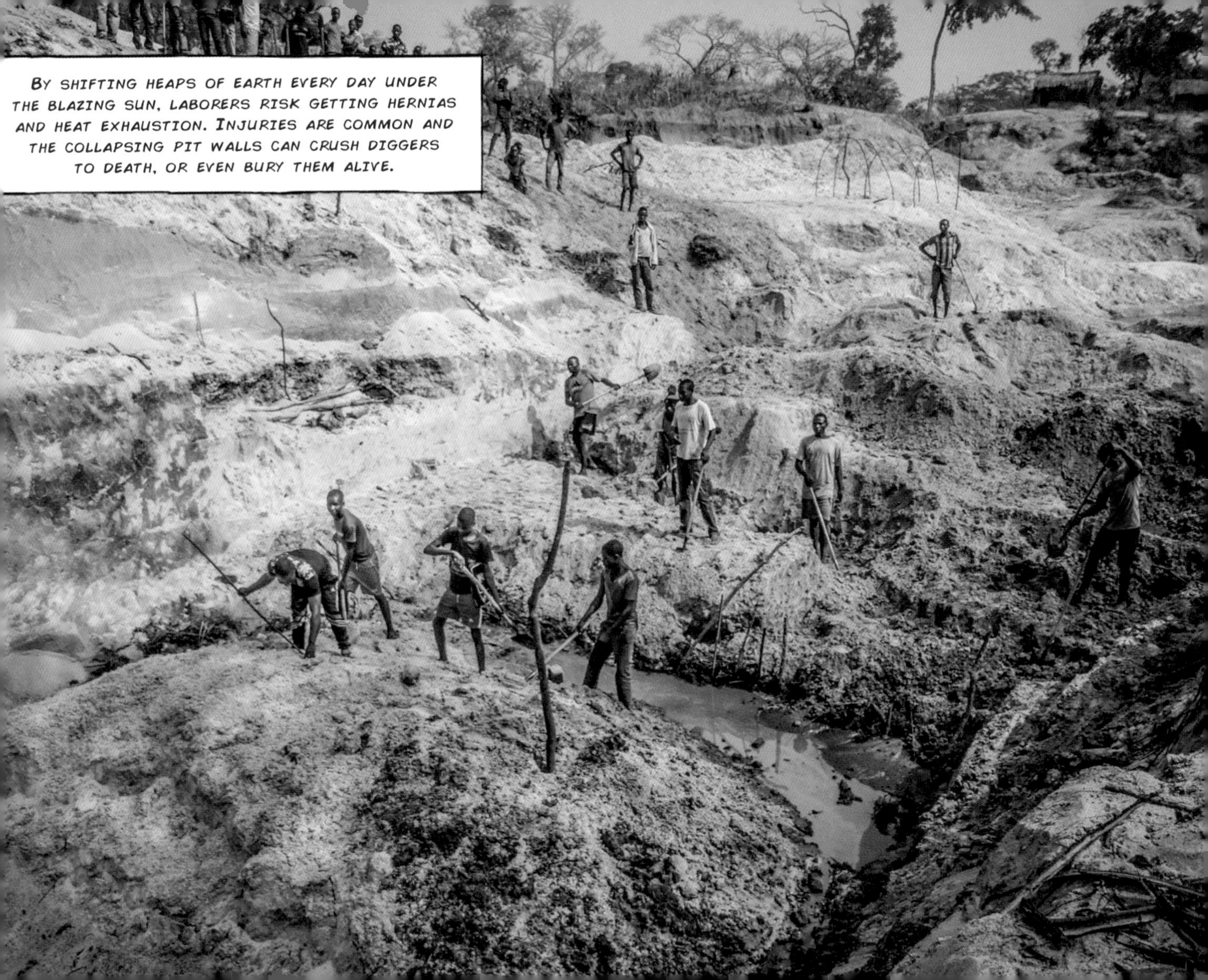
By shifting heaps of earth every day under the blazing sun, laborers risk getting hernias and heat exhaustion. Injuries are common and the collapsing pit walls can crush diggers to death, or even bury them alive.

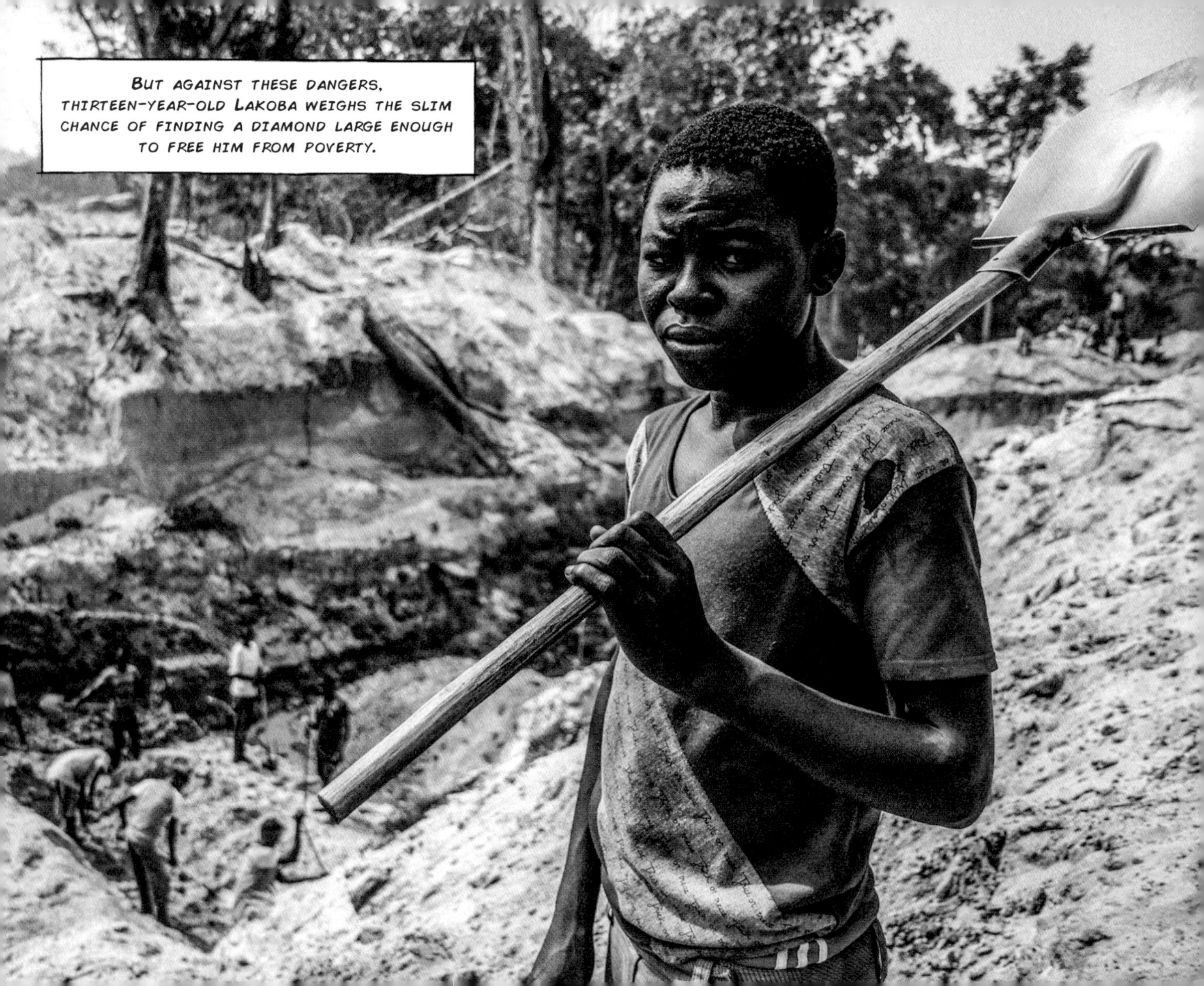
But against these dangers, thirteen-year-old Lakoba weighs the slim chance of finding a diamond large enough to free him from poverty.

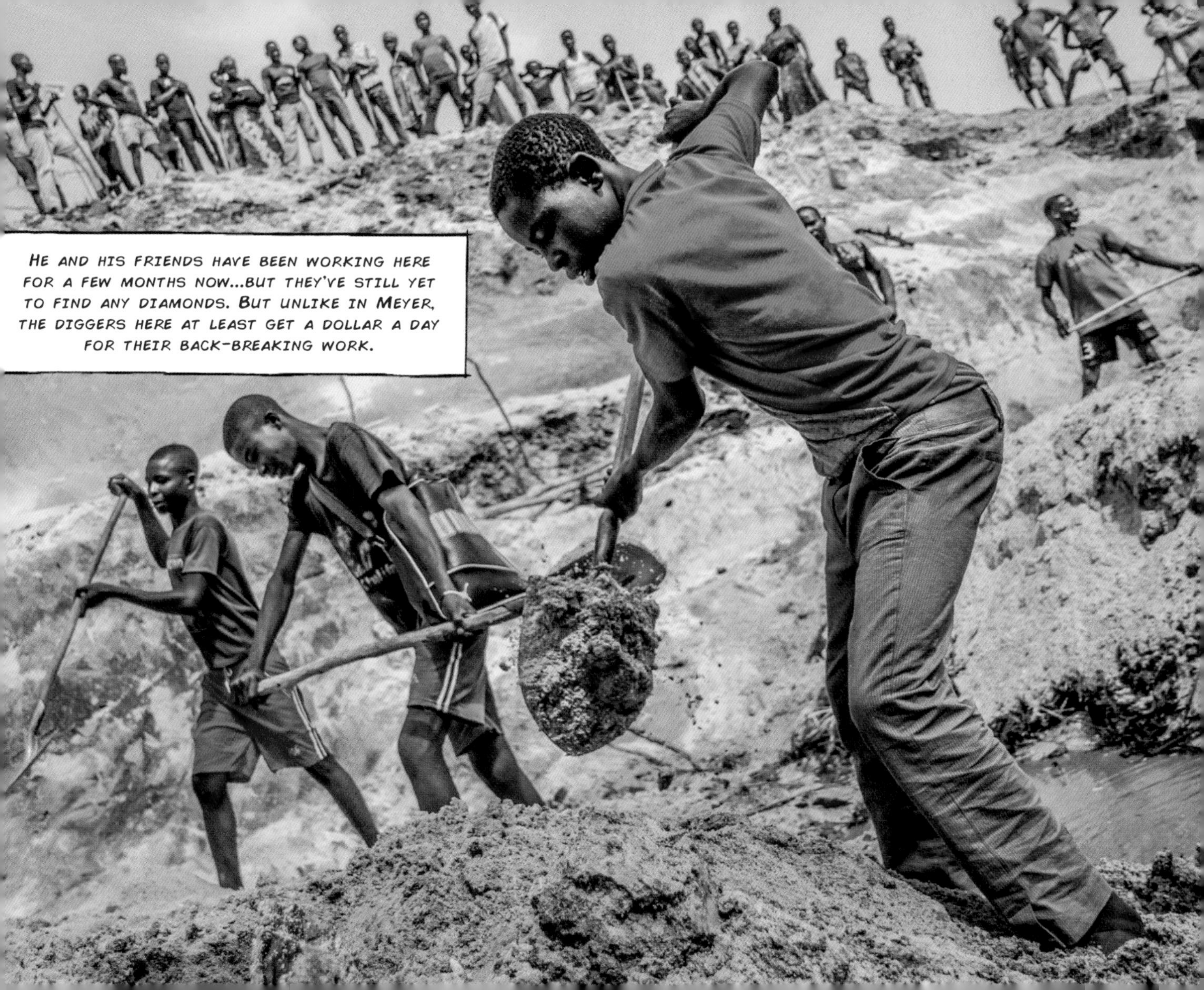
HE AND HIS FRIENDS HAVE BEEN WORKING HERE FOR A FEW MONTHS NOW...BUT THEY'VE STILL YET TO FIND ANY DIAMONDS. BUT UNLIKE IN MEYER, THE DIGGERS HERE AT LEAST GET A DOLLAR A DAY FOR THEIR BACK-BREAKING WORK.

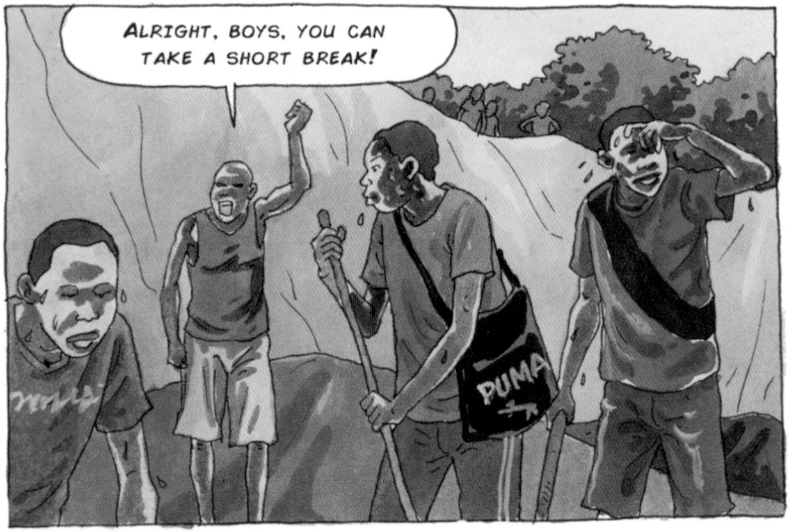
ALRIGHT, BOYS, YOU CAN TAKE A SHORT BREAK!
PUMA
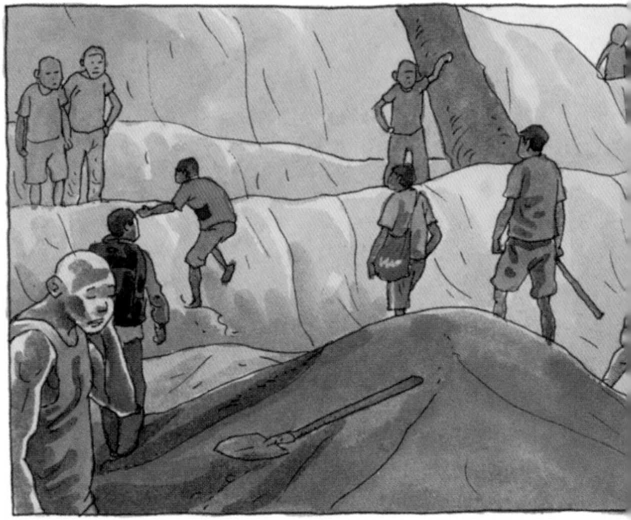
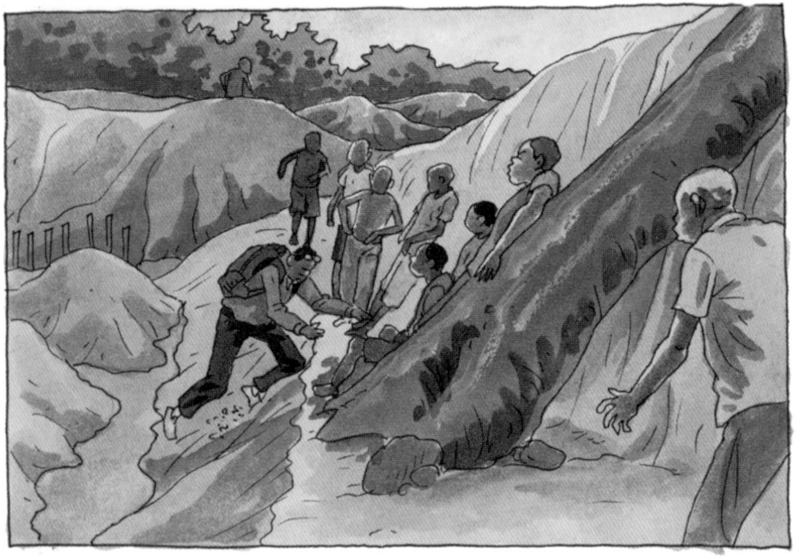
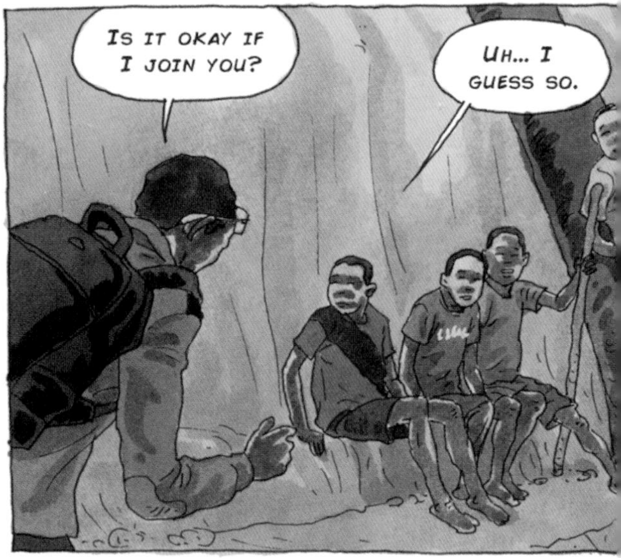
IS IT OKAY IF I JOIN YOU?
UH... I GUESS SO.

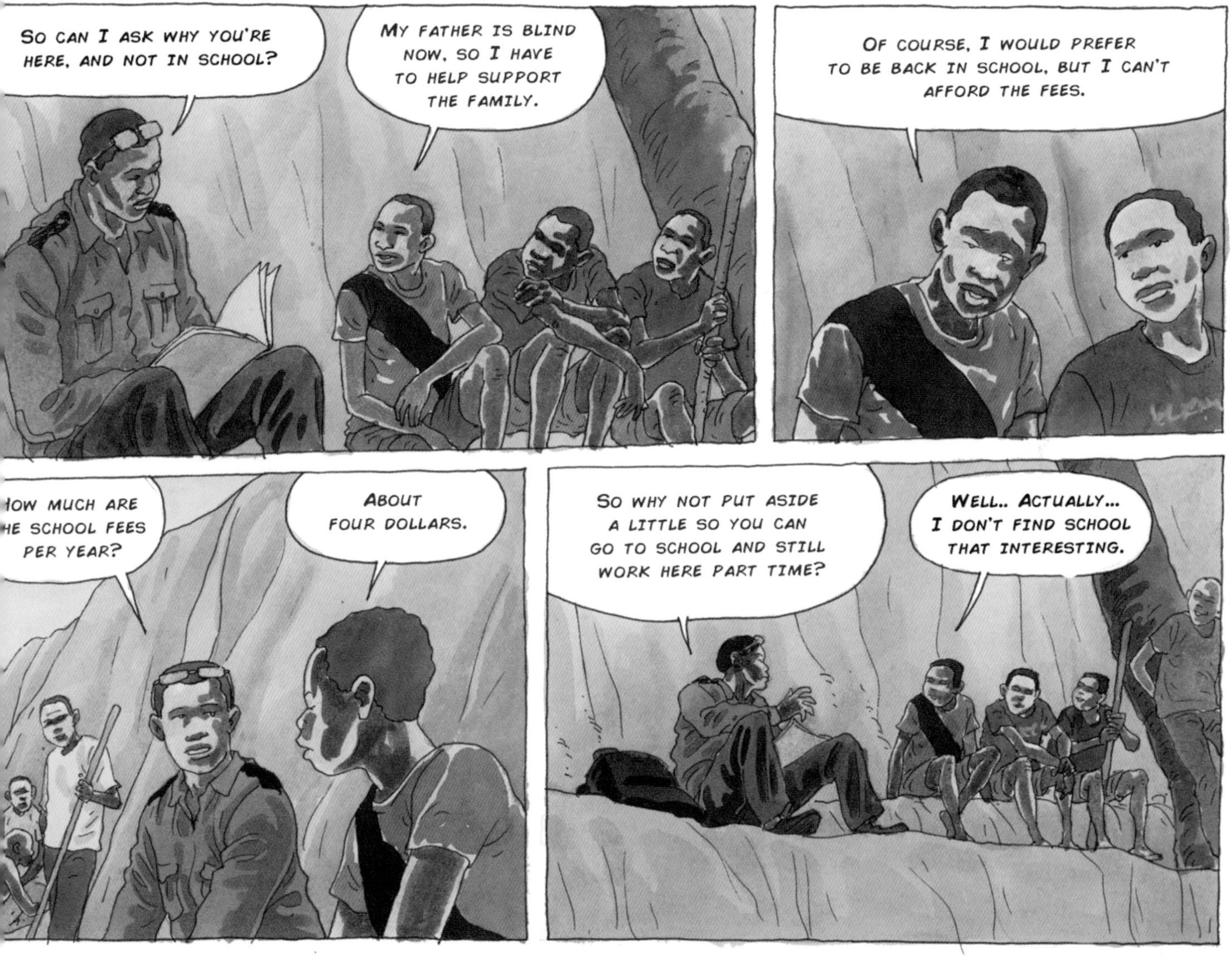
So can I ask why you're here, and not in school?
My father is blind now, so I have to help support the family.
Of course, I would prefer to be back in school, but I can't afford the fees.
ow much are he school fees per year?
About four dollars.
So why not put aside a little so you can go to school and still work here part time?
Well.. Actually... I don't find school that interesting.

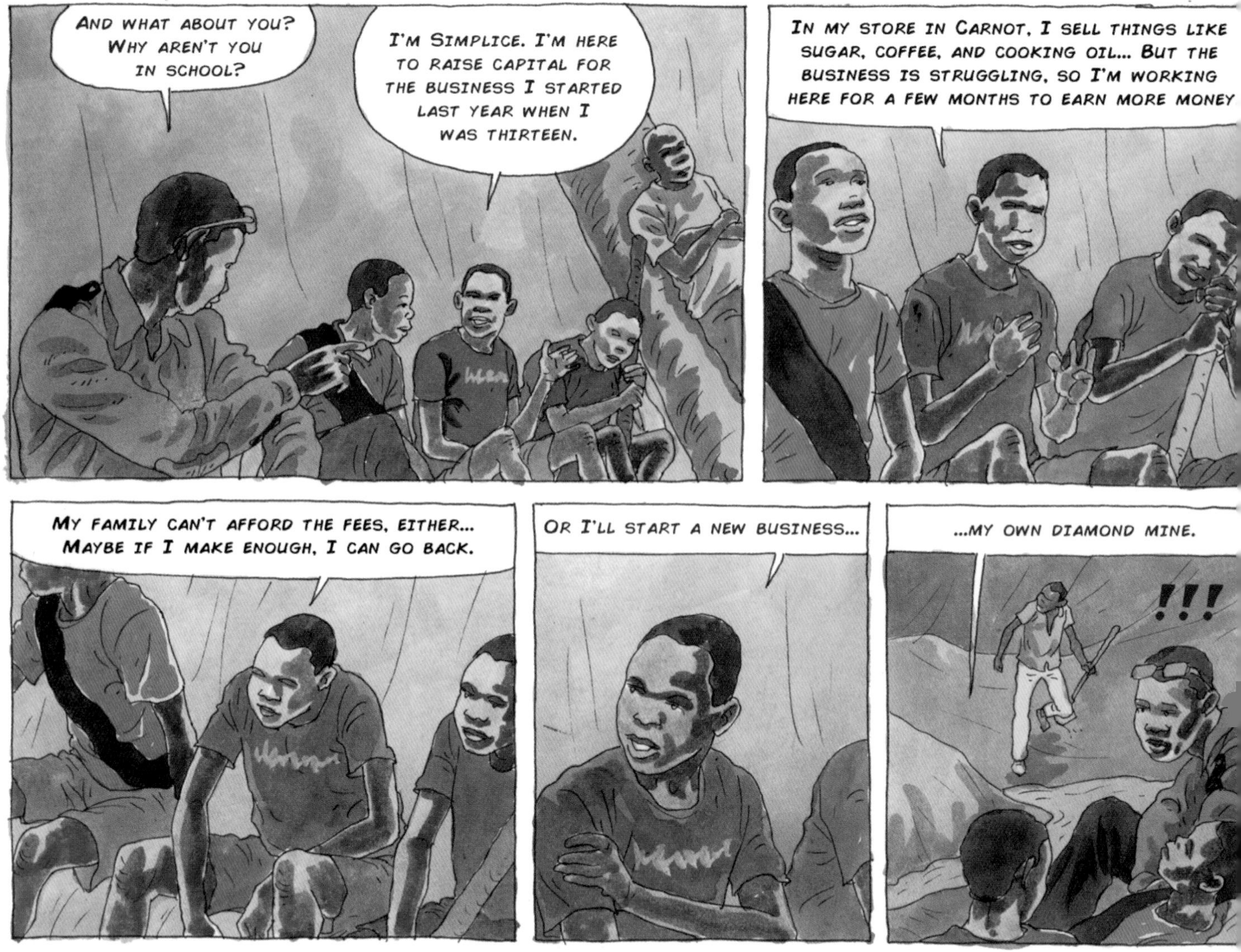
AND WHAT ABOUT YOU? WHY AREN'T YOU IN SCHOOL?
I'M SIMPLICE. I'M HERE TO RAISE CAPITAL FOR THE BUSINESS I STARTED LAST YEAR WHEN I WAS THIRTEEN.
IN MY STORE IN CARNOT, I SELL THINGS LIKE SUGAR, COFFEE, AND COOKING OIL... BUT THE BUSINESS IS STRUGGLING, SO I'M WORKING HERE FOR A FEW MONTHS TO EARN MORE MONEY
MY FAMILY CAN'T AFFORD THE FEES, EITHER... MAYBE IF I MAKE ENOUGH, I CAN GO BACK.
OR I'LL START A NEW BUSINESS...
...MY OWN DIAMOND MINE.
!!!

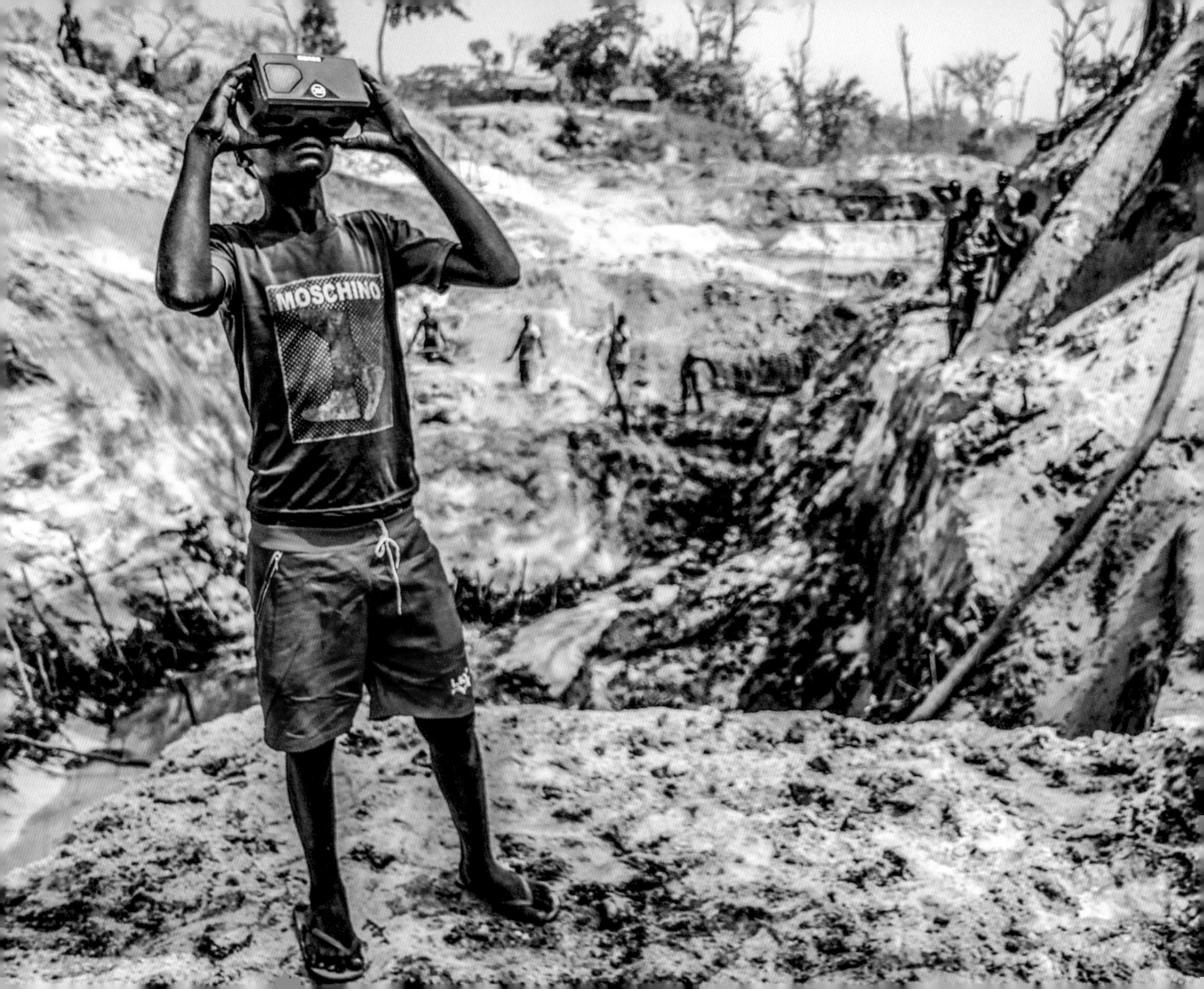
MOSCHINO

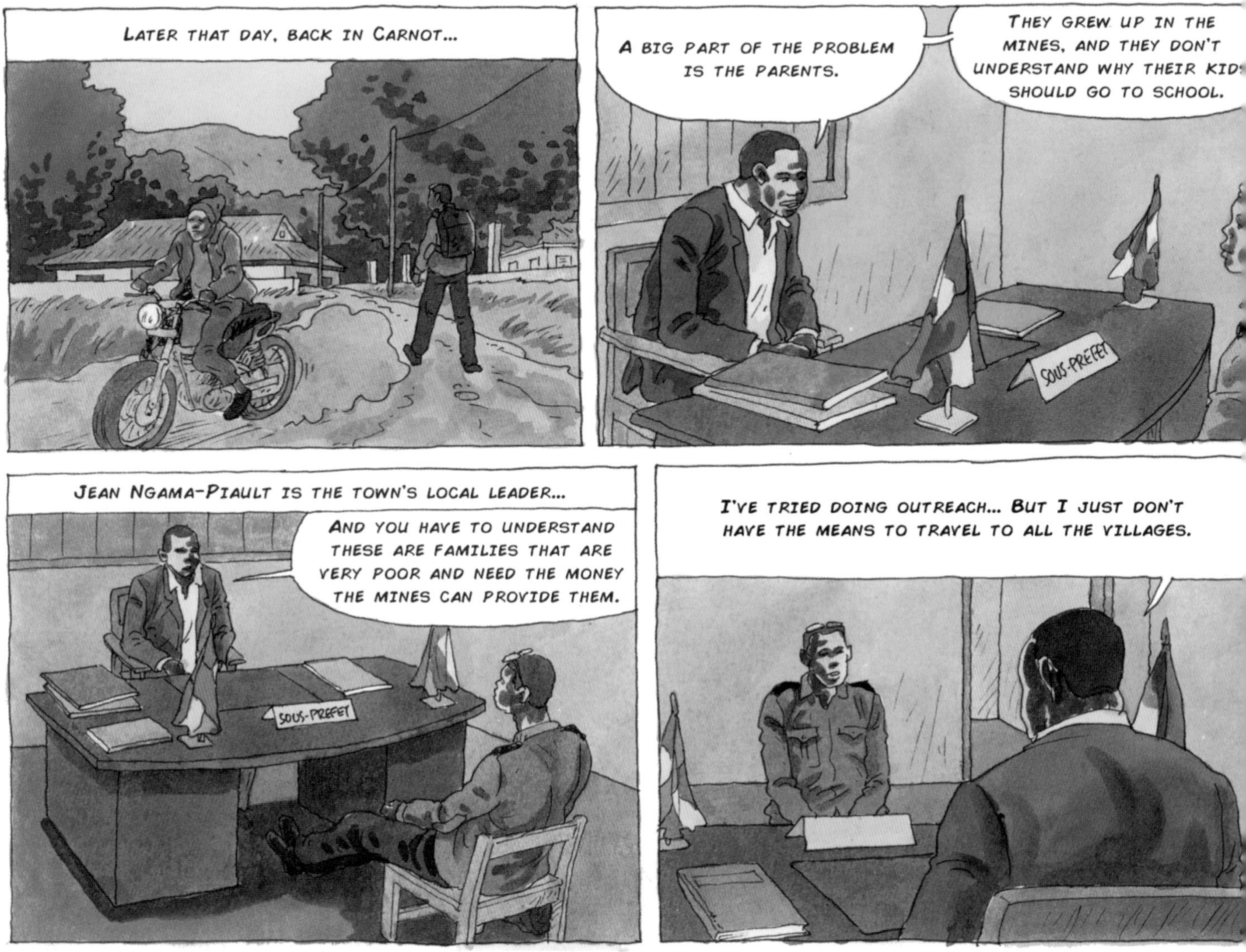
LATER THAT DAY, BACK IN CARNOT...
A BIG PART OF THE PROBLEM IS THE PARENTS.
THEY GREW UP IN THE MINES, AND THEY DON'T UNDERSTAND WHY THEIR KIDS SHOULD GO TO SCHOOL.
SOUS-PREFET
JEAN NGAMA-PIAULT IS THE TOWN'S LOCAL LEADER...
AND YOU HAVE TO UNDERSTAND THESE ARE FAMILIES THAT ARE VERY POOR AND NEED THE MONEY THE MINES CAN PROVIDE THEM.
SOUS-PREFET
I'VE TRIED DOING OUTREACH... BUT I JUST DON'T HAVE THE MEANS TO TRAVEL TO ALL THE VILLAGES.

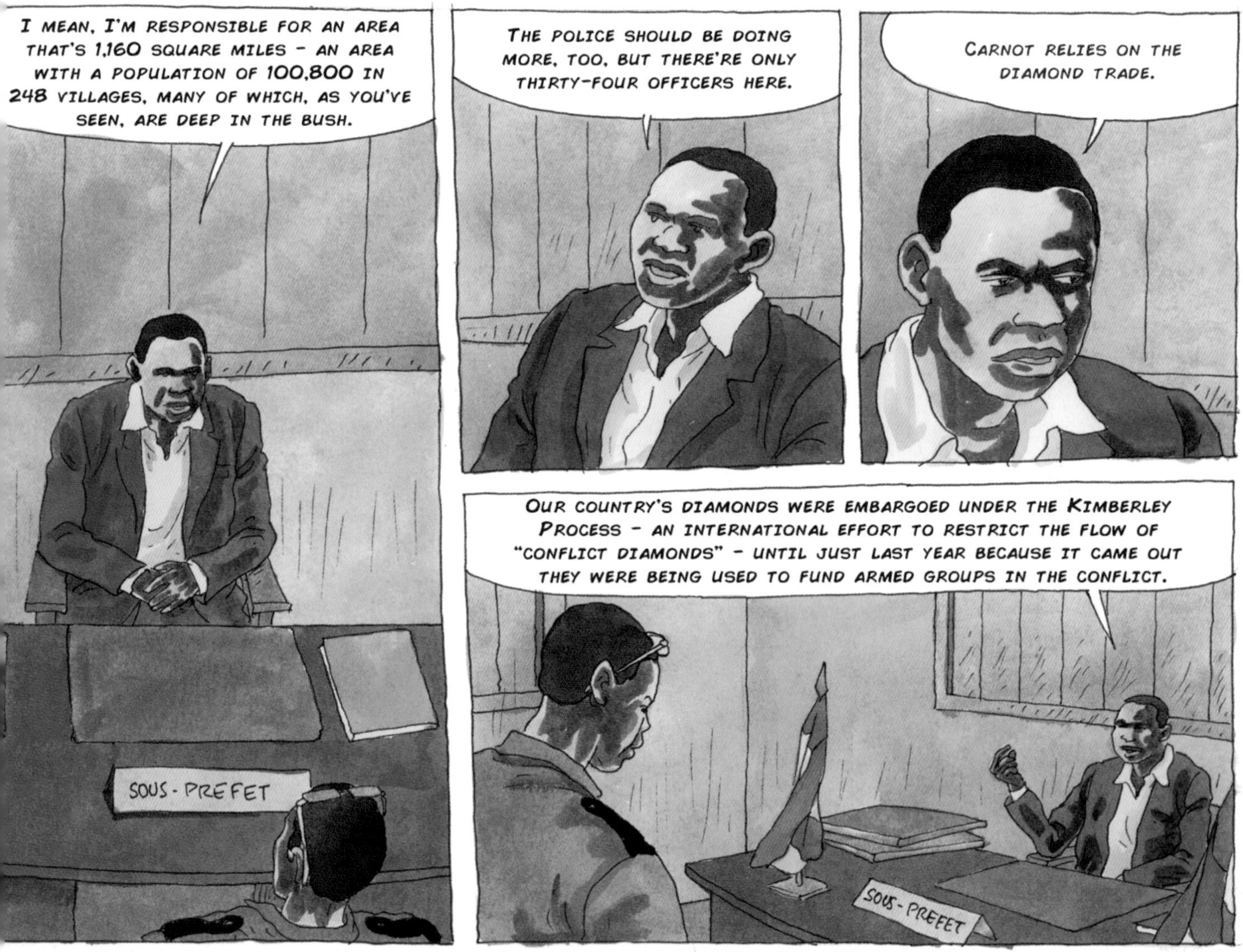
I MEAN, I'M RESPONSIBLE FOR AN AREA THAT'S 1,160 SQUARE MILES - AN AREA WITH A POPULATION OF 100,800 IN 248 VILLAGES, MANY OF WHICH, AS YOU'VE SEEN, ARE DEEP IN THE BUSH.
SOUS-PREFET
THE POLICE SHOULD BE DOING MORE, TOO, BUT THERE'RE ONLY THIRTY-FOUR OFFICERS HERE.
CARNOT RELIES ON THE DIAMOND TRADE.
OUR COUNTRY'S DIAMONDS WERE EMBARGOED UNDER THE KIMBERLEY PROCESS - AN INTERNATIONAL EFFORT TO RESTRICT THE FLOW OF "CONFLICT DIAMONDS" - UNTIL JUST LAST YEAR BECAUSE IT CAME OUT THEY WERE BEING USED TO FUND ARMED GROUPS IN THE CONFLICT.
SOUS-PREFET

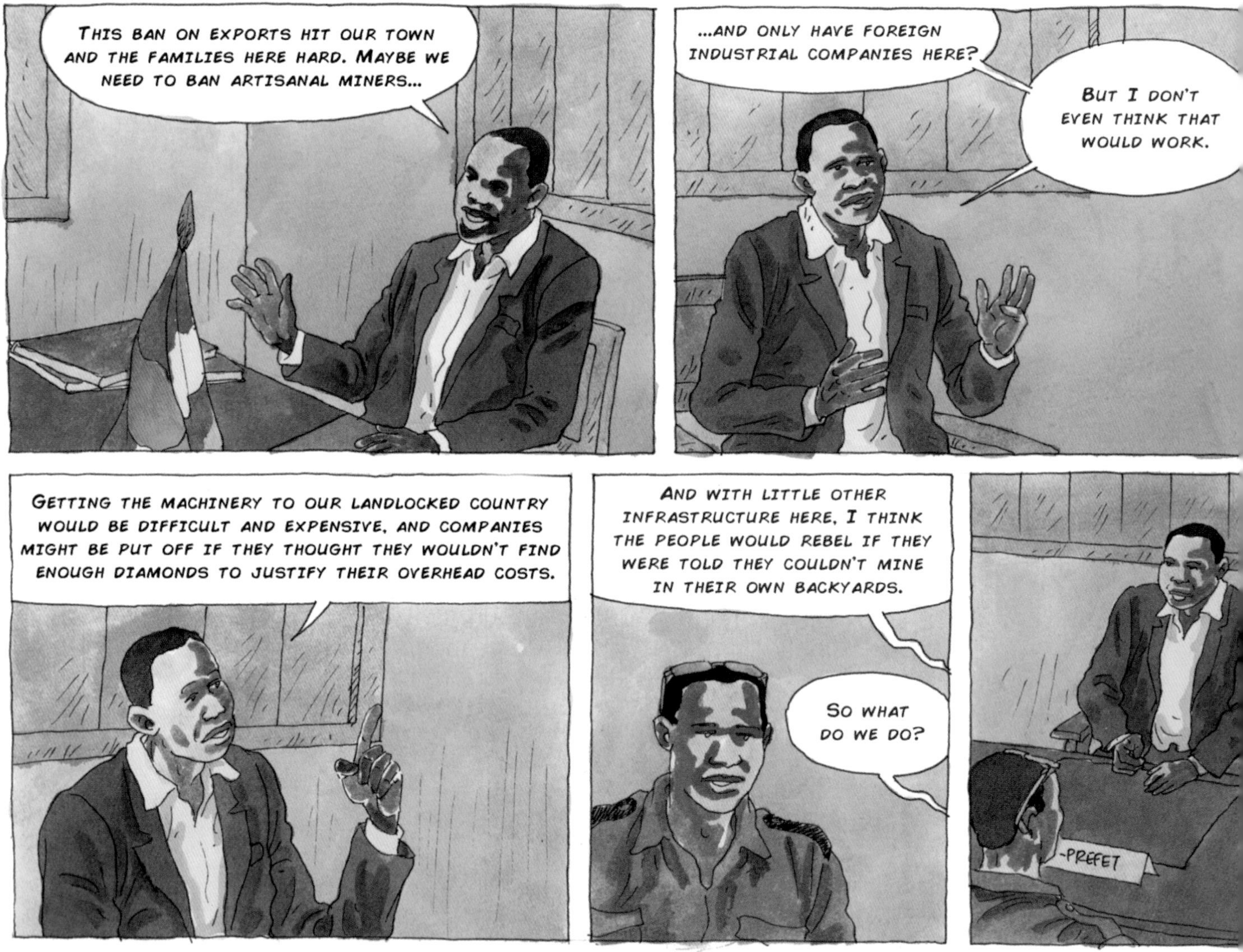
THIS BAN ON EXPORTS HIT OUR TOWN AND THE FAMILIES HERE HARD. MAYBE WE NEED TO BAN ARTISANAL MINERS...
...AND ONLY HAVE FOREIGN INDUSTRIAL COMPANIES HERE?
BUT I DON'T EVEN THINK THAT WOULD WORK.
GETTING THE MACHINERY TO OUR LANDLOCKED COUNTRY WOULD BE DIFFICULT AND EXPENSIVE, AND COMPANIES MIGHT BE PUT OFF IF THEY THOUGHT THEY WOULDN'T FIND ENOUGH DIAMONDS TO JUSTIFY THEIR OVERHEAD COSTS.
AND WITH LITTLE OTHER INFRASTRUCTURE HERE, I THINK THE PEOPLE WOULD REBEL IF THEY WERE TOLD THEY COULDN'T MINE IN THEIR OWN BACKYARDS.
SO WHAT DO WE DO?
-PREFET

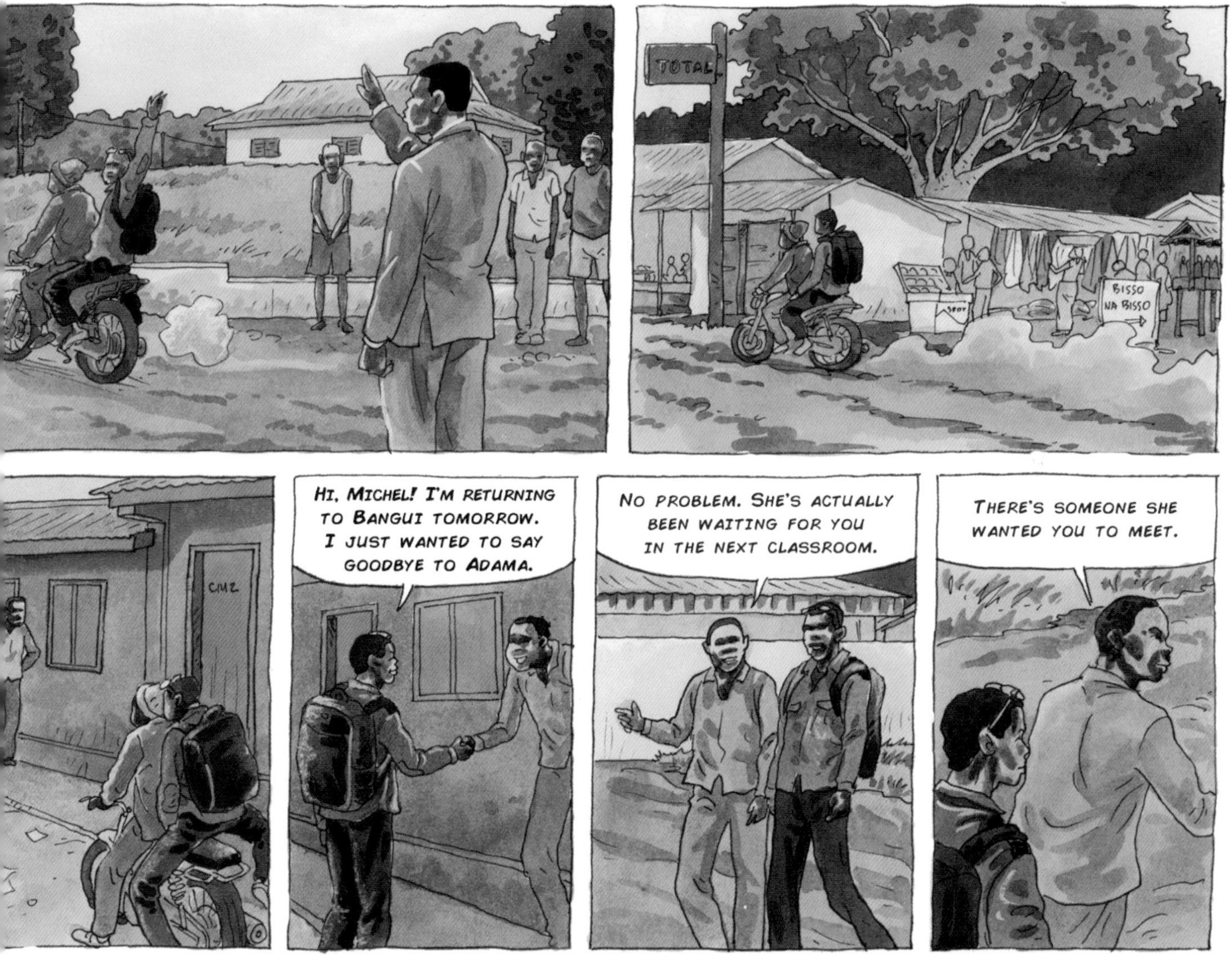
TOTAL
BISSO NA BISSO
CM2
HI, MICHEL! I'M RETURNING TO BANGUI TOMORROW. I JUST WANTED TO SAY GOODBYE TO ADAMA.
NO PROBLEM. SHE'S ACTUALLY BEEN WAITING FOR YOU IN THE NEXT CLASSROOM.
THERE'S SOMEONE SHE WANTED YOU TO MEET.

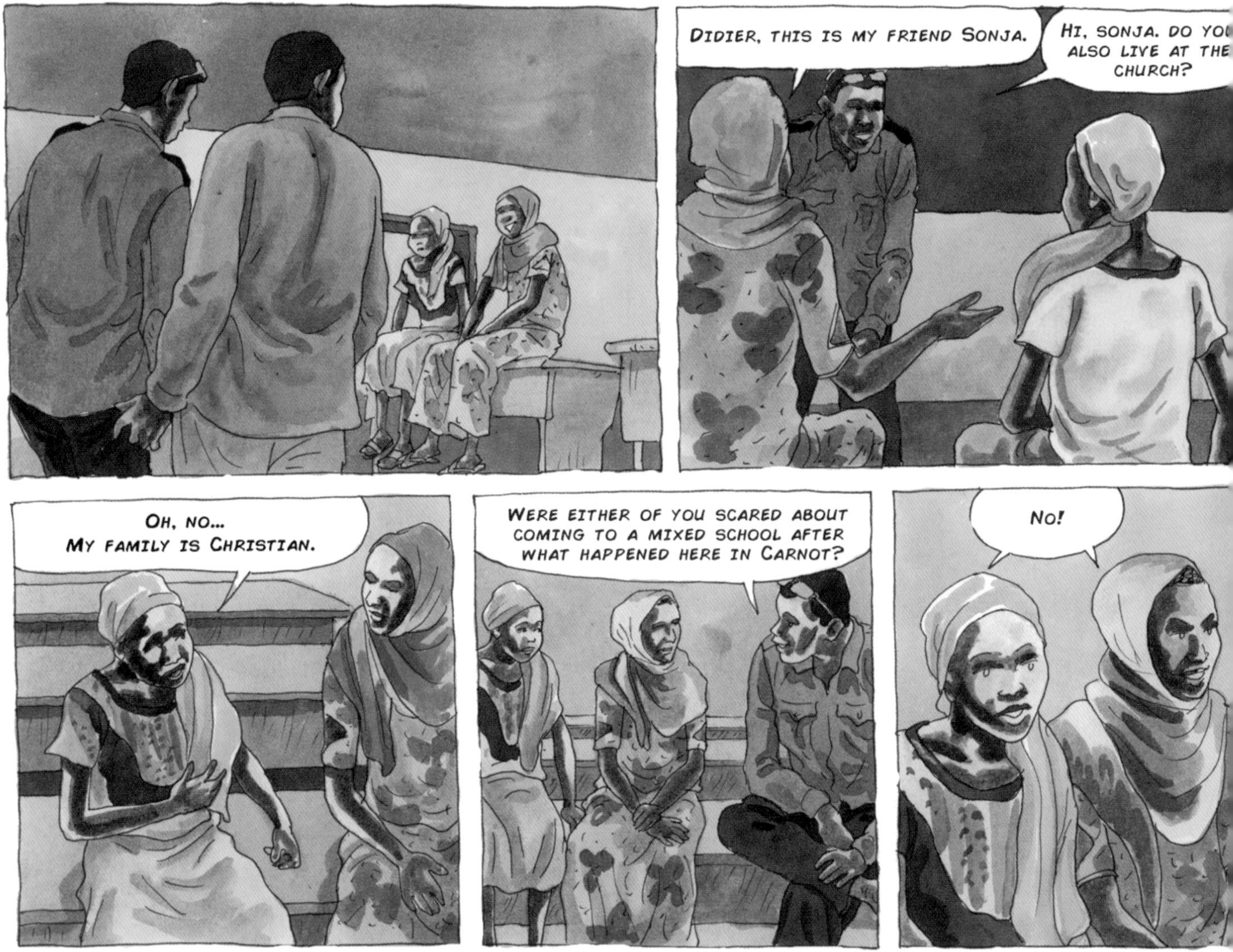
DIDIER, THIS IS MY FRIEND SONJA.
HI, SONJA. DO YO ALSO LIVE AT THE CHURCH?
OH, NO... MY FAMILY IS CHRISTIAN.
WERE EITHER OF YOU SCARED ABOUT COMING TO A MIXED SCHOOL AFTER WHAT HAPPENED HERE IN CARNOT?
NO!

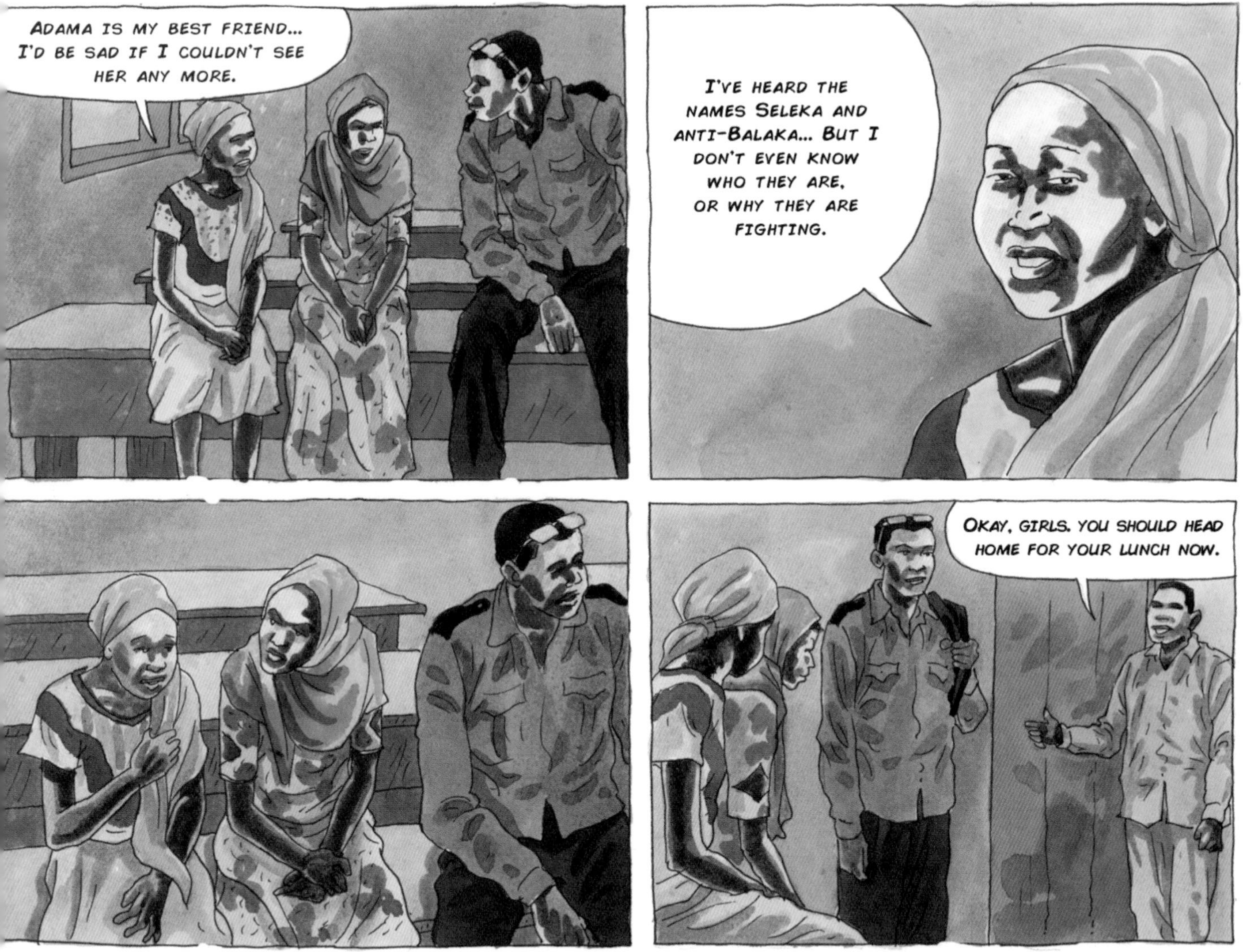
ADAMA IS MY BEST FRIEND... I'D BE SAD IF I COULDN'T SEE HER ANY MORE.
I'VE HEARD THE NAMES SELEKA AND ANTI-BALAKA... BUT I DON'T EVEN KNOW WHO THEY ARE, OR WHY THEY ARE FIGHTING.
OKAY, GIRLS. YOU SHOULD HEAD HOME FOR YOUR LUNCH NOW.

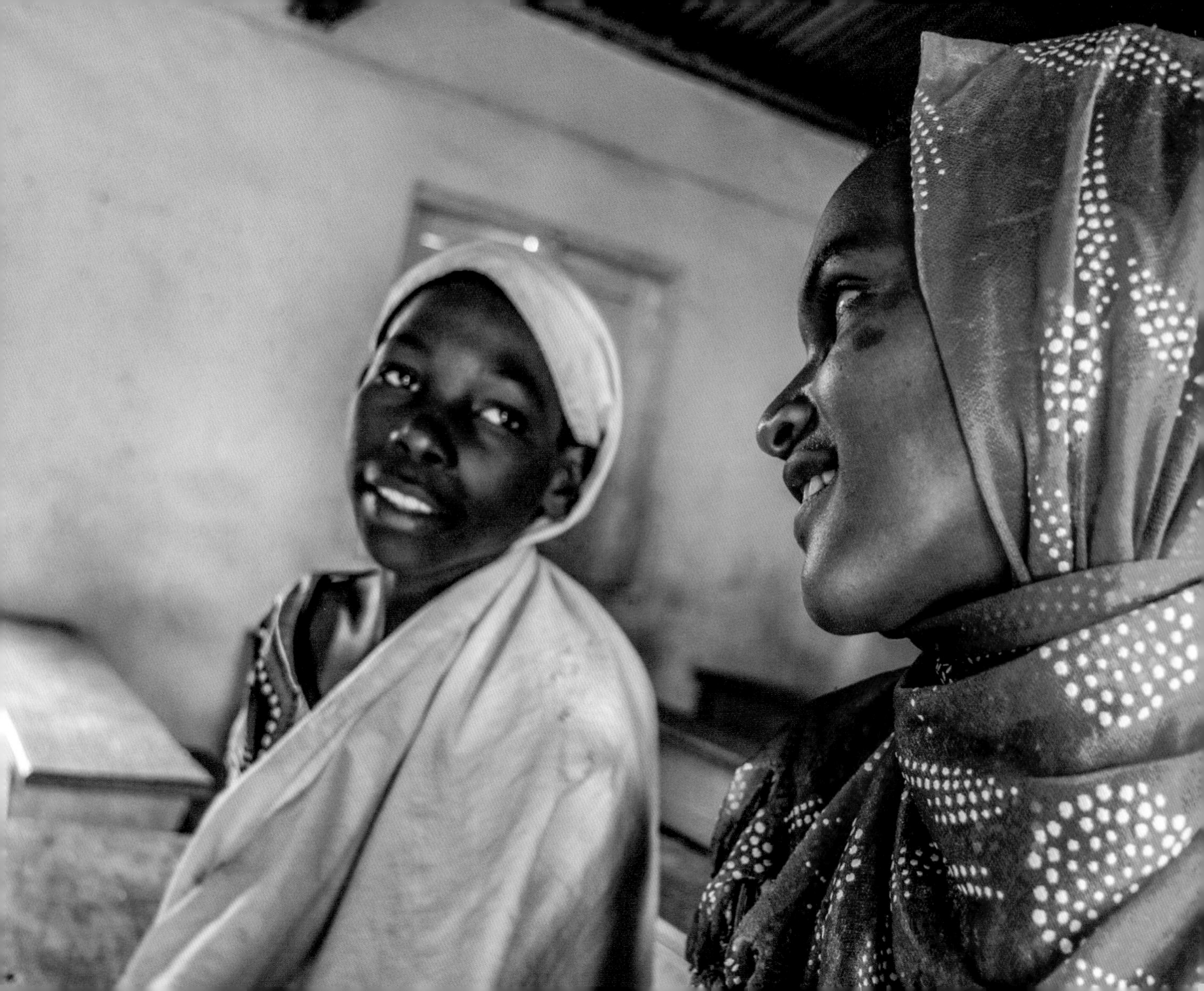

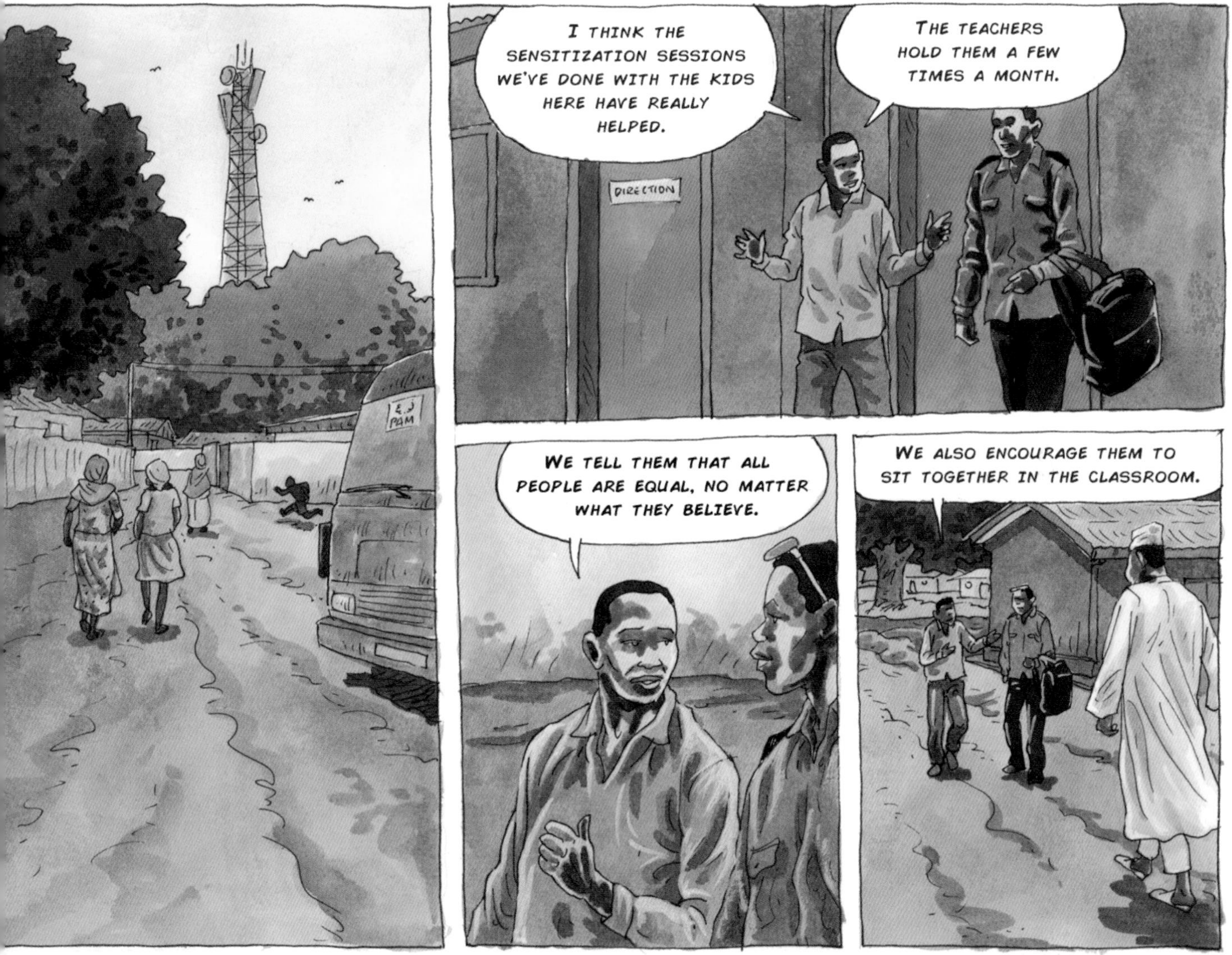
PAM
I THINK THE SENSITIZATION SESSIONS WE'VE DONE WITH THE KIDS HERE HAVE REALLY HELPED.
THE TEACHERS HOLD THEM A FEW TIMES A MONTH.
DIRECTION
WE TELL THEM THAT ALL PEOPLE ARE EQUAL, NO MATTER WHAT THEY BELIEVE.
WE ALSO ENCOURAGE THEM TO SIT TOGETHER IN THE CLASSROOM.

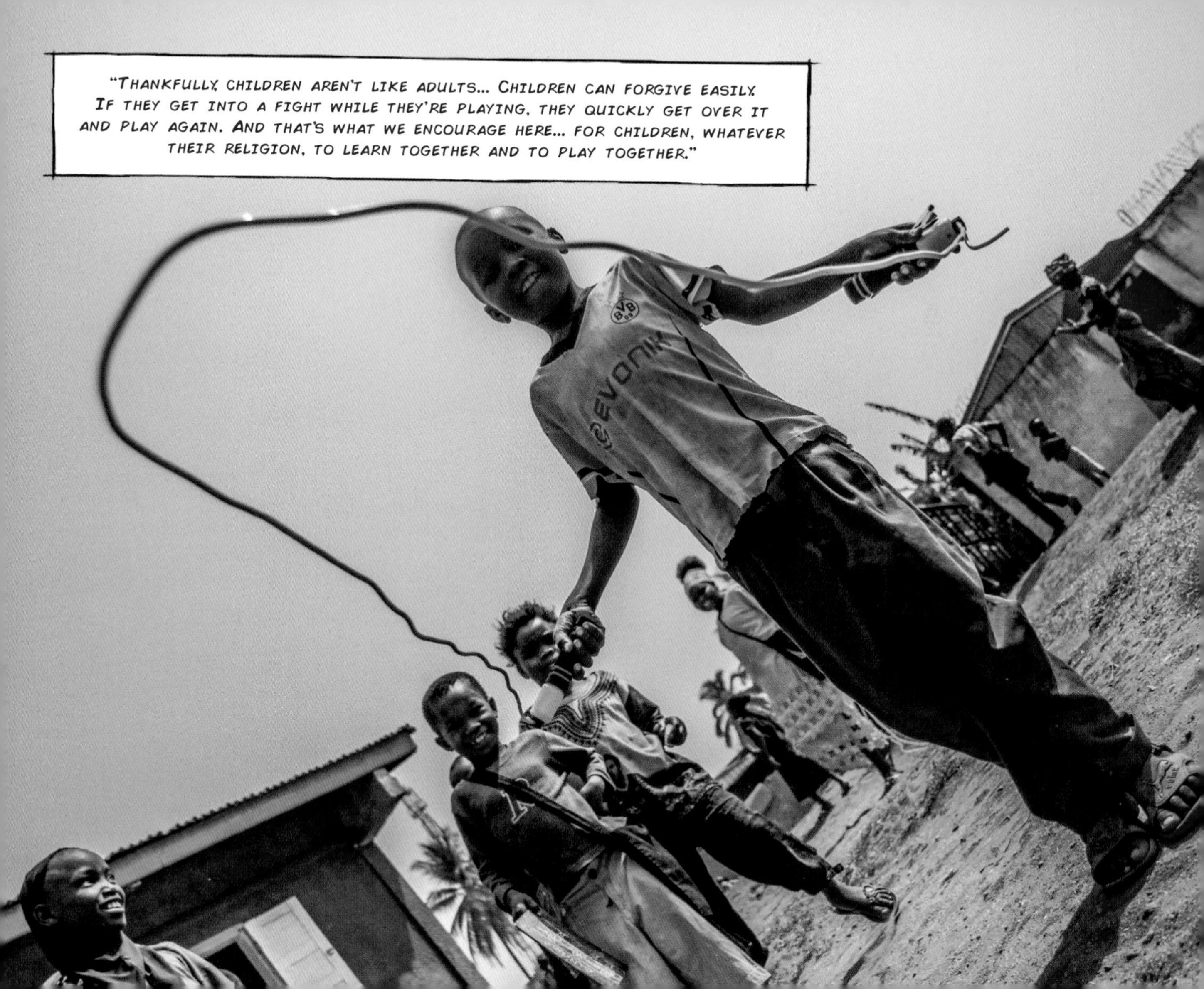
"THANKFULLY, CHILDREN AREN'T LIKE ADULTS... CHILDREN CAN FORGIVE EASILY. IF THEY GET INTO A FIGHT WHILE THEY'RE PLAYING, THEY QUICKLY GET OVER IT AND PLAY AGAIN. AND THAT'S WHAT WE ENCOURAGE HERE... FOR CHILDREN, WHATEVER THEIR RELIGION, TO LEARN TOGETHER AND TO PLAY TOGETHER."
EVONIK

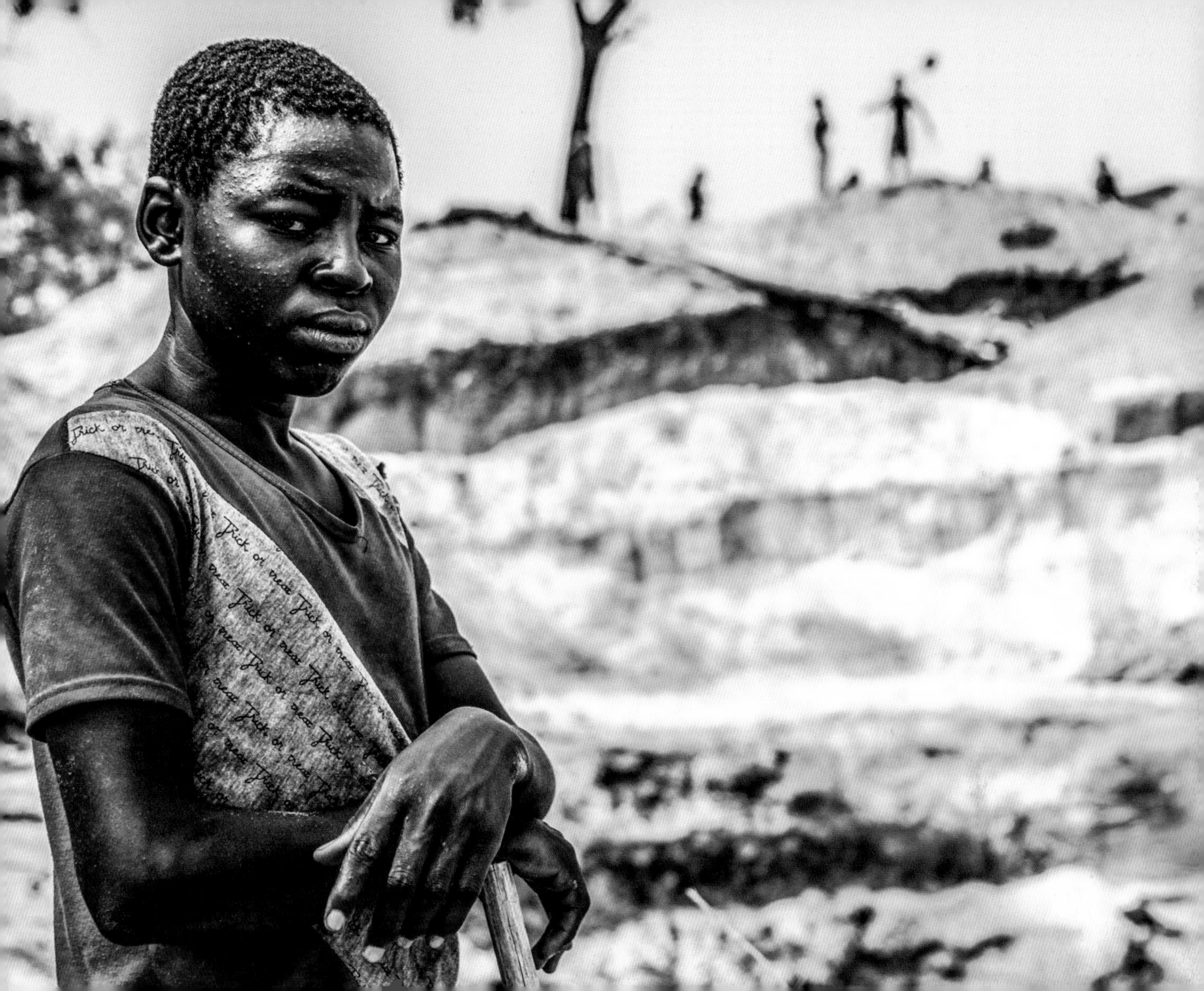
Trick or treat

A HOUSE WITHOUT WINDOWS

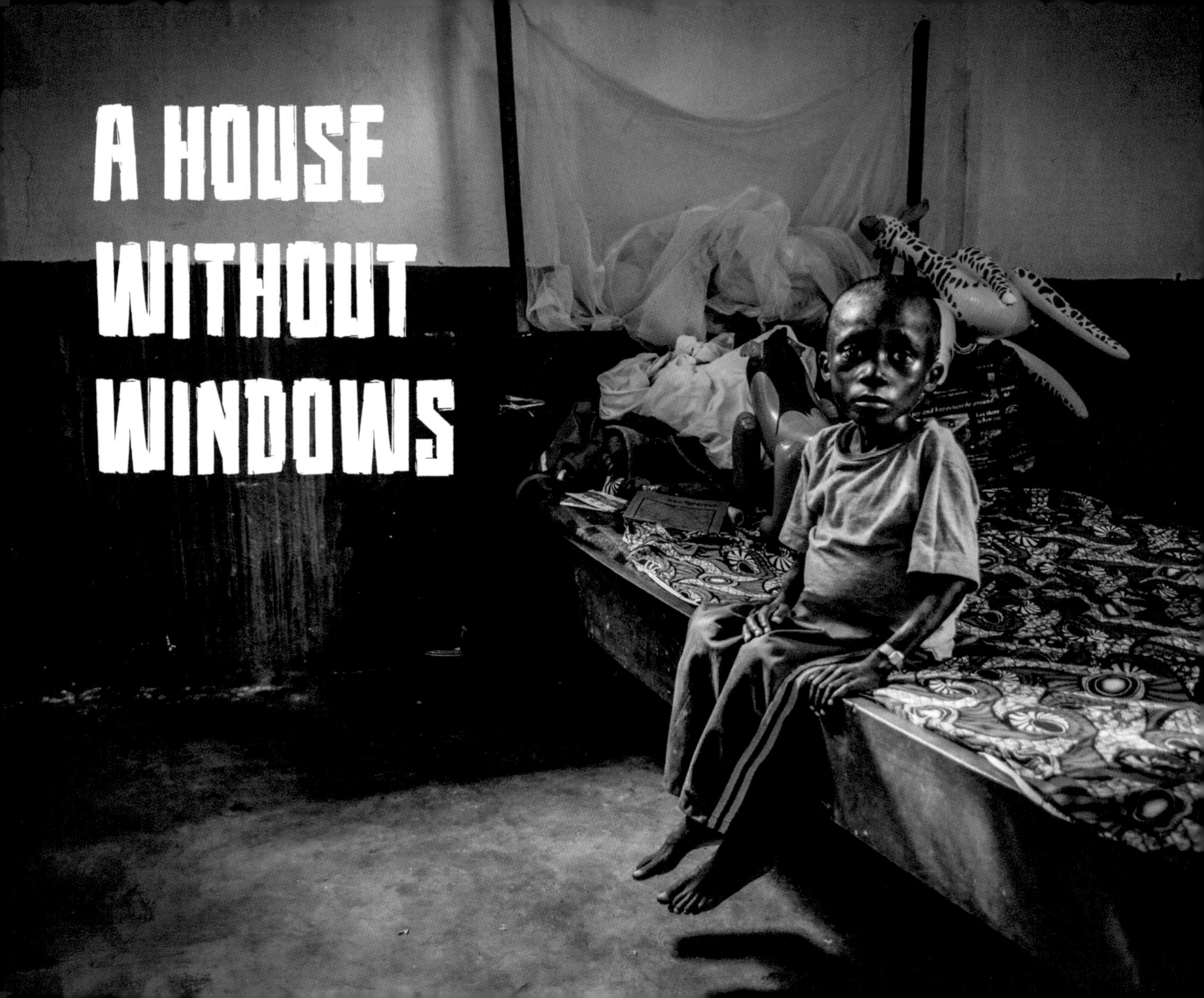

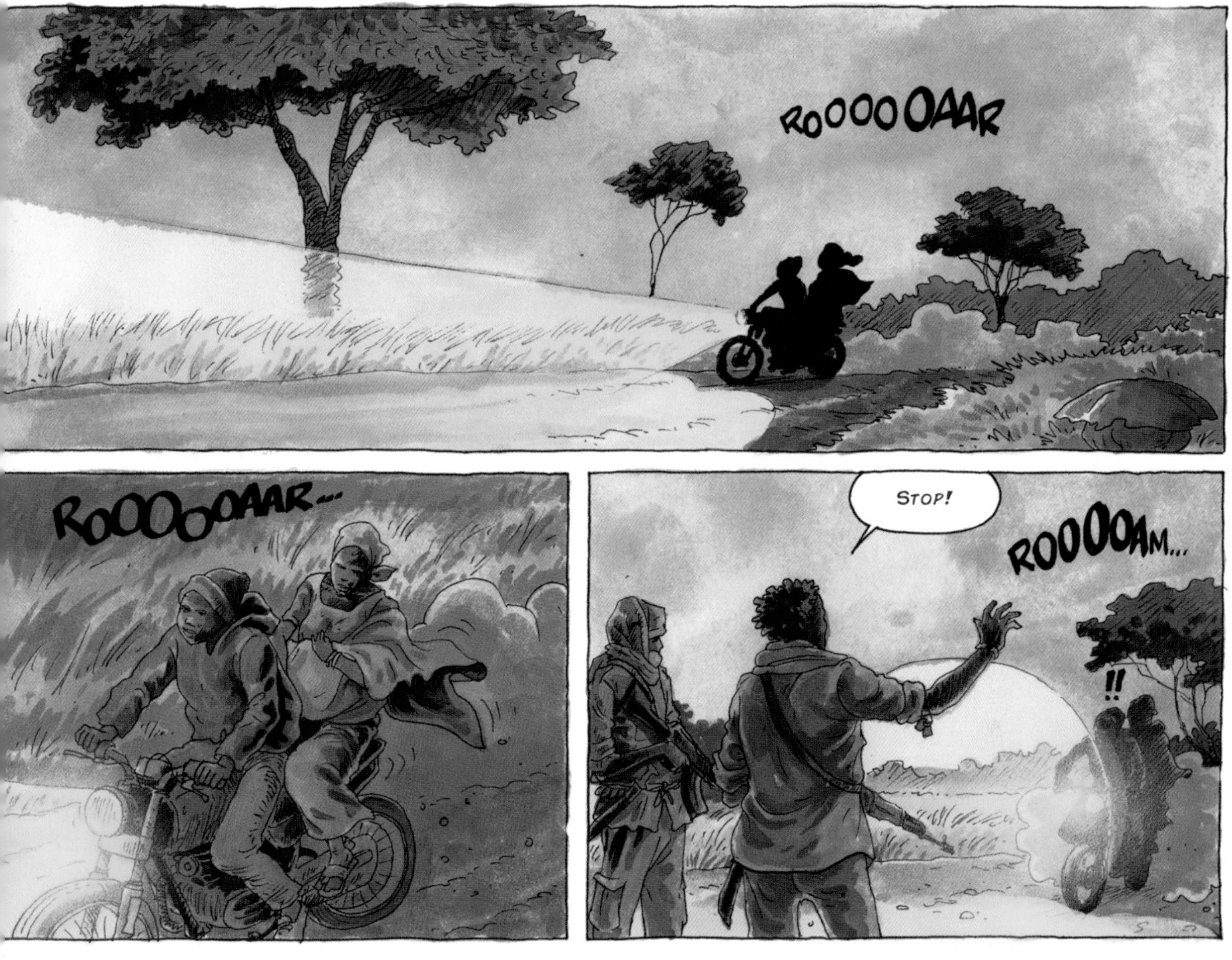
ROOOOOAAR
ROOOOOOAAR...
STOP!
ROOOOAM...
!!

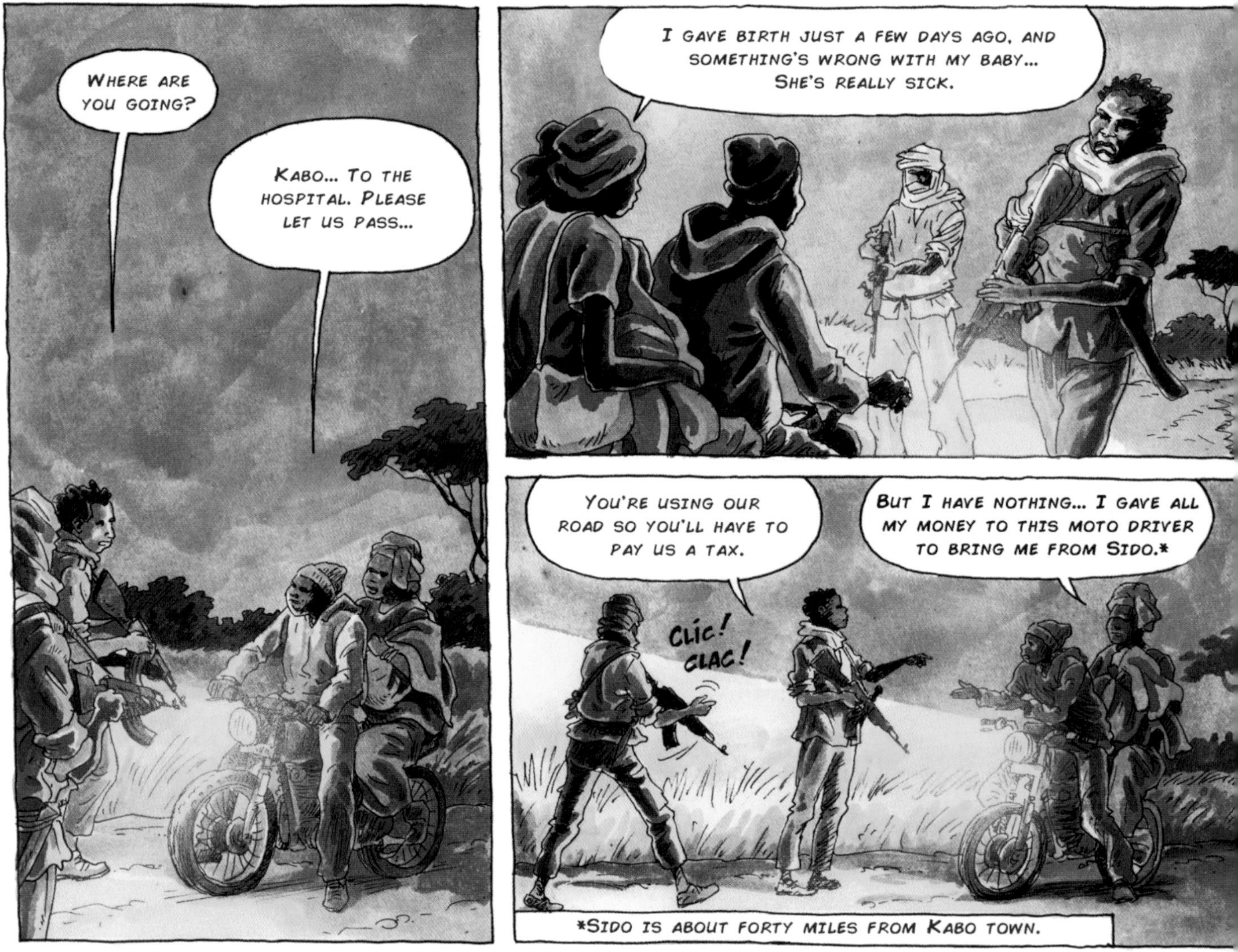
WHERE ARE YOU GOING?
KABO... TO THE HOSPITAL. PLEASE LET US PASS...
I GAVE BIRTH JUST A FEW DAYS AGO, AND SOMETHING'S WRONG WITH MY BABY... SHE'S REALLY SICK.
YOU'RE USING OUR ROAD SO YOU'LL HAVE TO PAY US A TAX.
CLIC! CLAC!
BUT I HAVE NOTHING... I GAVE ALL MY MONEY TO THIS MOTO DRIVER TO BRING ME FROM SIDO.*
*SIDO IS ABOUT FORTY MILES FROM KABO TOWN.

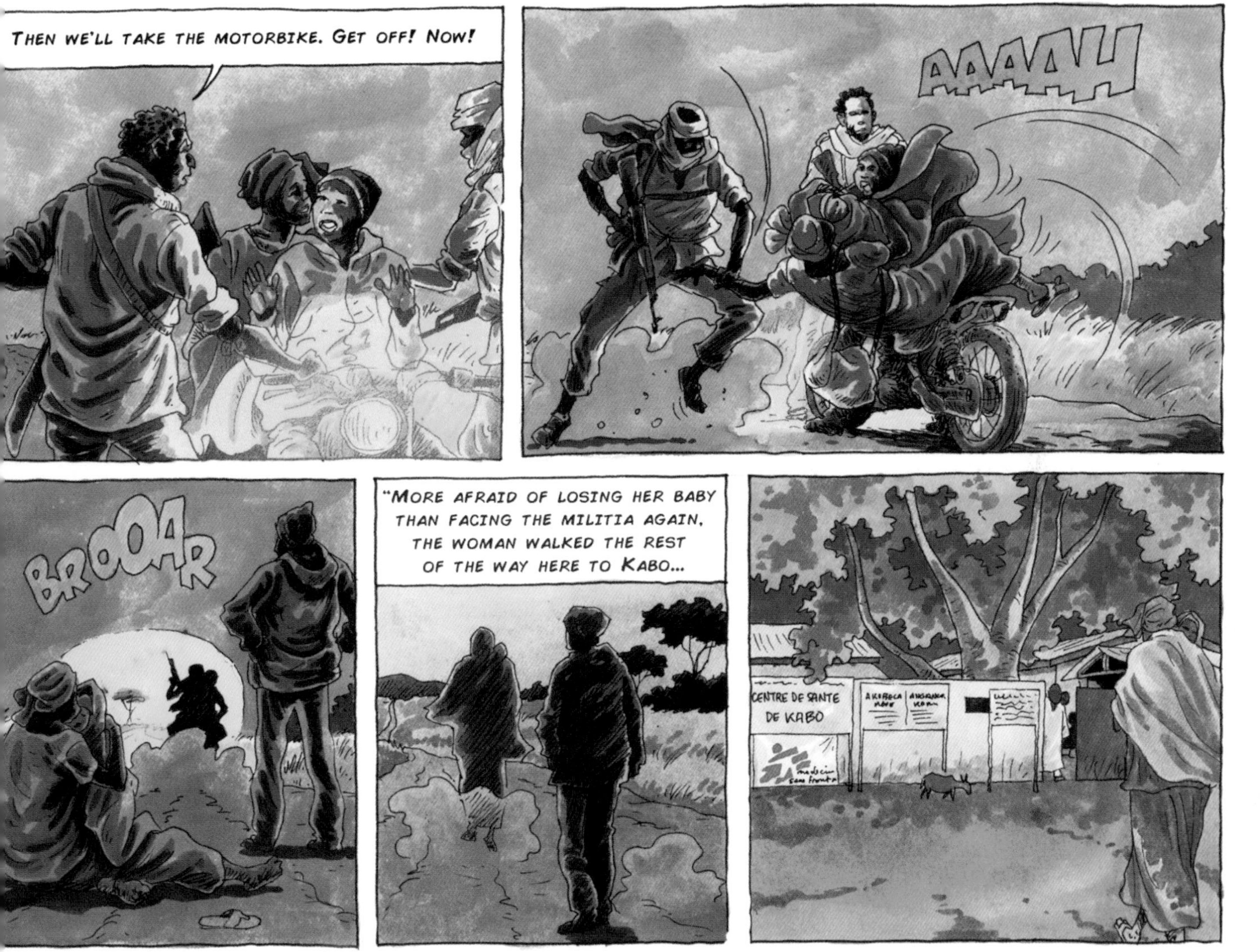
THEN WE'LL TAKE THE MOTORBIKE. GET OFF! NOW!
AAAAAH
BROOAR
"MORE AFRAID OF LOSING HER BABY THAN FACING THE MILITIA AGAIN, THE WOMAN WALKED THE REST OF THE WAY HERE TO KABO...
CENTRE DE SANTE DE KABO

BY THEN, THE BABY HAD DIED.

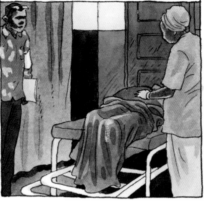

EMMANUELLE BAMONGO IS THE HEAD OF MATERNITY SERVICES AT THE KABO HOSPITAL WHICH IS RUN BY DOCTORS WITHOUT BORDERS.*

BUT THIS TYPE OF THING IS COMMON. IT'S THE REALITY HERE...

JUST RECENTLY, ANOTHER WOMAN – THIS ONE WAS PREGNANT – WAS FORCED OFF A MOTORBIKE AT GUNPOINT.

"SHE ENDED UP GIVING BIRTH ON THE SIDE OF A DIRT ROAD.

*MÉDECINS SANS FRONTIÈRES (MSF).

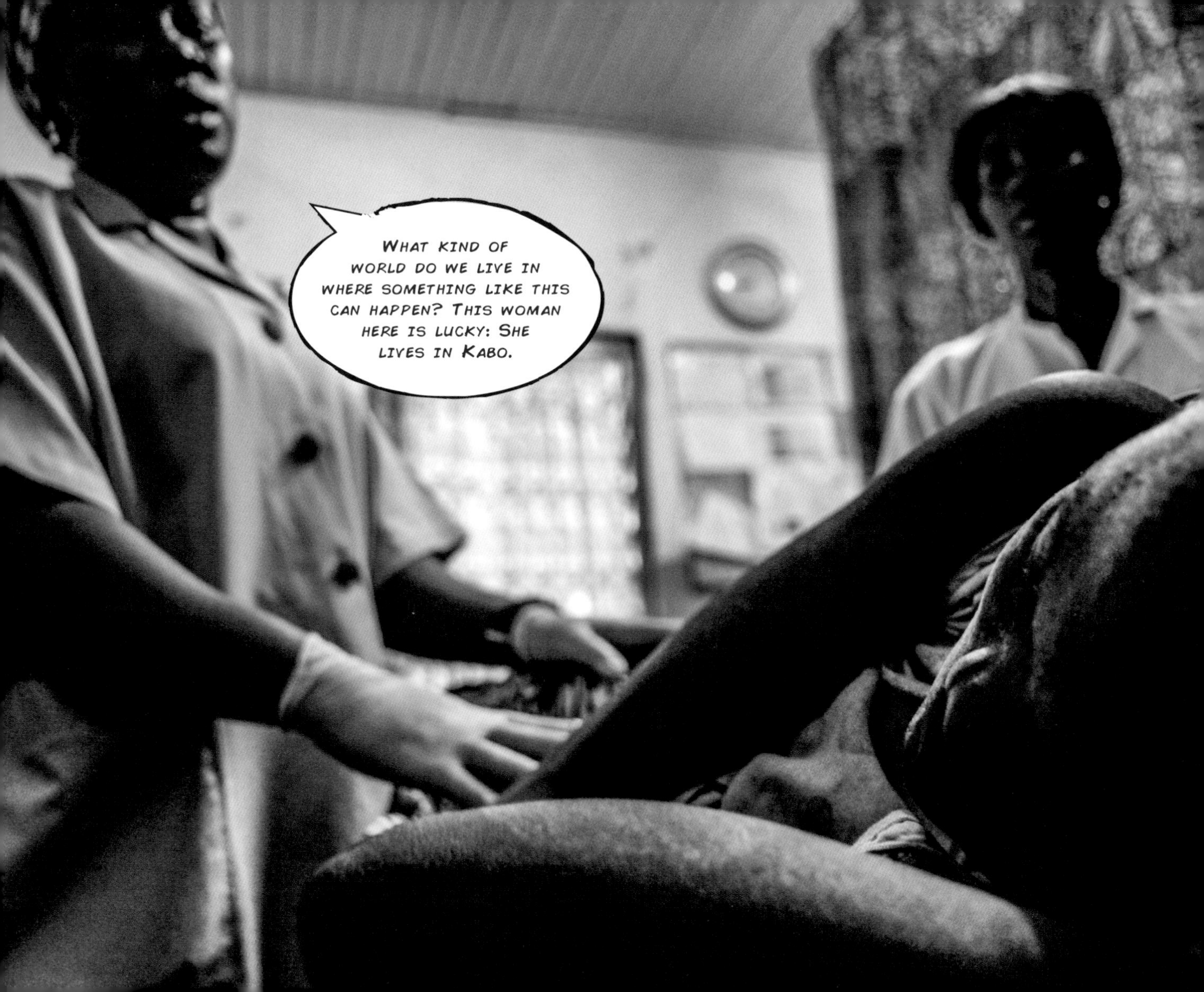
WHAT KIND OF WORLD DO WE LIVE IN WHERE SOMETHING LIKE THIS CAN HAPPEN? THIS WOMAN HERE IS LUCKY: SHE LIVES IN KABO.

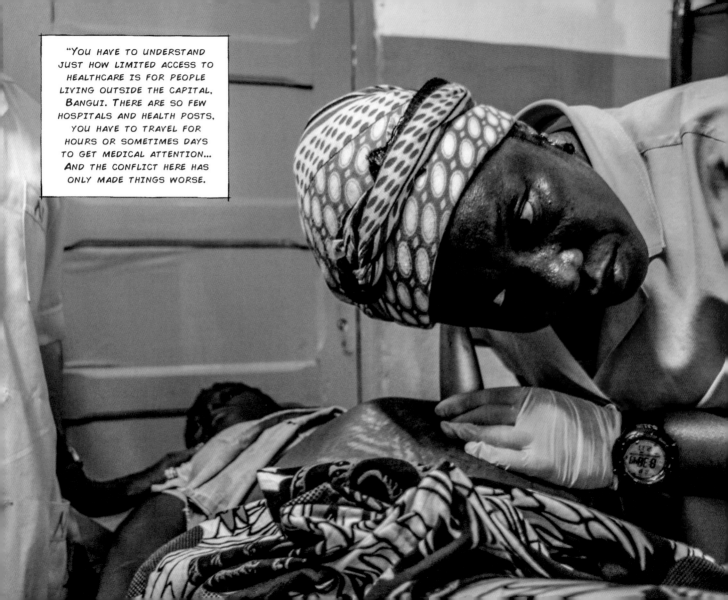

"YOU HAVE TO UNDERSTAND JUST HOW LIMITED ACCESS TO HEALTHCARE IS FOR PEOPLE LIVING OUTSIDE THE CAPITAL, BANGUI. THERE ARE SO FEW HOSPITALS AND HEALTH POSTS, YOU HAVE TO TRAVEL FOR HOURS OR SOMETIMES DAYS TO GET MEDICAL ATTENTION... AND THE CONFLICT HERE HAS ONLY MADE THINGS WORSE.

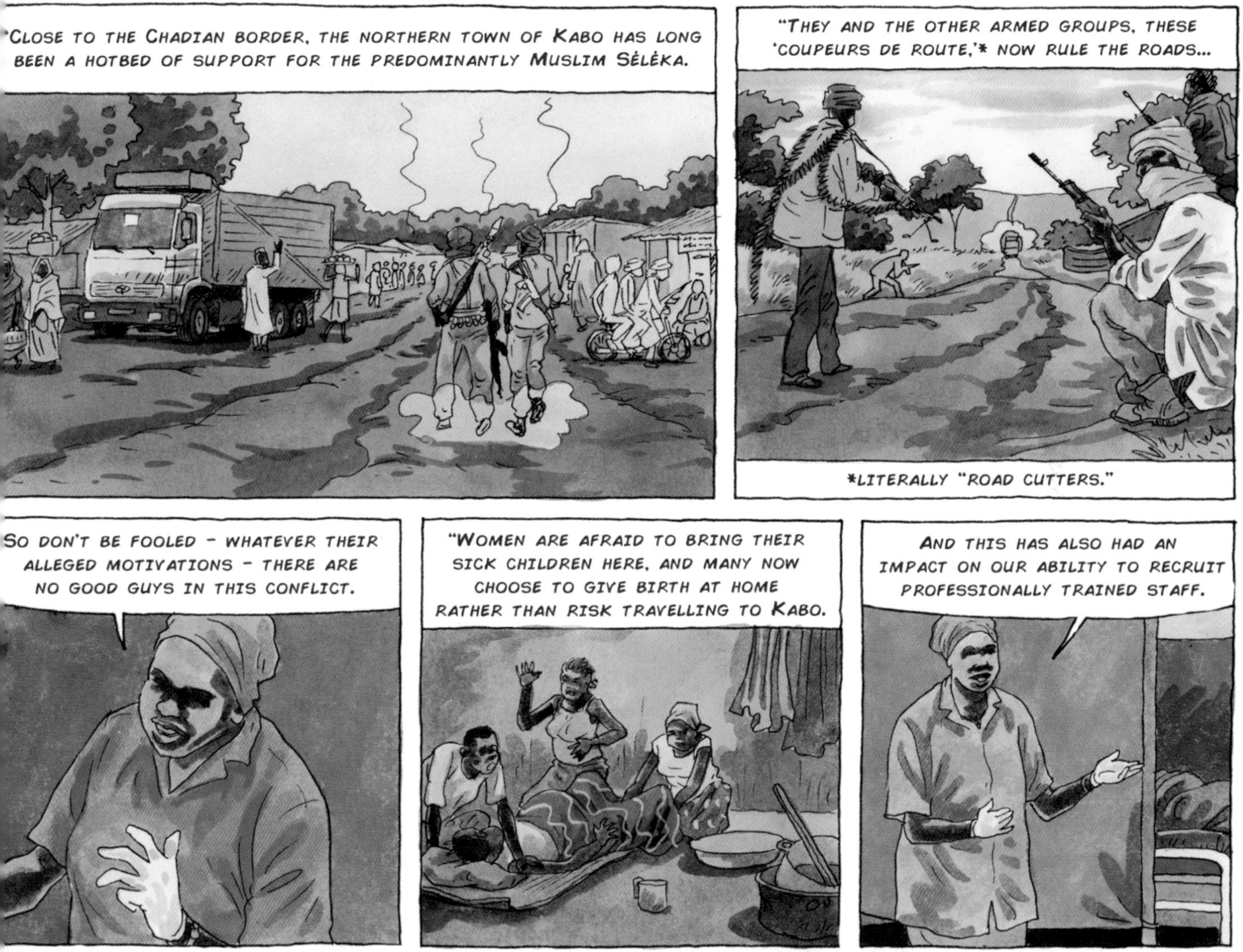
"CLOSE TO THE CHADIAN BORDER, THE NORTHERN TOWN OF KABO HAS LONG BEEN A HOTBED OF SUPPORT FOR THE PREDOMINANTLY MUSLIM SÉLÉKA.
"THEY AND THE OTHER ARMED GROUPS, THESE 'COUPEURS DE ROUTE,'* NOW RULE THE ROADS...
*LITERALLY "ROAD CUTTERS."
SO DON'T BE FOOLED - WHATEVER THEIR ALLEGED MOTIVATIONS - THERE ARE NO GOOD GUYS IN THIS CONFLICT.
"WOMEN ARE AFRAID TO BRING THEIR SICK CHILDREN HERE, AND MANY NOW CHOOSE TO GIVE BIRTH AT HOME RATHER THAN RISK TRAVELLING TO KABO.
AND THIS HAS ALSO HAD AN IMPACT ON OUR ABILITY TO RECRUIT PROFESSIONALLY TRAINED STAFF.

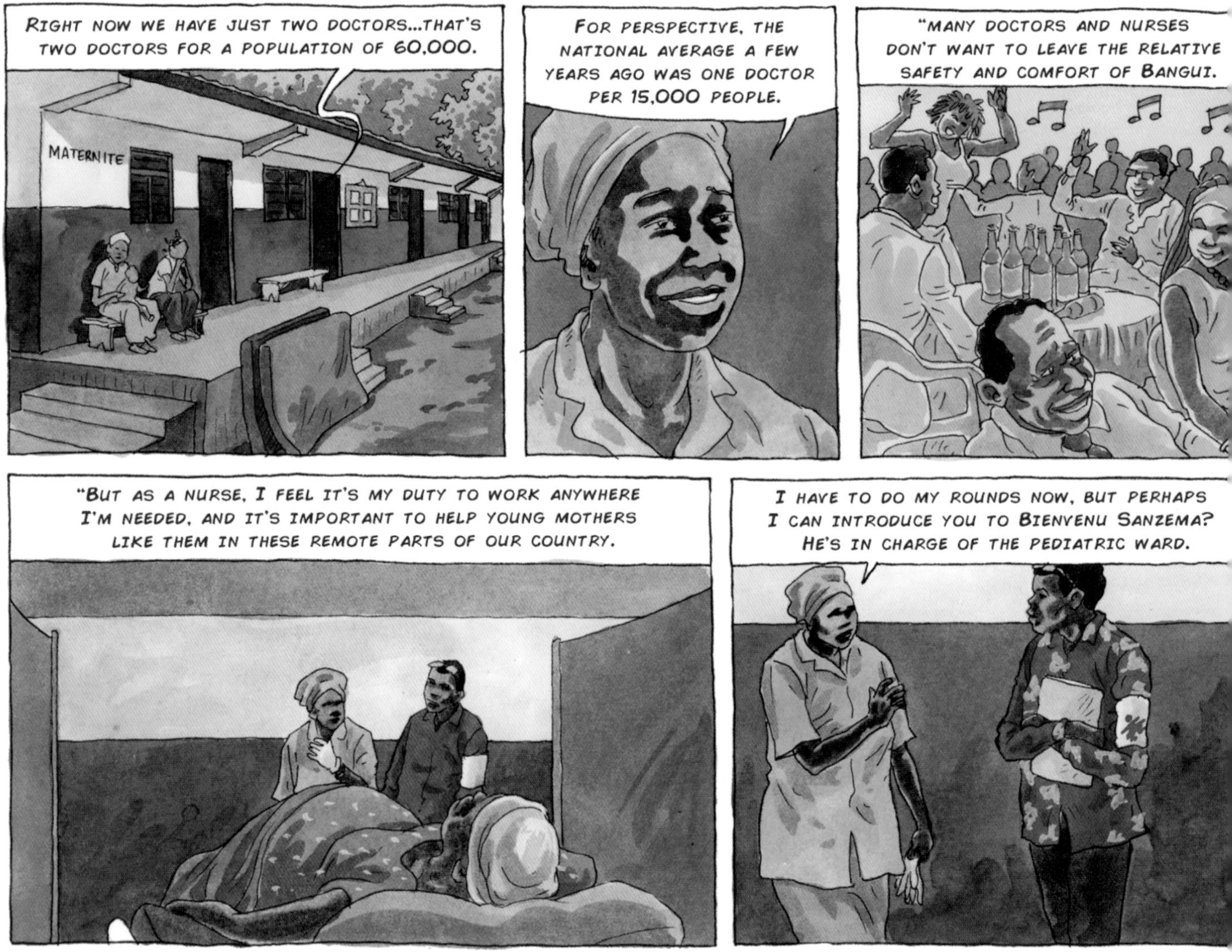
RIGHT NOW WE HAVE JUST TWO DOCTORS...THAT'S TWO DOCTORS FOR A POPULATION OF 60,000.
MATERNITE
FOR PERSPECTIVE, THE NATIONAL AVERAGE A FEW YEARS AGO WAS ONE DOCTOR PER 15,000 PEOPLE.
"MANY DOCTORS AND NURSES DON'T WANT TO LEAVE THE RELATIVE SAFETY AND COMFORT OF BANGUI.
"BUT AS A NURSE, I FEEL IT'S MY DUTY TO WORK ANYWHERE I'M NEEDED, AND IT'S IMPORTANT TO HELP YOUNG MOTHERS LIKE THEM IN THESE REMOTE PARTS OF OUR COUNTRY.
I HAVE TO DO MY ROUNDS NOW, BUT PERHAPS I CAN INTRODUCE YOU TO BIENVENU SANZEMA? HE'S IN CHARGE OF THE PEDIATRIC WARD.

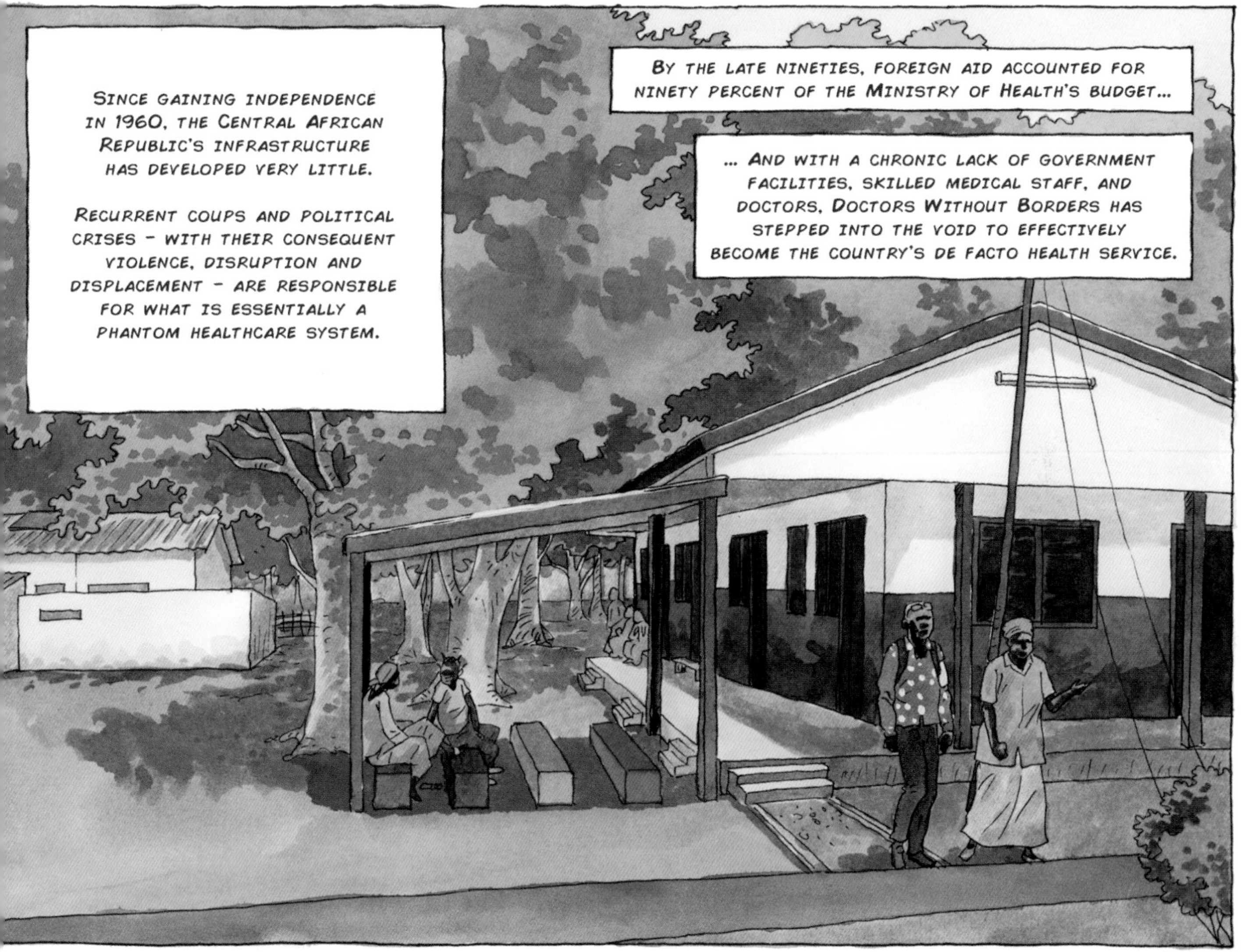
SINCE GAINING INDEPENDENCE IN 1960, THE CENTRAL AFRICAN REPUBLIC'S INFRASTRUCTURE HAS DEVELOPED VERY LITTLE.
RECURRENT COUPS AND POLITICAL CRISES - WITH THEIR CONSEQUENT VIOLENCE, DISRUPTION AND DISPLACEMENT - ARE RESPONSIBLE FOR WHAT IS ESSENTIALLY A PHANTOM HEALTHCARE SYSTEM.
BY THE LATE NINETIES, FOREIGN AID ACCOUNTED FOR NINETY PERCENT OF THE MINISTRY OF HEALTH'S BUDGET...
... AND WITH A CHRONIC LACK OF GOVERNMENT FACILITIES, SKILLED MEDICAL STAFF, AND DOCTORS, DOCTORS WITHOUT BORDERS HAS STEPPED INTO THE VOID TO EFFECTIVELY BECOME THE COUNTRY'S DE FACTO HEALTH SERVICE.

HI, BIENVENU — THIS IS DIDIER. HE'S AN ARTIST RESEARCHING CHILDREN'S HEALTH. DO YOU MIND TALKING WITH HIM?

SURE! NO PROBLEM.

SO WHY ARE THESE PARTICULAR CHILDREN HERE?

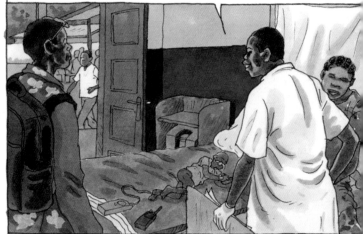

WELL, THIS IS THE INTENSIVE CARE SECTION OF OUR PEDIATRIC WARD

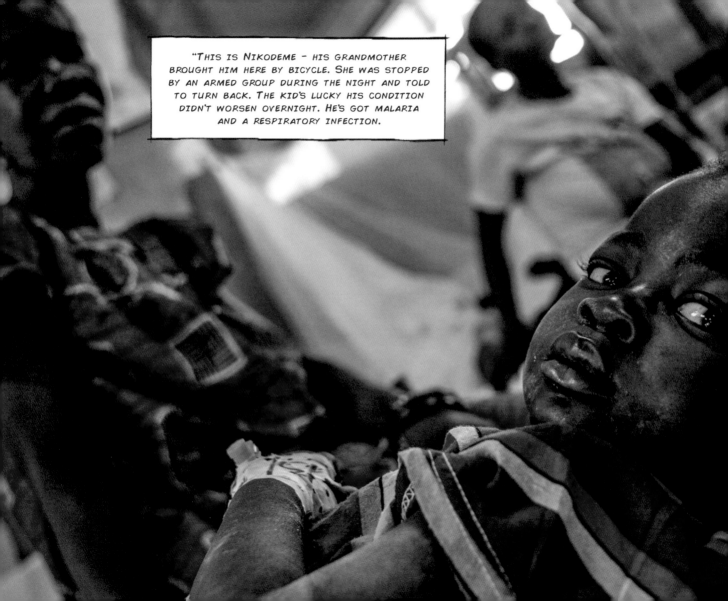

"THIS IS NIKODEME — HIS GRANDMOTHER BROUGHT HIM HERE BY BICYCLE. SHE WAS STOPPED BY AN ARMED GROUP DURING THE NIGHT AND TOLD TO TURN BACK. THE KID'S LUCKY HIS CONDITION DIDN'T WORSEN OVERNIGHT. HE'S GOT MALARIA AND A RESPIRATORY INFECTION.

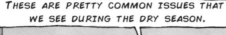
THESE ARE PRETTY COMMON ISSUES THAT WE SEE DURING THE DRY SEASON.

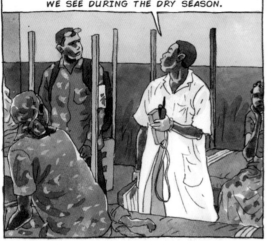

IT'S SO HOT THAT PEOPLE SLEEP OUTSIDE WITHOUT MOSQUITO NETS.

BUT I'VE SEEN AN INCREAS[E] IN KIDS BEING ADMITTED SINCE THE CRISIS STARTED.

"MANY FAMILIES HAVE HAD TO FLEE THEIR HOMES SUDDENLY, WITHOUT THE TIME TO PACK CLOTHES... LET ALONE THEIR MOSQUITO NETS.

"THEY SLEEP OUTDOORS IN THE BUSH, OR CRAM INTO TARPAULIN TENTS IN UNHYGIENIC HOMELESS CAMPS.

"THOSE THAT HAVE FLED ARE NO[W] IN MORE REMOTE AREAS...SO I[F] YOU NEED HELP, BY THE TIME YO[U] GET HERE, YOUR CONDITION WIL[L] HAVE WORSENED SIGNIFICANTL[Y]

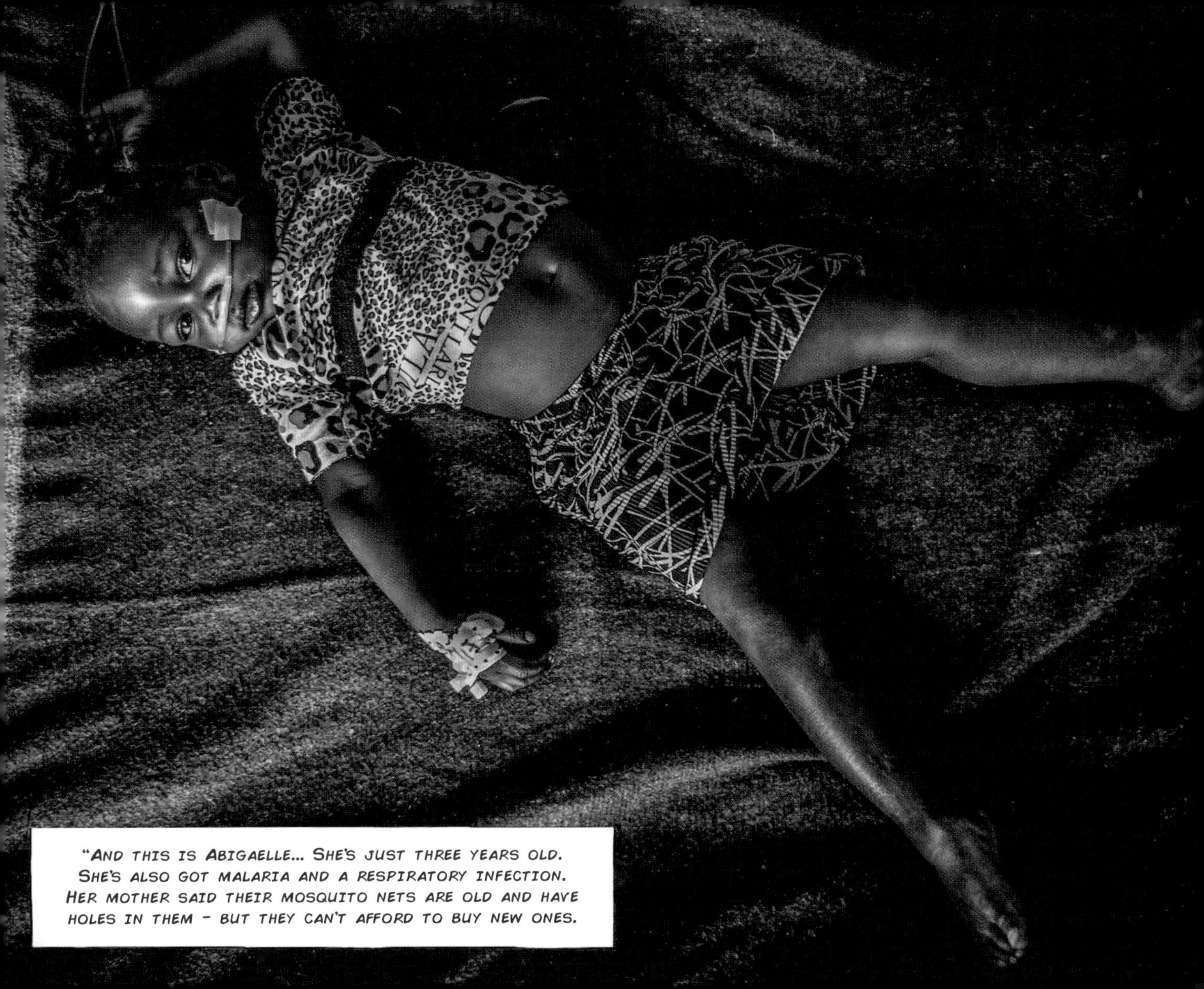
"AND THIS IS ABIGAELLE... SHE'S JUST THREE YEARS OLD. SHE'S ALSO GOT MALARIA AND A RESPIRATORY INFECTION. HER MOTHER SAID THEIR MOSQUITO NETS ARE OLD AND HAVE HOLES IN THEM - BUT THEY CAN'T AFFORD TO BUY NEW ONES.

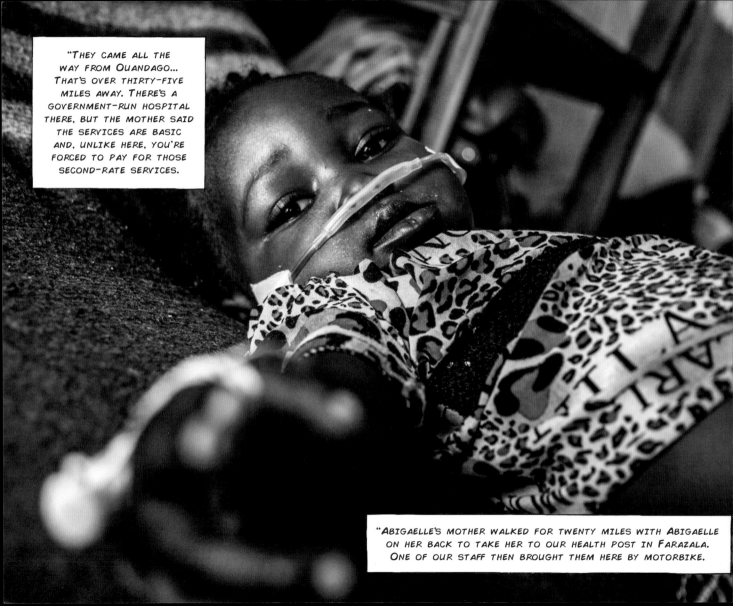

"THEY CAME ALL THE WAY FROM OUANDAGO... THAT'S OVER THIRTY-FIVE MILES AWAY. THERE'S A GOVERNMENT-RUN HOSPITAL THERE, BUT THE MOTHER SAID THE SERVICES ARE BASIC AND, UNLIKE HERE, YOU'RE FORCED TO PAY FOR THOSE SECOND-RATE SERVICES.

"ABIGAELLE'S MOTHER WALKED FOR TWENTY MILES WITH ABIGAELLE ON HER BACK TO TAKE HER TO OUR HEALTH POST IN FARAZALA. ONE OF OUR STAFF THEN BROUGHT THEM HERE BY MOTORBIKE.

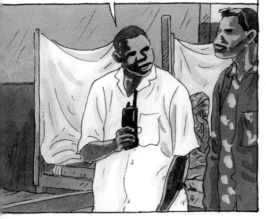

THERE WAS A REPORT A FEW YEARS AGO THAT SHOWED MORE PEOPLE HAD DIED FROM THE ABSENCE OF HEALTH SERVICES THAN THE WAR ITSELF.

IF WE WEREN'T HERE, I DON'T KNOW WHAT WOULD HAVE HAPPENED TO THESE CHILDREN.

I'VE BEEN MEANING TO ASK...WHEN I CAME INTO THE HOSPITAL THIS MORNING I NOTICED AN AREA WITH COLORED BENCHES. WHAT ARE THEY FOR?

OH, YOU MEAN THE PEDIATRIC OUTPATIENTS BUILDING. LET'S HEAD OVER THERE NOW.

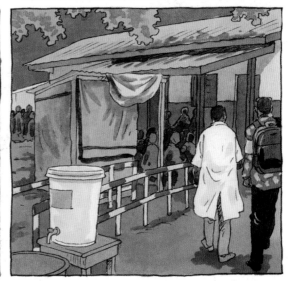

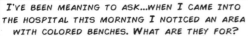

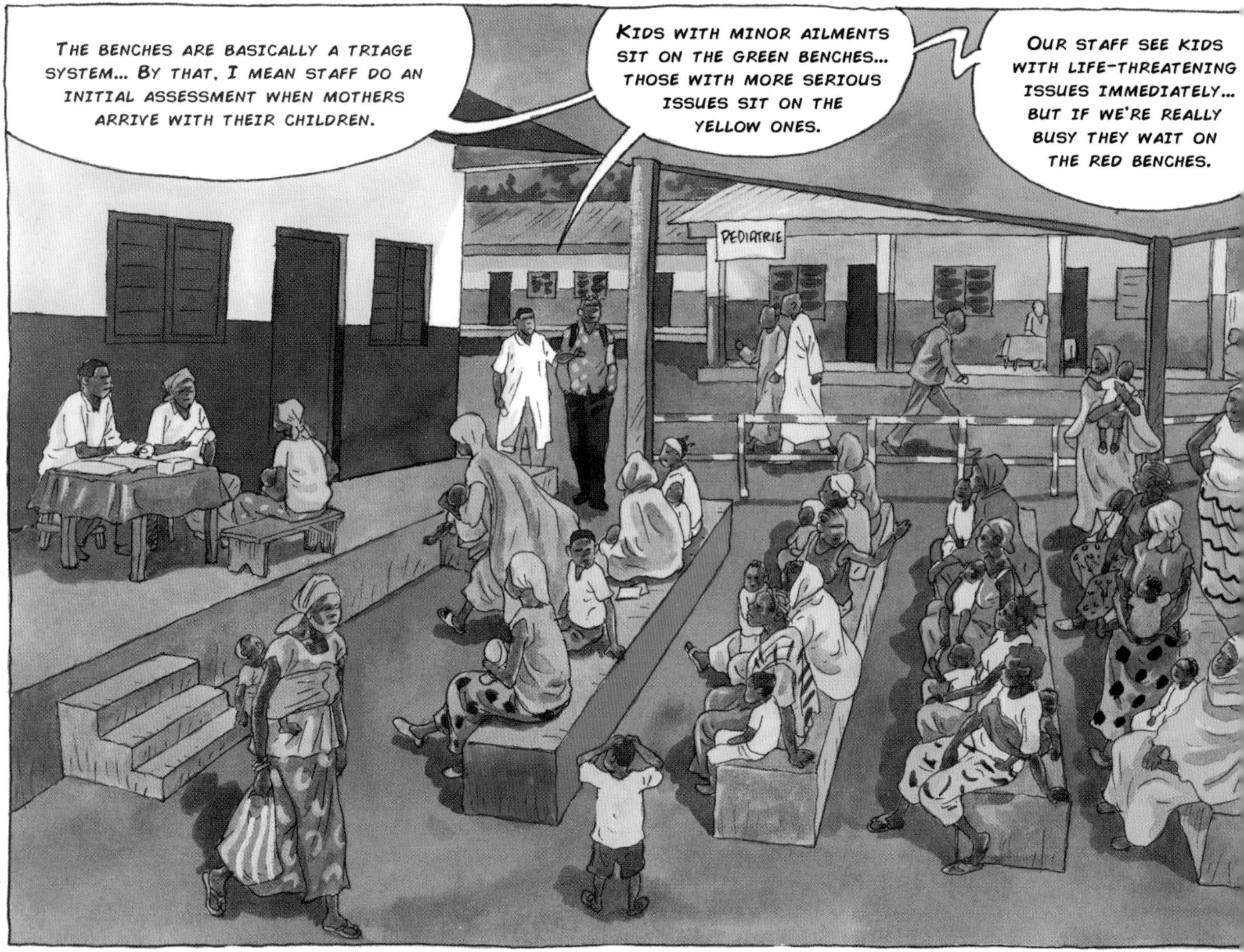
THE BENCHES ARE BASICALLY A TRIAGE SYSTEM... BY THAT, I MEAN STAFF DO AN INITIAL ASSESSMENT WHEN MOTHERS ARRIVE WITH THEIR CHILDREN.
KIDS WITH MINOR AILMENTS SIT ON THE GREEN BENCHES... THOSE WITH MORE SERIOUS ISSUES SIT ON THE YELLOW ONES.
OUR STAFF SEE KIDS WITH LIFE-THREATENING ISSUES IMMEDIATELY... BUT IF WE'RE REALLY BUSY THEY WAIT ON THE RED BENCHES.
PEDIATRIE

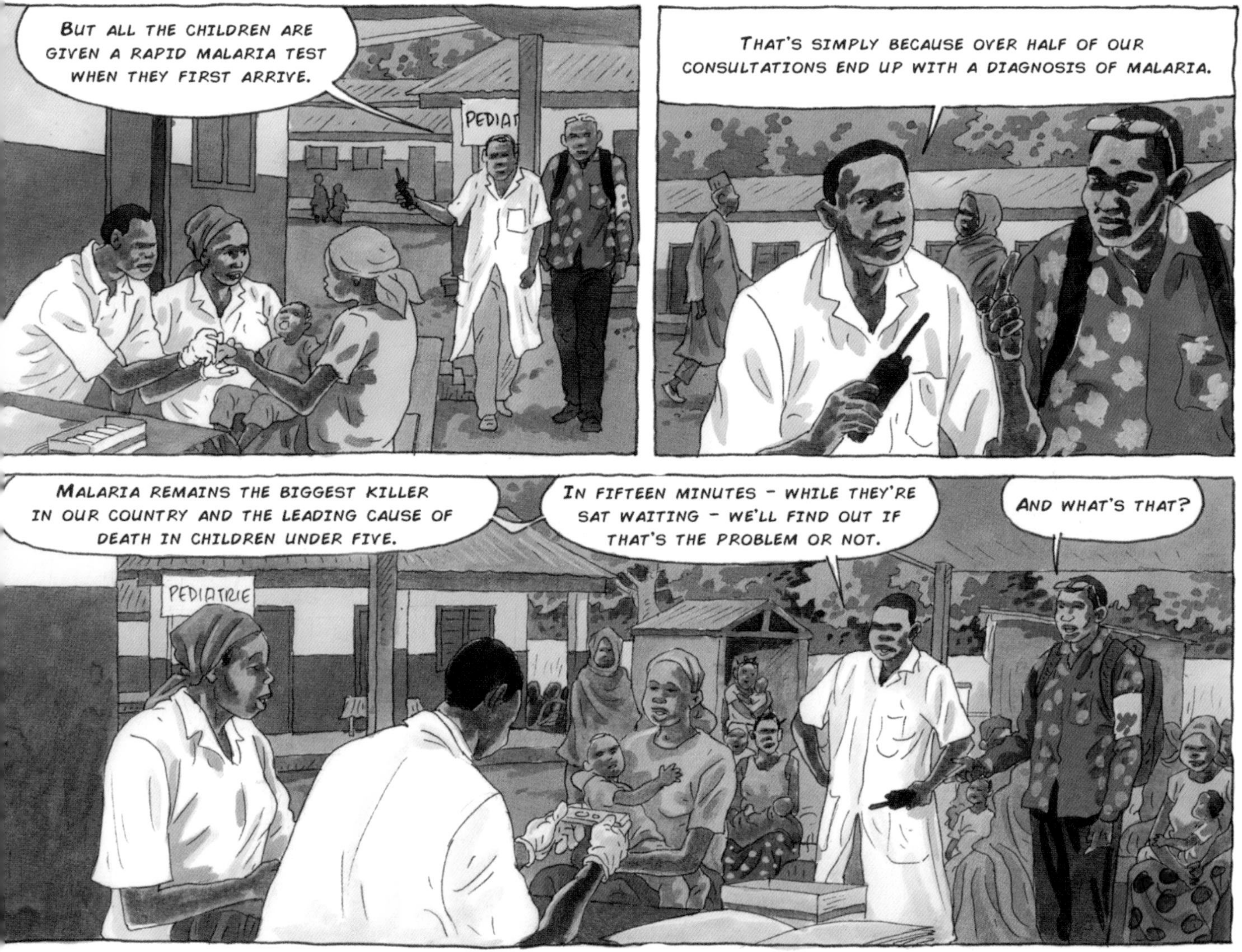
BUT ALL THE CHILDREN ARE GIVEN A RAPID MALARIA TEST WHEN THEY FIRST ARRIVE.
PEDIAT
THAT'S SIMPLY BECAUSE OVER HALF OF OUR CONSULTATIONS END UP WITH A DIAGNOSIS OF MALARIA.
MALARIA REMAINS THE BIGGEST KILLER IN OUR COUNTRY AND THE LEADING CAUSE OF DEATH IN CHILDREN UNDER FIVE.
IN FIFTEEN MINUTES - WHILE THEY'RE SAT WAITING - WE'LL FIND OUT IF THAT'S THE PROBLEM OR NOT.
AND WHAT'S THAT?
PEDIATRIE

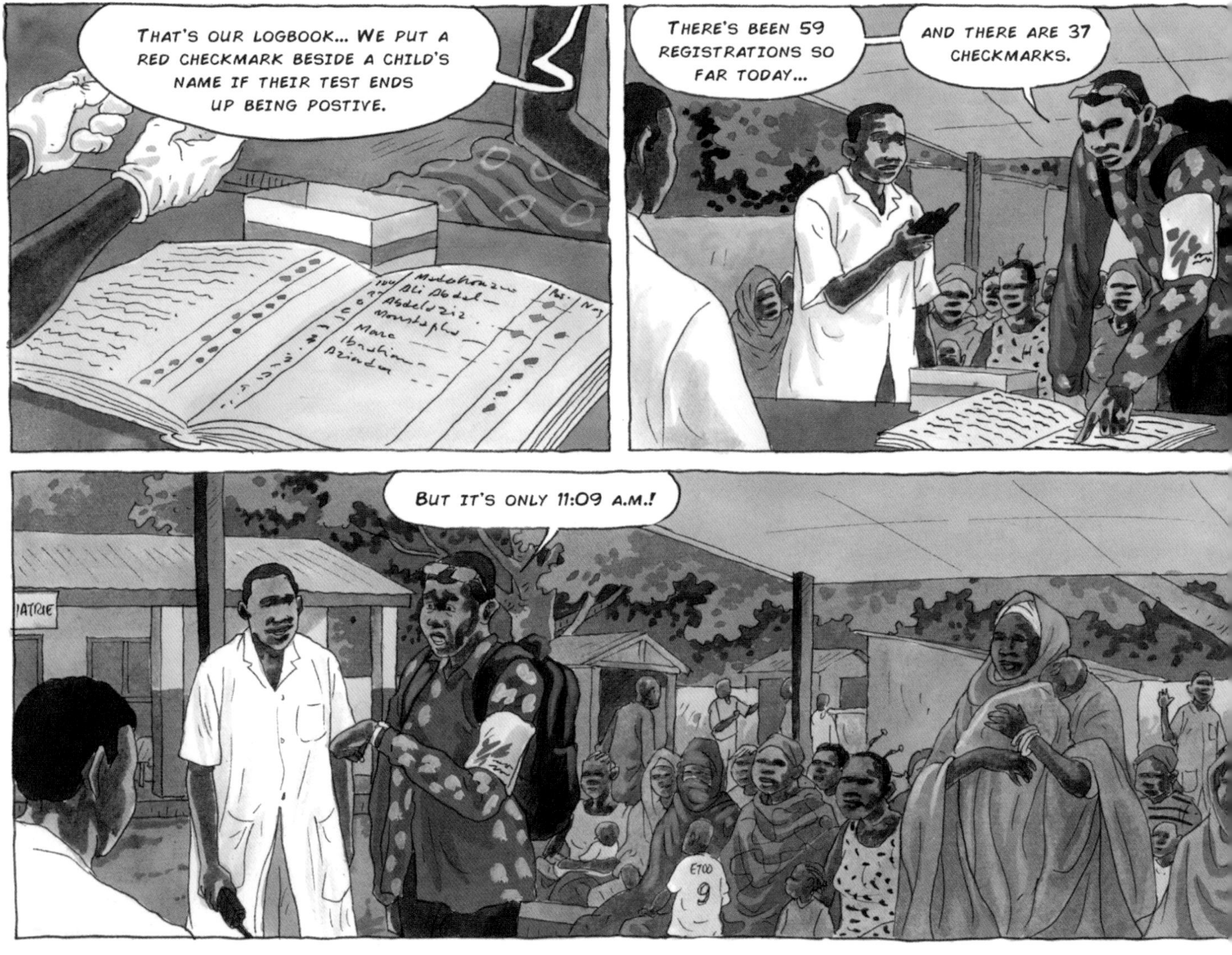
THAT'S OUR LOGBOOK... WE PUT A RED CHECKMARK BESIDE A CHILD'S NAME IF THEIR TEST ENDS UP BEING POSTIVE.
THERE'S BEEN 59 REGISTRATIONS SO FAR TODAY...
AND THERE ARE 37 CHECKMARKS.
BUT IT'S ONLY 11:09 A.M.!

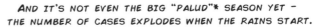

YEAH, IT'S NOT UNUSUAL FOR OVER HALF OF THE 1,200 TESTS WE DO A WEEK TO TURN OUT POSITIVE.

AND IT'S NOT EVEN THE BIG "PALUD"* SEASON YET — THE NUMBER OF CASES EXPLODES WHEN THE RAINS START.

*FRENCH SLANG FOR MALARIA.

BUT MALNUTRITION IS ALSO A MAJOR ISSUE THAT AFFECTS CHILDREN HERE...

...SO MUCH SO THAT WE HAVE A SEPARATE BUILDING FOR THEM.

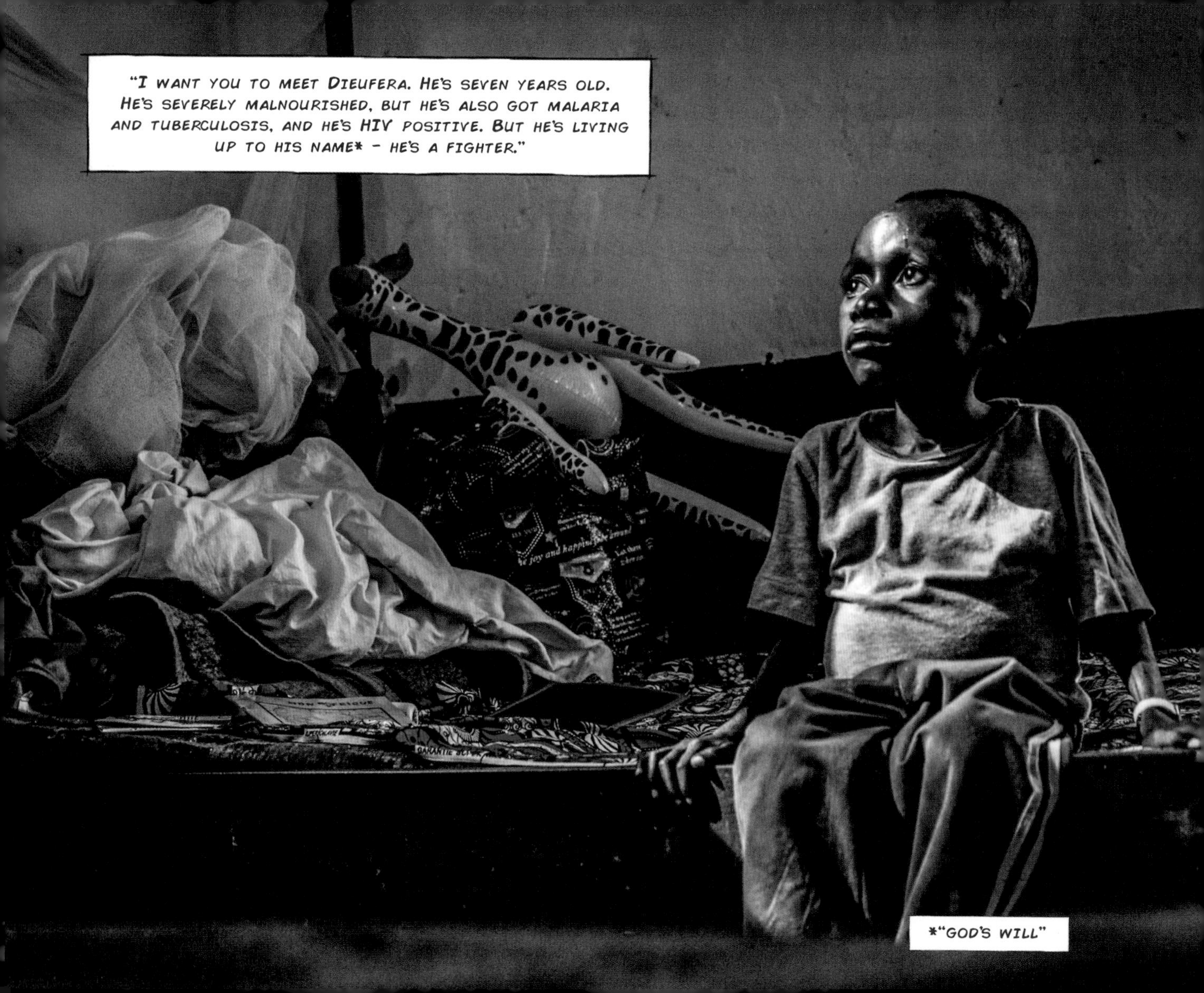
"I WANT YOU TO MEET DIEUFERA. HE'S SEVEN YEARS OLD. HE'S SEVERELY MALNOURISHED, BUT HE'S ALSO GOT MALARIA AND TUBERCULOSIS, AND HE'S HIV POSITIVE. BUT HE'S LIVING UP TO HIS NAME* - HE'S A FIGHTER."
*"GOD'S WILL"

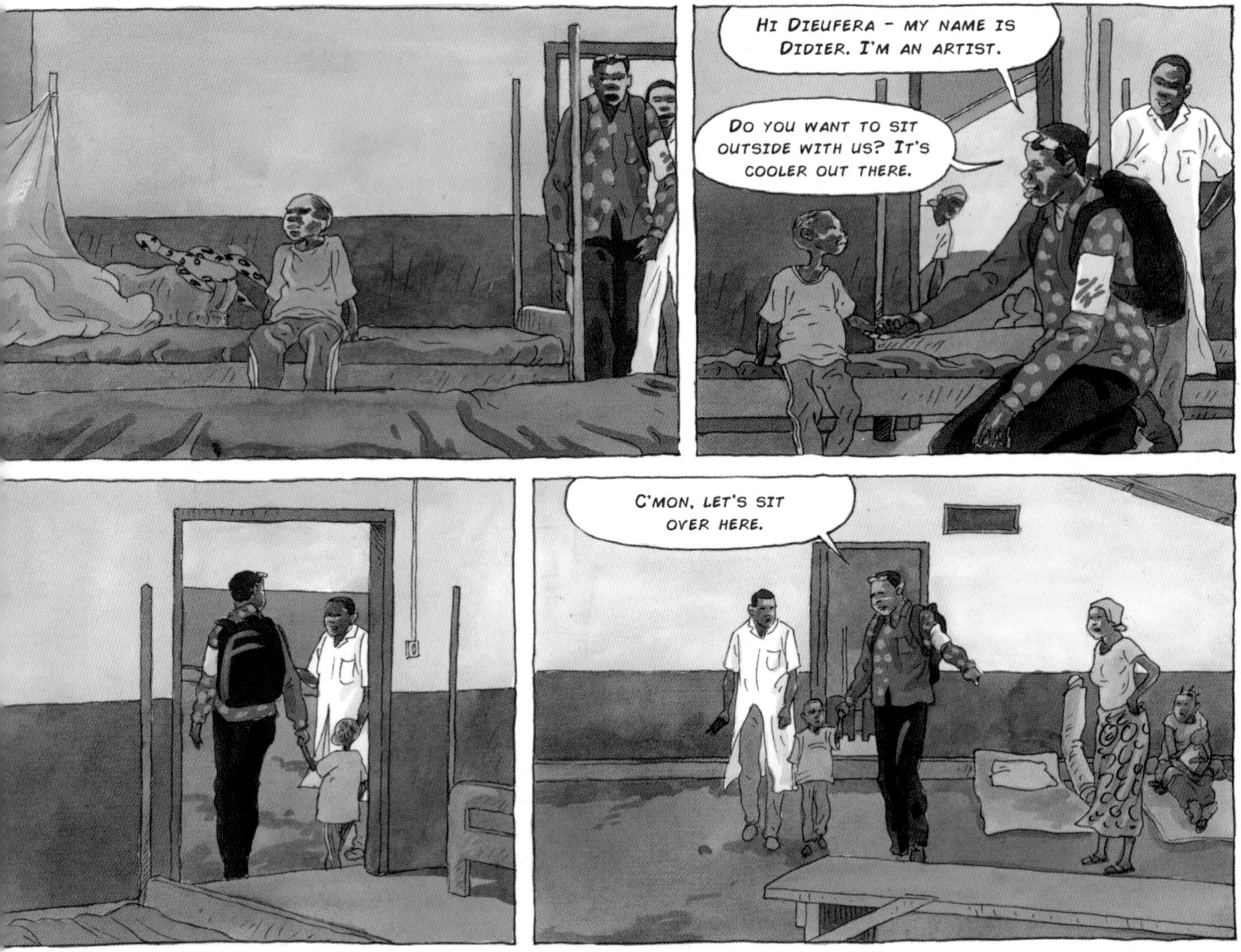
HI DIEUFERA - MY NAME IS DIDIER. I'M AN ARTIST.
DO YOU WANT TO SIT OUTSIDE WITH US? IT'S COOLER OUT THERE.
C'MON, LET'S SIT OVER HERE.

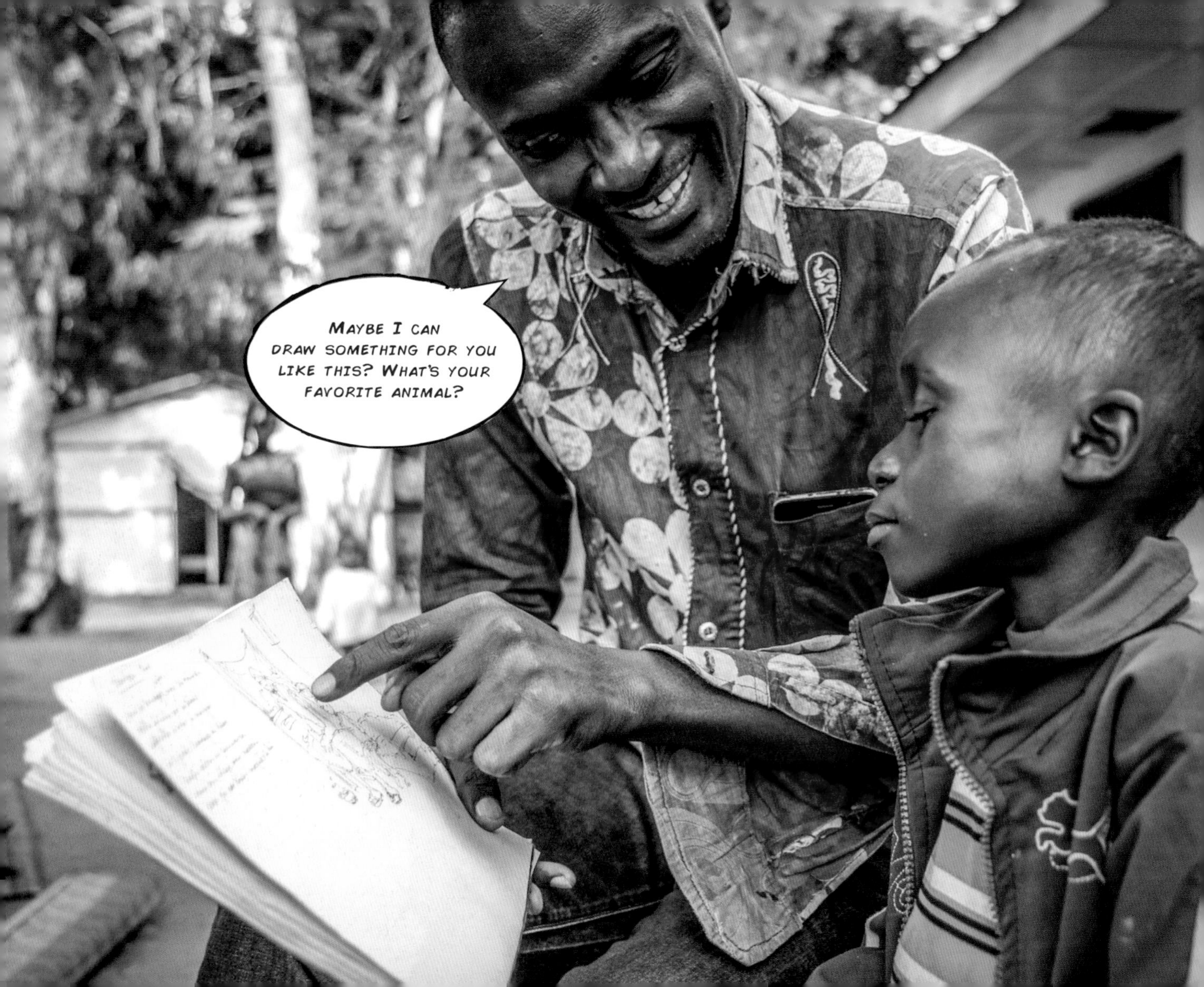
MAYBE I CAN DRAW SOMETHING FOR YOU LIKE THIS? WHAT'S YOUR FAVORITE ANIMAL?

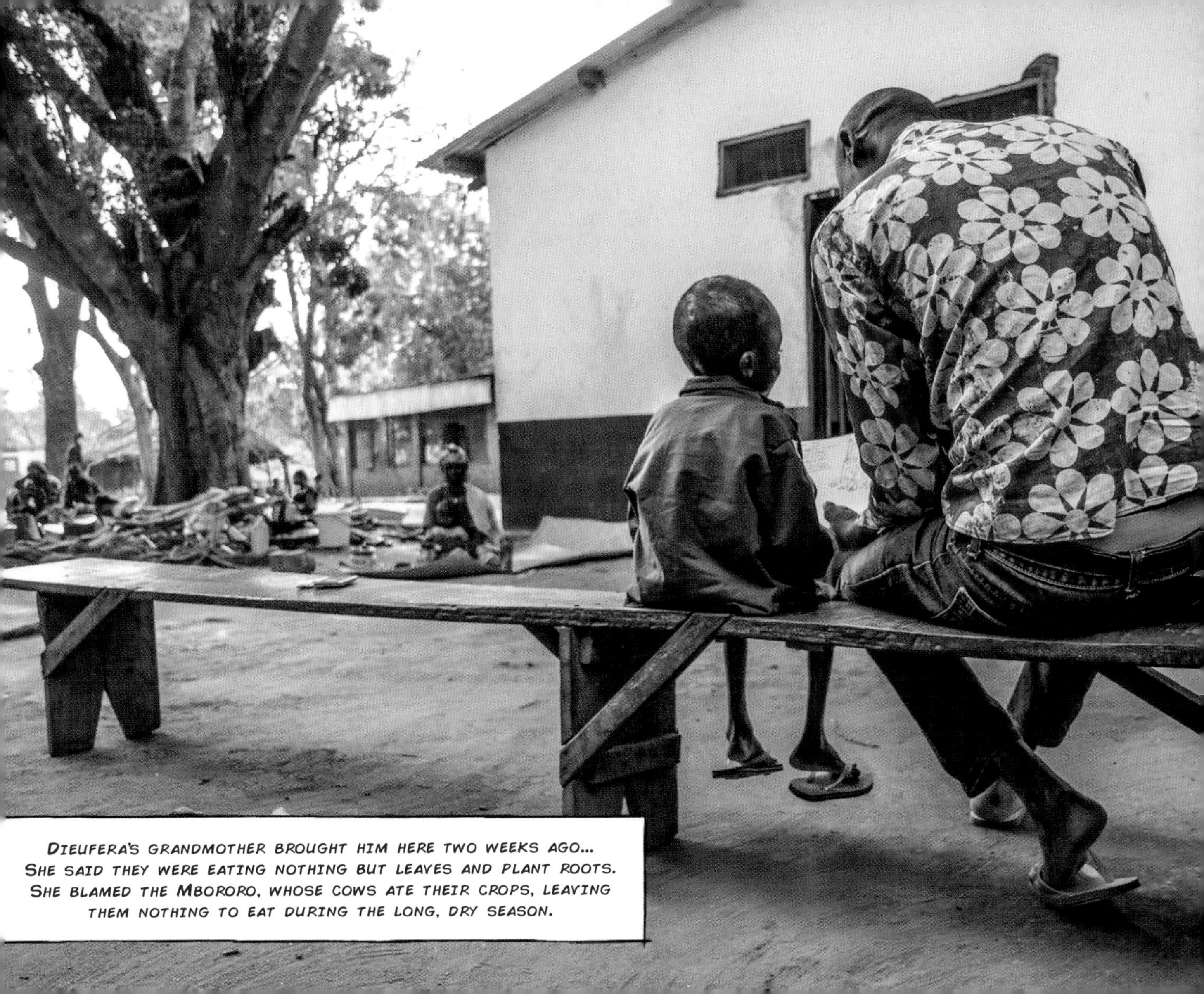
DIEUFERA'S GRANDMOTHER BROUGHT HIM HERE TWO WEEKS AGO... SHE SAID THEY WERE EATING NOTHING BUT LEAVES AND PLANT ROOTS. SHE BLAMED THE MBORORO, WHOSE COWS ATE THEIR CROPS, LEAVING THEM NOTHING TO EAT DURING THE LONG, DRY SEASON.

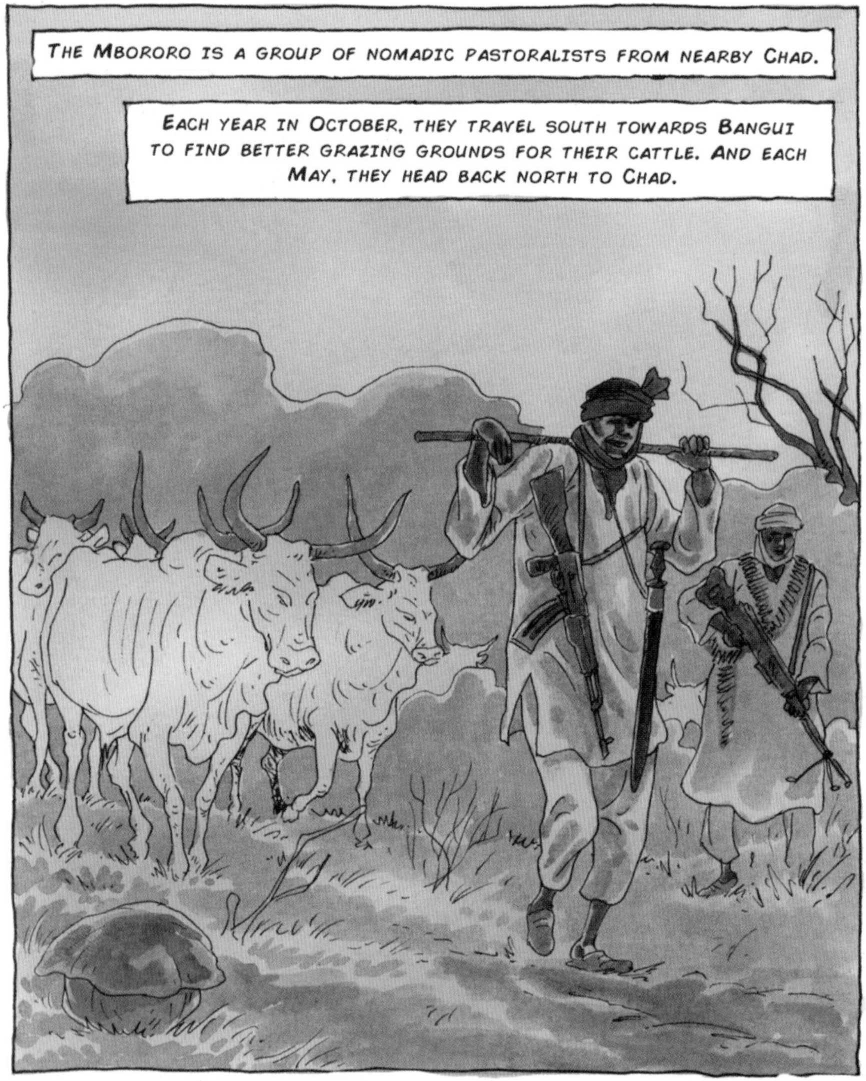
The Mbororo is a group of nomadic pastoralists from nearby Chad.
Each year in October, they travel south towards Bangui to find better grazing grounds for their cattle. And each May, they head back north to Chad.

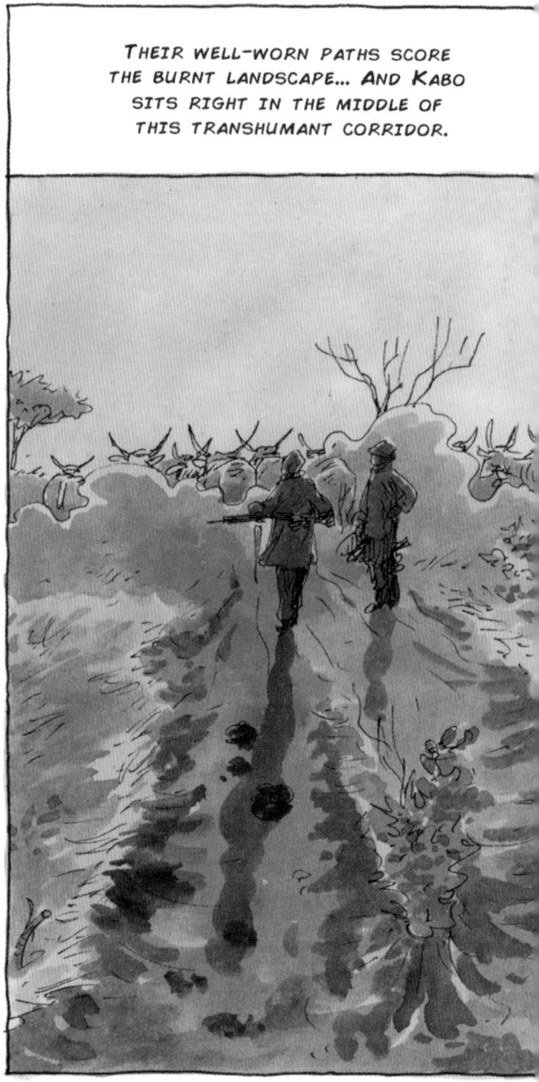
Their well-worn paths score the burnt landscape... And Kabo sits right in the middle of this transhumant corridor.

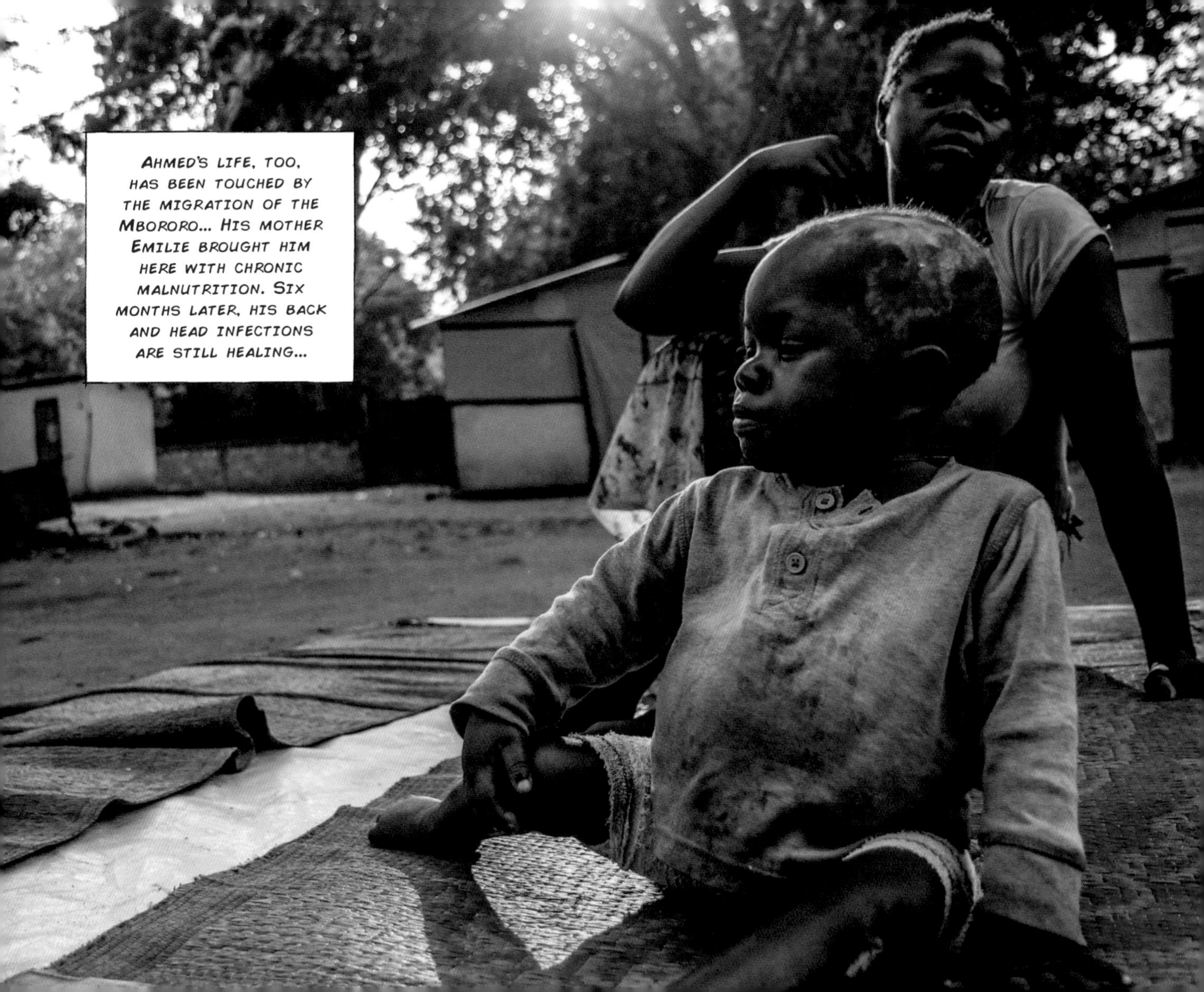
AHMED'S LIFE, TOO, HAS BEEN TOUCHED BY THE MIGRATION OF THE MBORORO... HIS MOTHER EMILIE BROUGHT HIM HERE WITH CHRONIC MALNUTRITION. SIX MONTHS LATER, HIS BACK AND HEAD INFECTIONS ARE STILL HEALING...

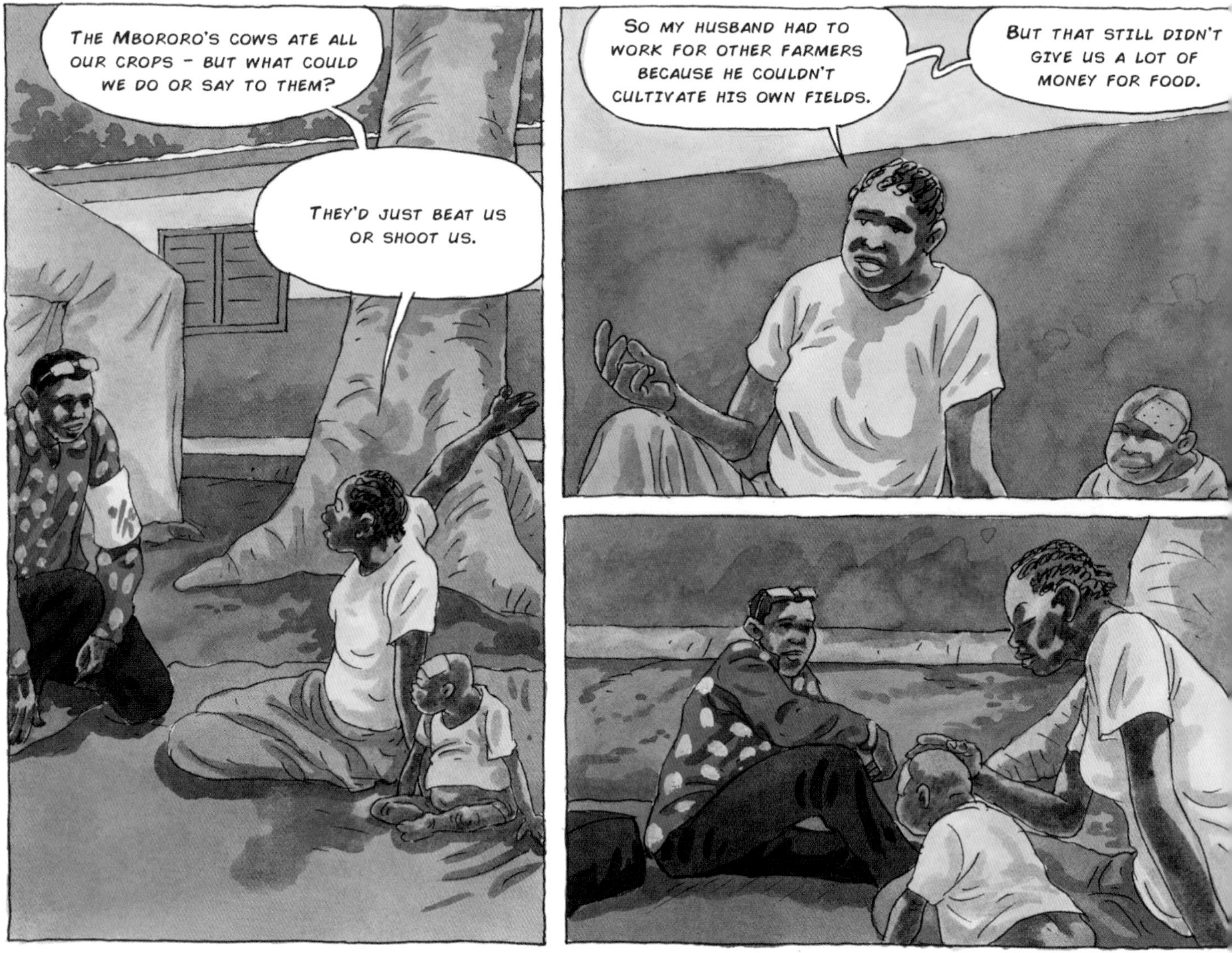
THE MBORORO'S COWS ATE ALL OUR CROPS - BUT WHAT COULD WE DO OR SAY TO THEM?
THEY'D JUST BEAT US OR SHOOT US.
SO MY HUSBAND HAD TO WORK FOR OTHER FARMERS BECAUSE HE COULDN'T CULTIVATE HIS OWN FIELDS.
BUT THAT STILL DIDN'T GIVE US A LOT OF MONEY FOR FOOD.

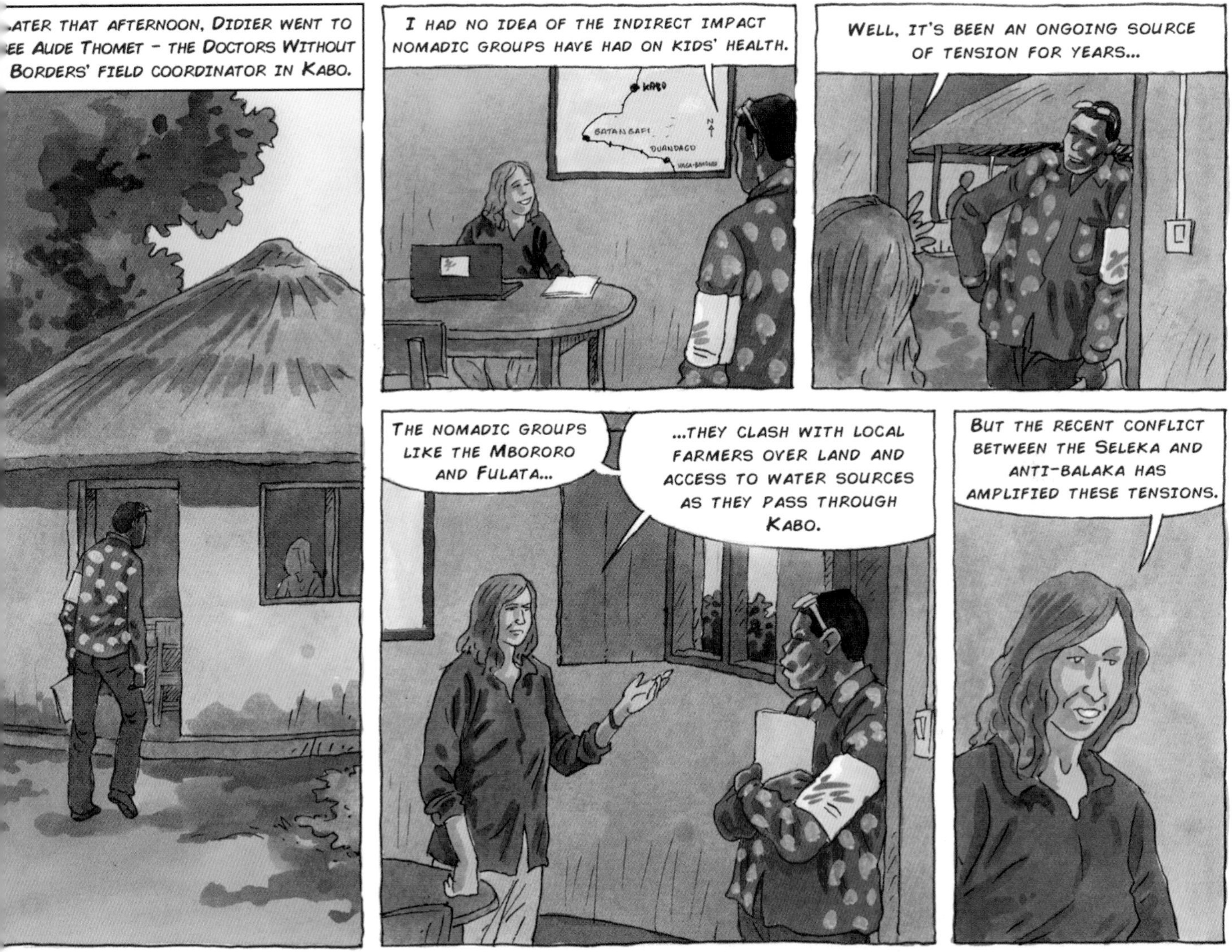
ATER THAT AFTERNOON, DIDIER WENT TO EE AUDE THOMET – THE DOCTORS WITHOUT BORDERS' FIELD COORDINATOR IN KABO.
I HAD NO IDEA OF THE INDIRECT IMPACT NOMADIC GROUPS HAVE HAD ON KIDS' HEALTH.
WELL, IT'S BEEN AN ONGOING SOURCE OF TENSION FOR YEARS...
THE NOMADIC GROUPS LIKE THE MBORORO AND FULATA...
...THEY CLASH WITH LOCAL FARMERS OVER LAND AND ACCESS TO WATER SOURCES AS THEY PASS THROUGH KABO.
BUT THE RECENT CONFLICT BETWEEN THE SELEKA AND ANTI-BALAKA HAS AMPLIFIED THESE TENSIONS.

HOW SO?

HMM... IT'S PROBABLY EASIER TO EXPLAIN WITH A DRAWING...

BEFORE THE CONFLICT, THESE GROUPS HAD ROUGHLY AN AREA OF TWENTY-FIVE SQUARE MILES OF DECENT GRASSLAND IN WHICH TO LET THEIR CATTLE GRAZE...

SCRITCH! SCRITCH!

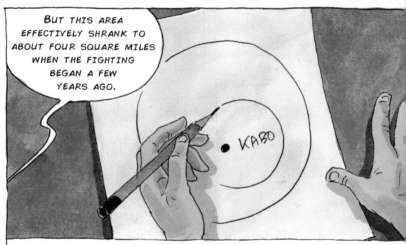

BUT THIS AREA EFFECTIVELY SHRANK TO ABOUT FOUR SQUARE MILES WHEN THE FIGHTING BEGAN A FEW YEARS AGO.

KABO

LIKE THE CONCENTRIC RINGS OF A TREE TRUNK CUT IN HALF, THESE EVER-DECREASING CIRCLES MARK THE INCREASE OF VIOLENCE IN THE REGION.

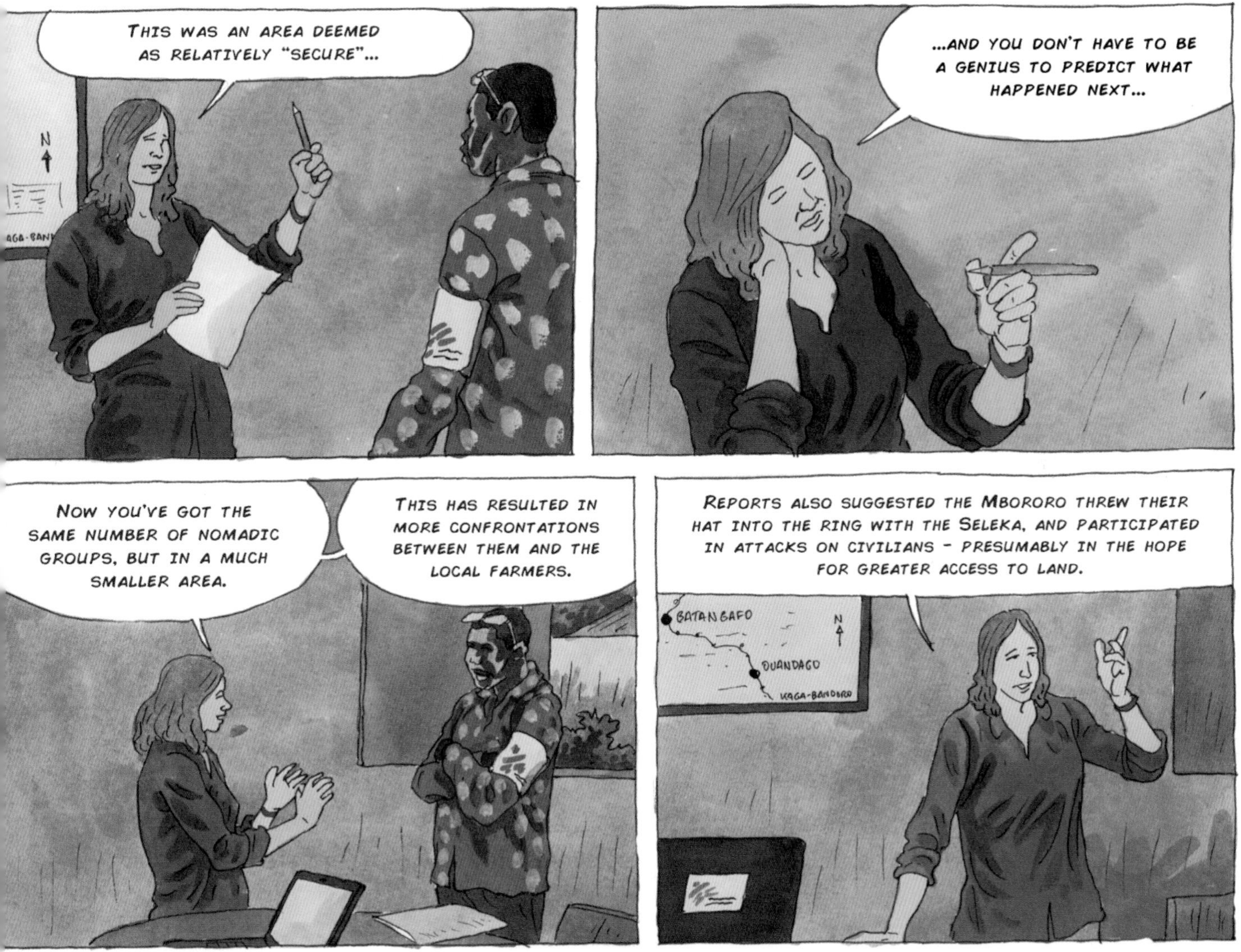
THIS WAS AN AREA DEEMED AS RELATIVELY "SECURE"...
...AND YOU DON'T HAVE TO BE A GENIUS TO PREDICT WHAT HAPPENED NEXT...
NOW YOU'VE GOT THE SAME NUMBER OF NOMADIC GROUPS, BUT IN A MUCH SMALLER AREA.
THIS HAS RESULTED IN MORE CONFRONTATIONS BETWEEN THEM AND THE LOCAL FARMERS.
REPORTS ALSO SUGGESTED THE MBORORO THREW THEIR HAT INTO THE RING WITH THE SELEKA, AND PARTICIPATED IN ATTACKS ON CIVILIANS - PRESUMABLY IN THE HOPE FOR GREATER ACCESS TO LAND.
BATANGAFO
N
OUANDAGO
KAGA-BANDORO

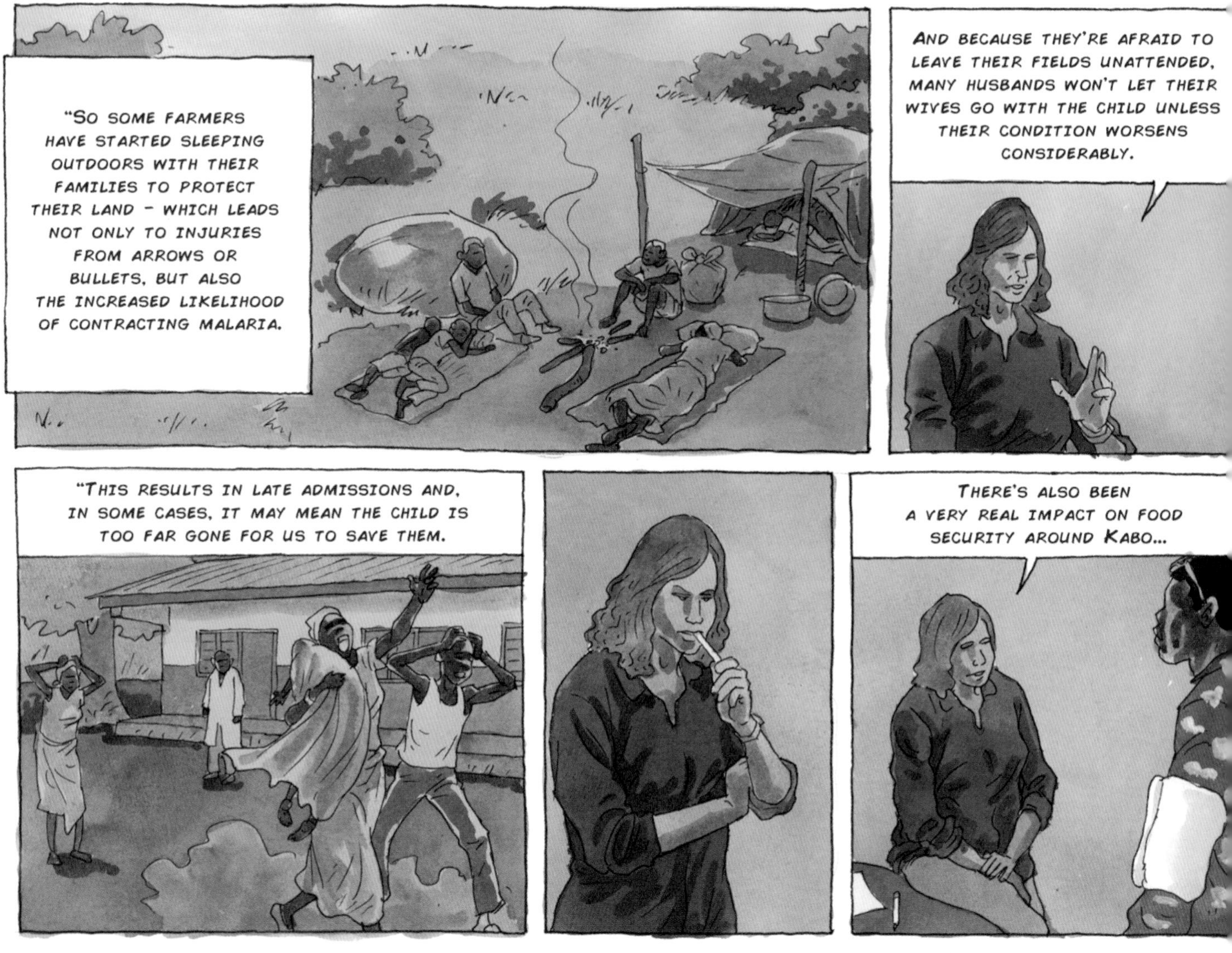
"SO SOME FARMERS HAVE STARTED SLEEPING OUTDOORS WITH THEIR FAMILIES TO PROTECT THEIR LAND - WHICH LEADS NOT ONLY TO INJURIES FROM ARROWS OR BULLETS, BUT ALSO THE INCREASED LIKELIHOOD OF CONTRACTING MALARIA.
AND BECAUSE THEY'RE AFRAID TO LEAVE THEIR FIELDS UNATTENDED, MANY HUSBANDS WON'T LET THEIR WIVES GO WITH THE CHILD UNLESS THEIR CONDITION WORSENS CONSIDERABLY.
"THIS RESULTS IN LATE ADMISSIONS AND, IN SOME CASES, IT MAY MEAN THE CHILD IS TOO FAR GONE FOR US TO SAVE THEM.
THERE'S ALSO BEEN A VERY REAL IMPACT ON FOOD SECURITY AROUND KABO...

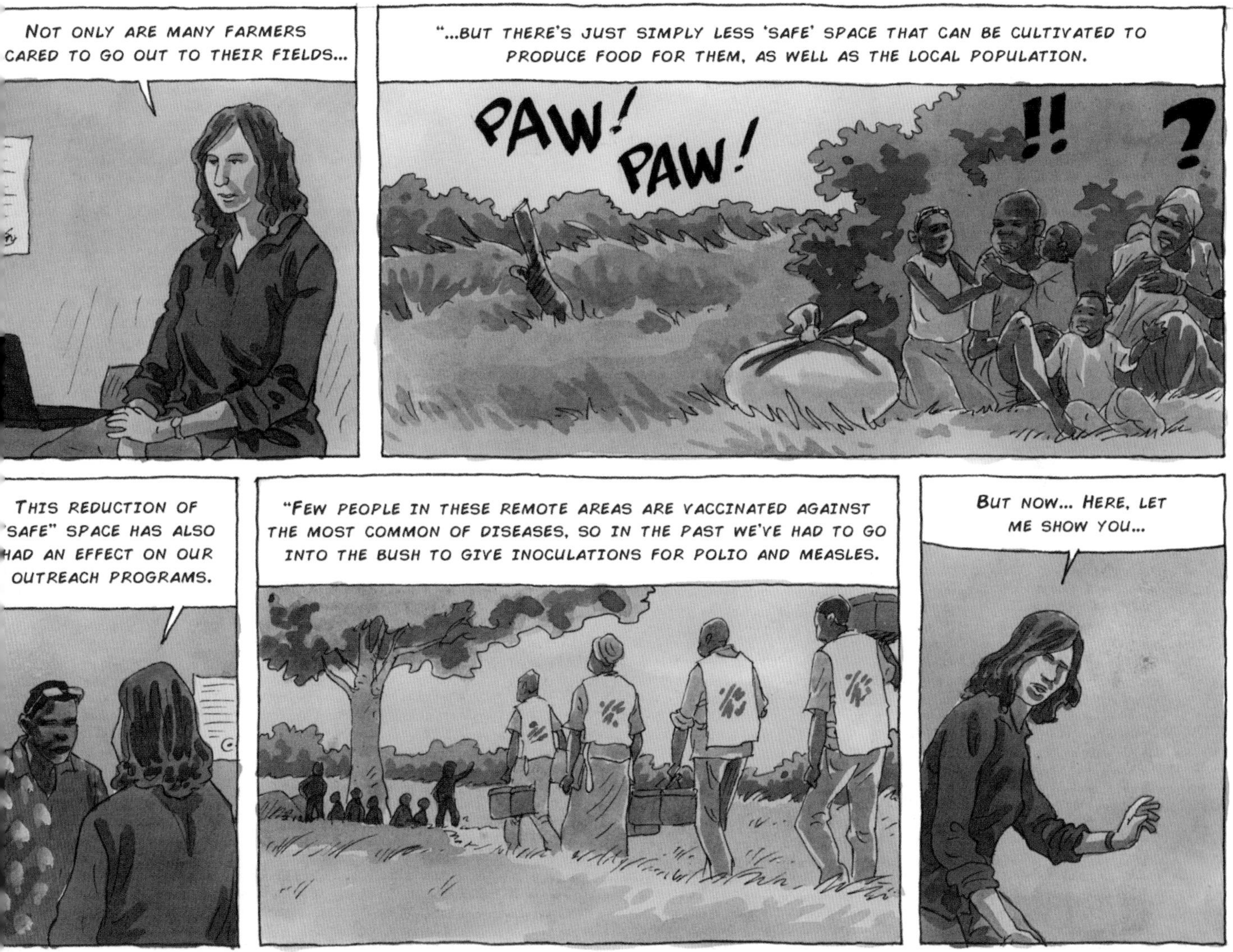
NOT ONLY ARE MANY FARMERS CARED TO GO OUT TO THEIR FIELDS...
"...BUT THERE'S JUST SIMPLY LESS 'SAFE' SPACE THAT CAN BE CULTIVATED TO PRODUCE FOOD FOR THEM, AS WELL AS THE LOCAL POPULATION.
PAW!
PAW!
!!
?
THIS REDUCTION OF "SAFE" SPACE HAS ALSO HAD AN EFFECT ON OUR OUTREACH PROGRAMS.
"FEW PEOPLE IN THESE REMOTE AREAS ARE VACCINATED AGAINST THE MOST COMMON OF DISEASES, SO IN THE PAST WE'VE HAD TO GO INTO THE BUSH TO GIVE INOCULATIONS FOR POLIO AND MEASLES.
BUT NOW... HERE, LET ME SHOW YOU...

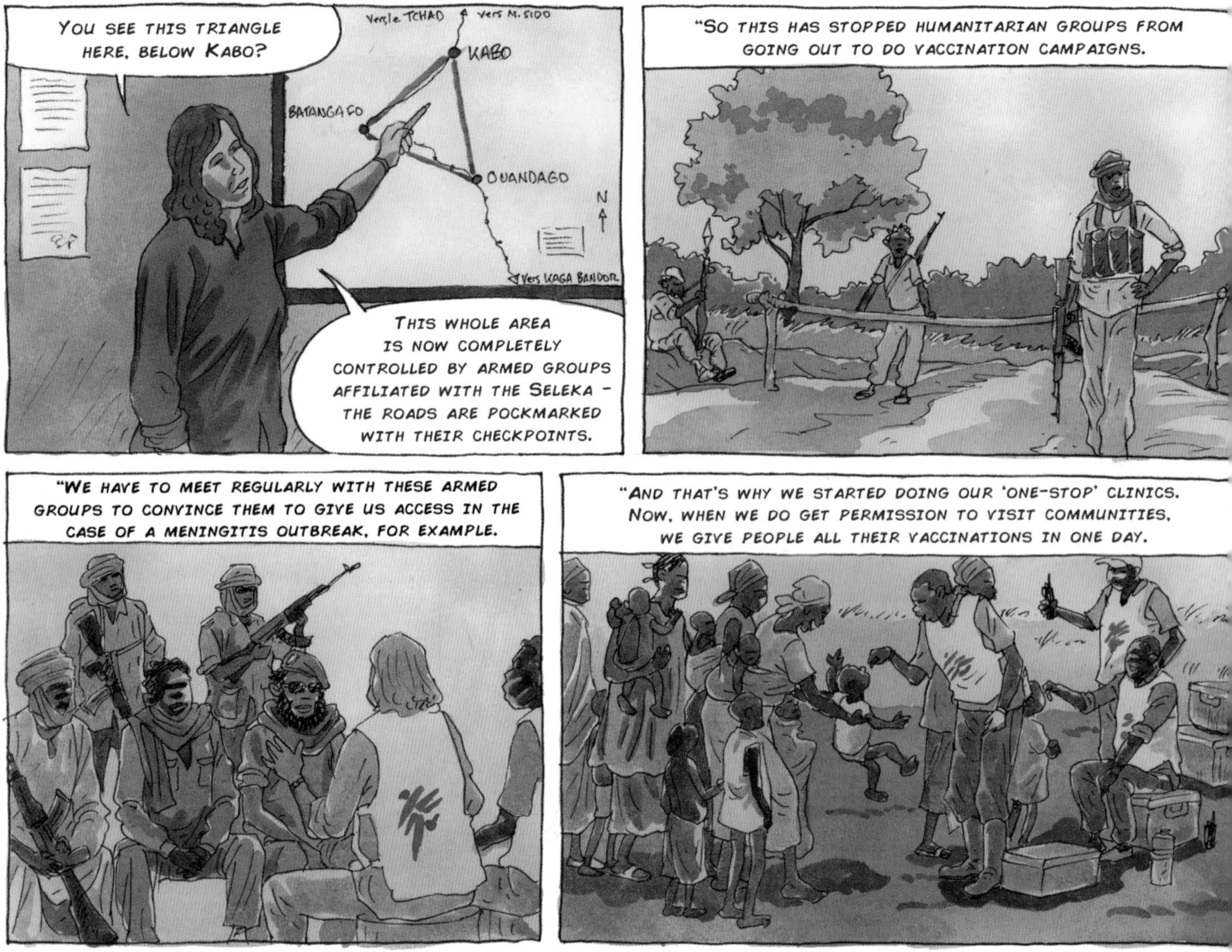
YOU SEE THIS TRIANGLE HERE, BELOW KABO?
Vers le TCHAD
vers M. SIDO
KABO
BATANGAFO
OUANDAGO
N
Vers KAGA BANDOR
THIS WHOLE AREA IS NOW COMPLETELY CONTROLLED BY ARMED GROUPS AFFILIATED WITH THE SELEKA – THE ROADS ARE POCKMARKED WITH THEIR CHECKPOINTS.
"SO THIS HAS STOPPED HUMANITARIAN GROUPS FROM GOING OUT TO DO VACCINATION CAMPAIGNS.
"WE HAVE TO MEET REGULARLY WITH THESE ARMED GROUPS TO CONVINCE THEM TO GIVE US ACCESS IN THE CASE OF A MENINGITIS OUTBREAK, FOR EXAMPLE.
"AND THAT'S WHY WE STARTED DOING OUR 'ONE-STOP' CLINICS. NOW, WHEN WE DO GET PERMISSION TO VISIT COMMUNITIES, WE GIVE PEOPLE ALL THEIR VACCINATIONS IN ONE DAY.

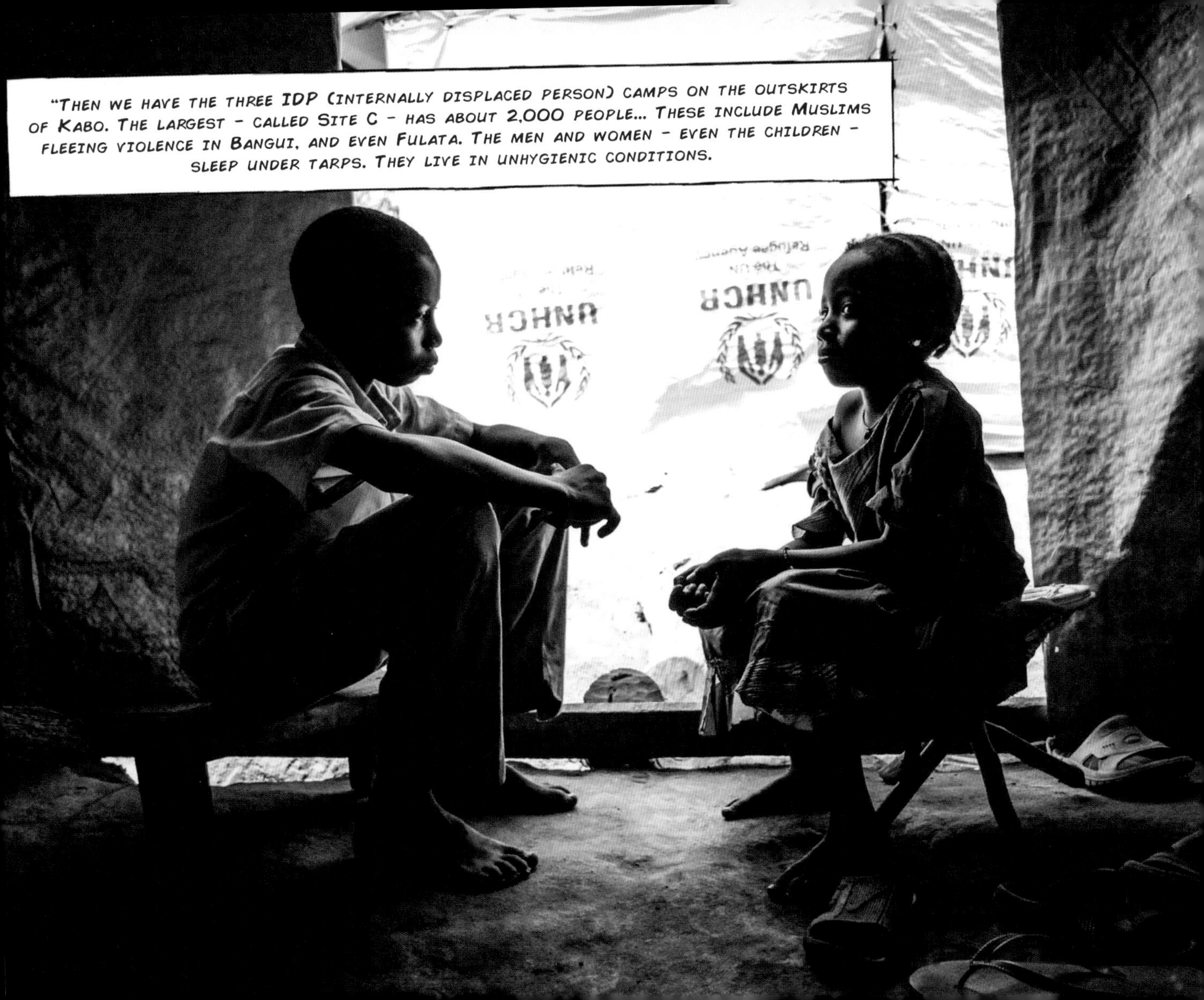
"THEN WE HAVE THE THREE IDP (INTERNALLY DISPLACED PERSON) CAMPS ON THE OUTSKIRTS OF KABO. THE LARGEST - CALLED SITE C - HAS ABOUT 2,000 PEOPLE... THESE INCLUDE MUSLIMS FLEEING VIOLENCE IN BANGUI, AND EVEN FULATA. THE MEN AND WOMEN - EVEN THE CHILDREN - SLEEP UNDER TARPS. THEY LIVE IN UNHYGIENIC CONDITIONS.

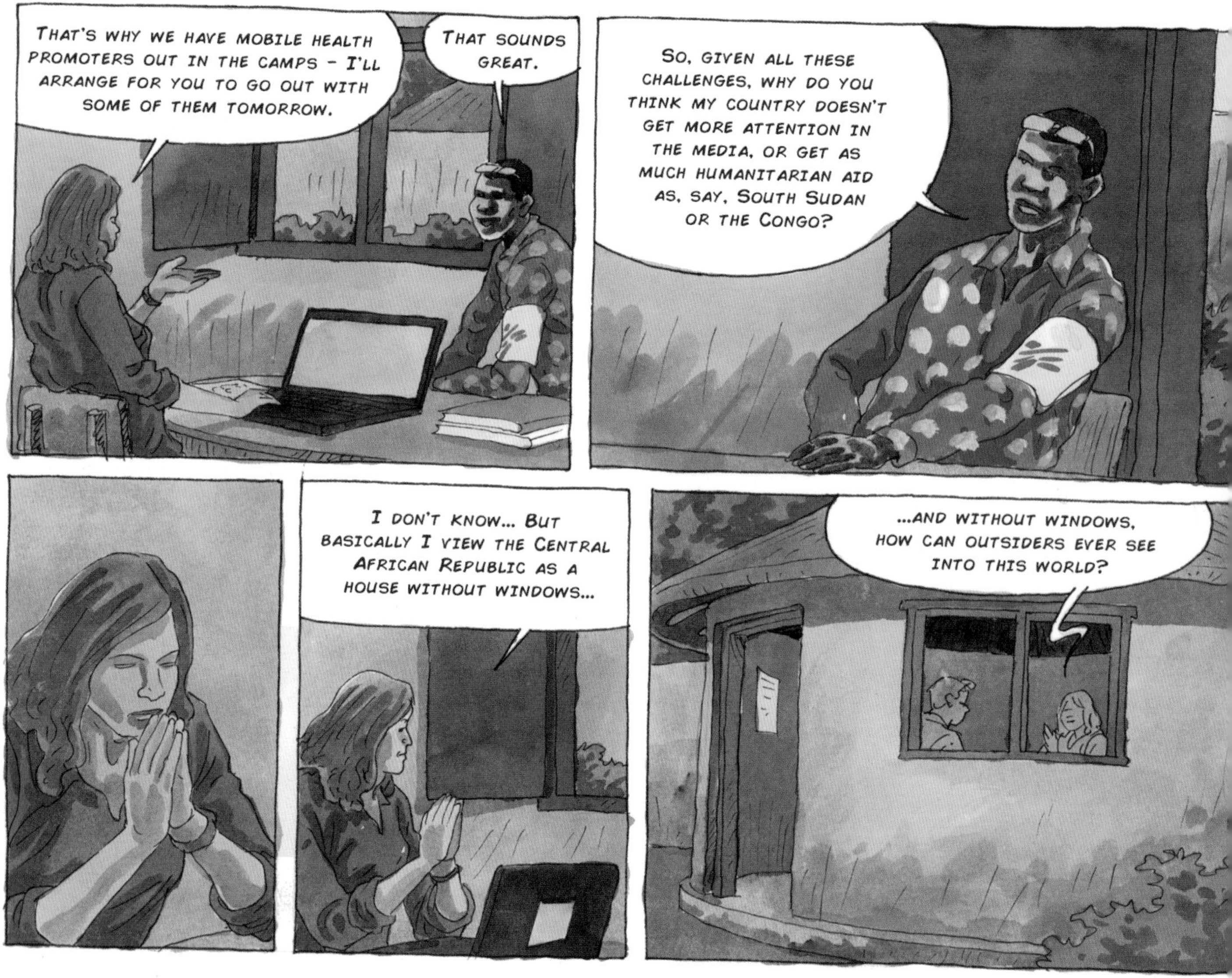
THAT'S WHY WE HAVE MOBILE HEALTH PROMOTERS OUT IN THE CAMPS - I'LL ARRANGE FOR YOU TO GO OUT WITH SOME OF THEM TOMORROW.
THAT SOUNDS GREAT.
SO, GIVEN ALL THESE CHALLENGES, WHY DO YOU THINK MY COUNTRY DOESN'T GET MORE ATTENTION IN THE MEDIA, OR GET AS MUCH HUMANITARIAN AID AS, SAY, SOUTH SUDAN OR THE CONGO?
I DON'T KNOW... BUT BASICALLY I VIEW THE CENTRAL AFRICAN REPUBLIC AS A HOUSE WITHOUT WINDOWS...
...AND WITHOUT WINDOWS, HOW CAN OUTSIDERS EVER SEE INTO THIS WORLD?

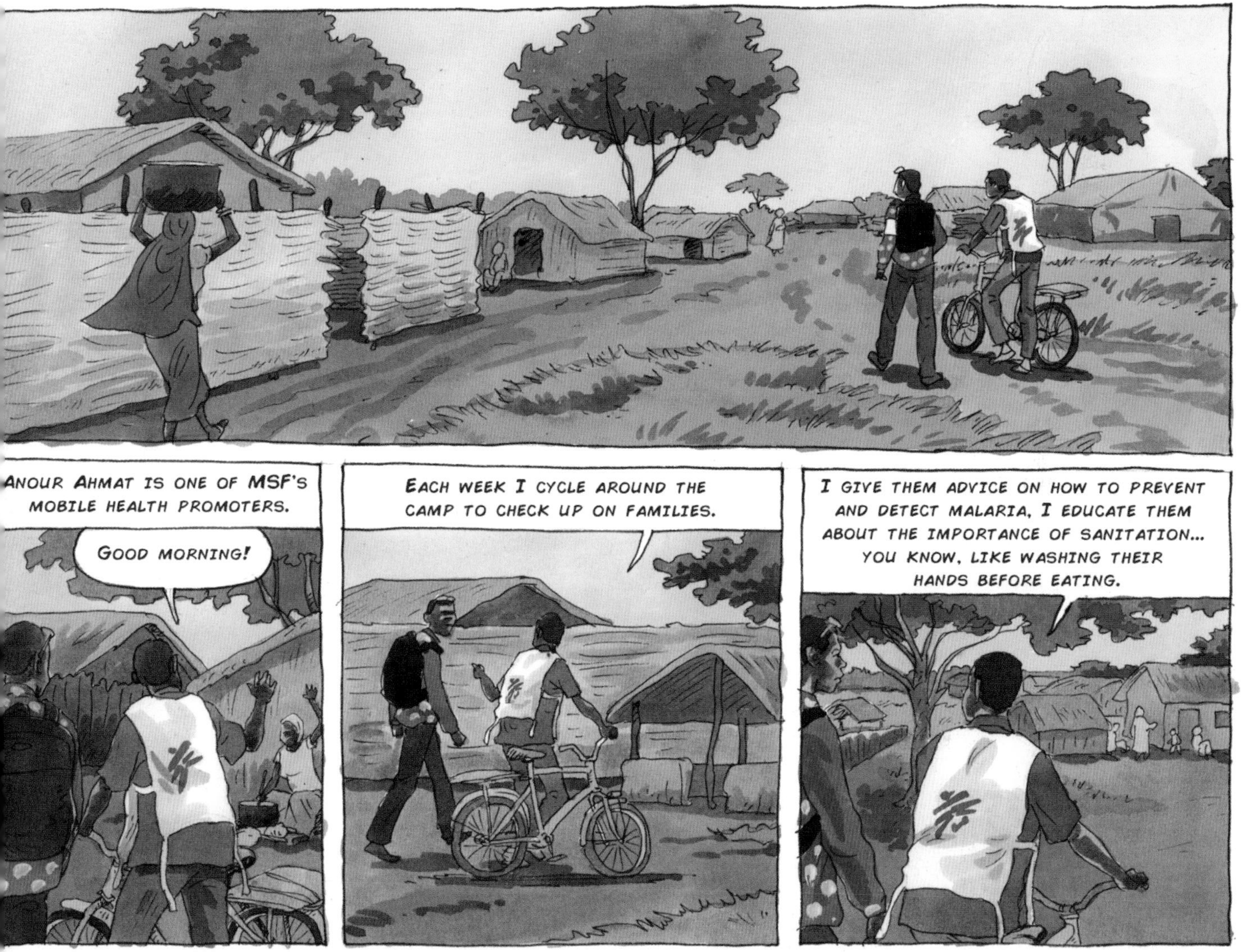
ANOUR AHMAT IS ONE OF MSF'S MOBILE HEALTH PROMOTERS.
GOOD MORNING!
EACH WEEK I CYCLE AROUND THE CAMP TO CHECK UP ON FAMILIES.
I GIVE THEM ADVICE ON HOW TO PREVENT AND DETECT MALARIA. I EDUCATE THEM ABOUT THE IMPORTANCE OF SANITATION... YOU KNOW, LIKE WASHING THEIR HANDS BEFORE EATING.

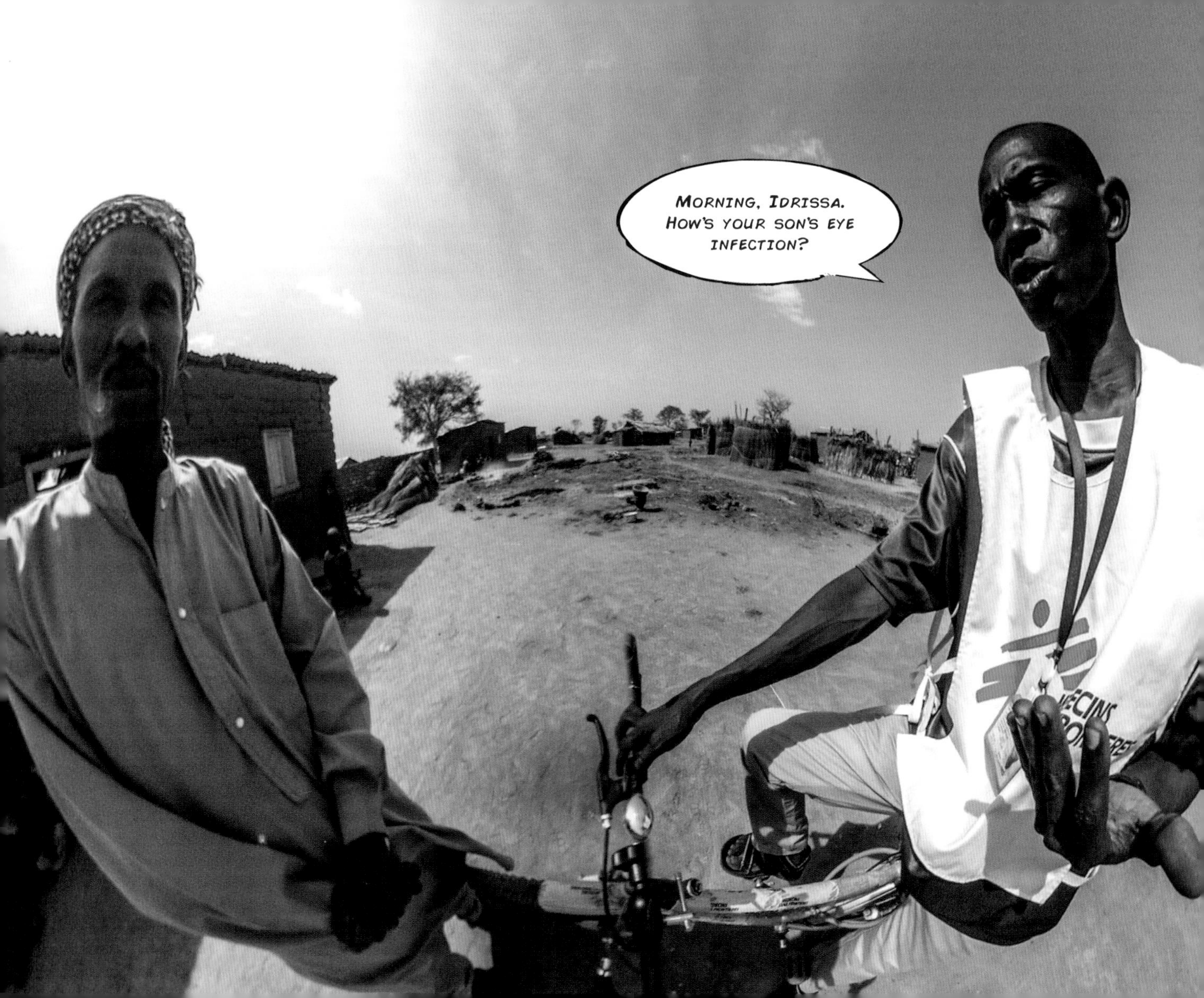
Morning, Idrissa. How's your son's eye infection?

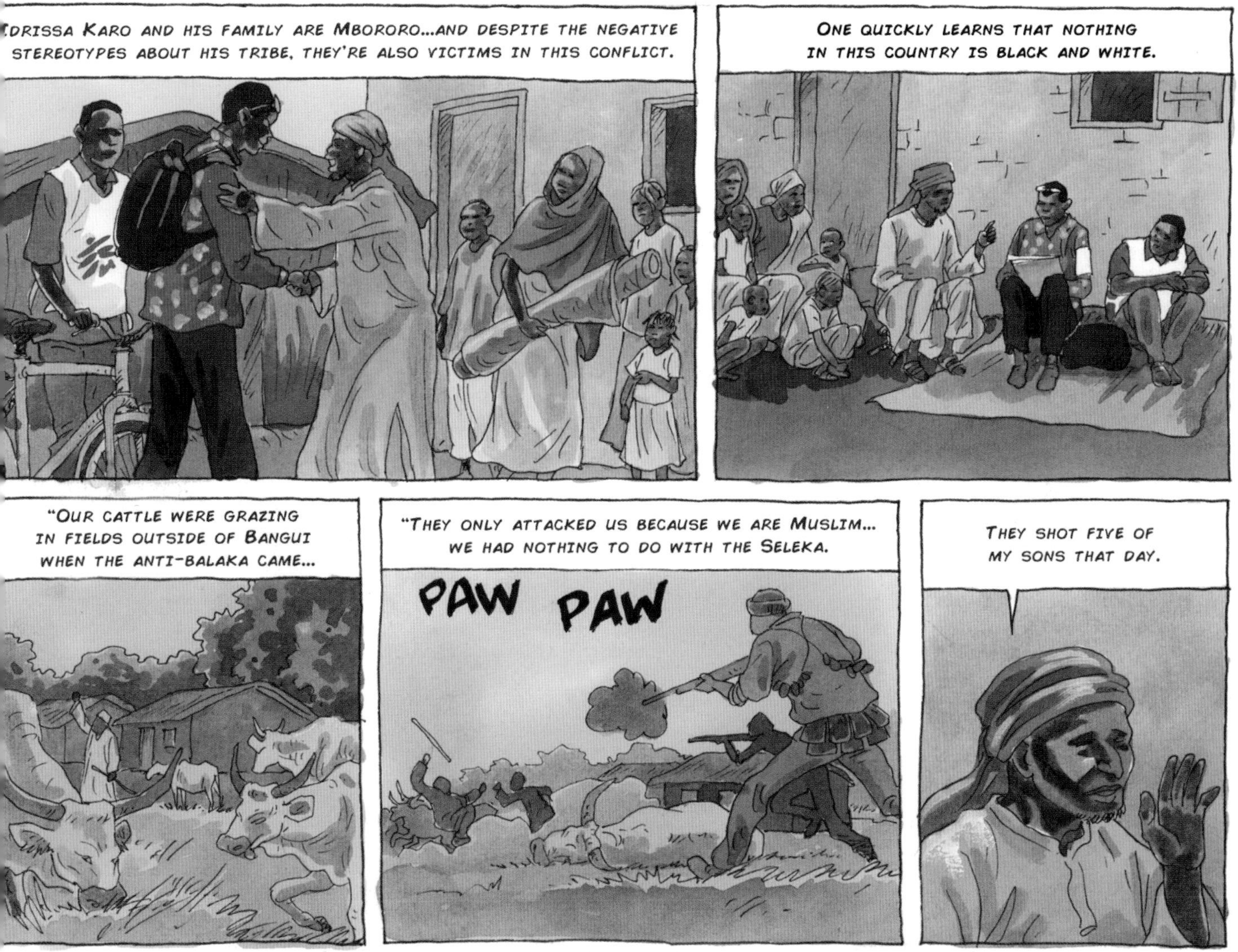
IDRISSA KARO AND HIS FAMILY ARE MBORORO...AND DESPITE THE NEGATIVE STEREOTYPES ABOUT HIS TRIBE, THEY'RE ALSO VICTIMS IN THIS CONFLICT.
ONE QUICKLY LEARNS THAT NOTHING IN THIS COUNTRY IS BLACK AND WHITE.
"OUR CATTLE WERE GRAZING IN FIELDS OUTSIDE OF BANGUI WHEN THE ANTI-BALAKA CAME...
"THEY ONLY ATTACKED US BECAUSE WE ARE MUSLIM... WE HAD NOTHING TO DO WITH THE SELEKA.
PAW PAW
THEY SHOT FIVE OF MY SONS THAT DAY.

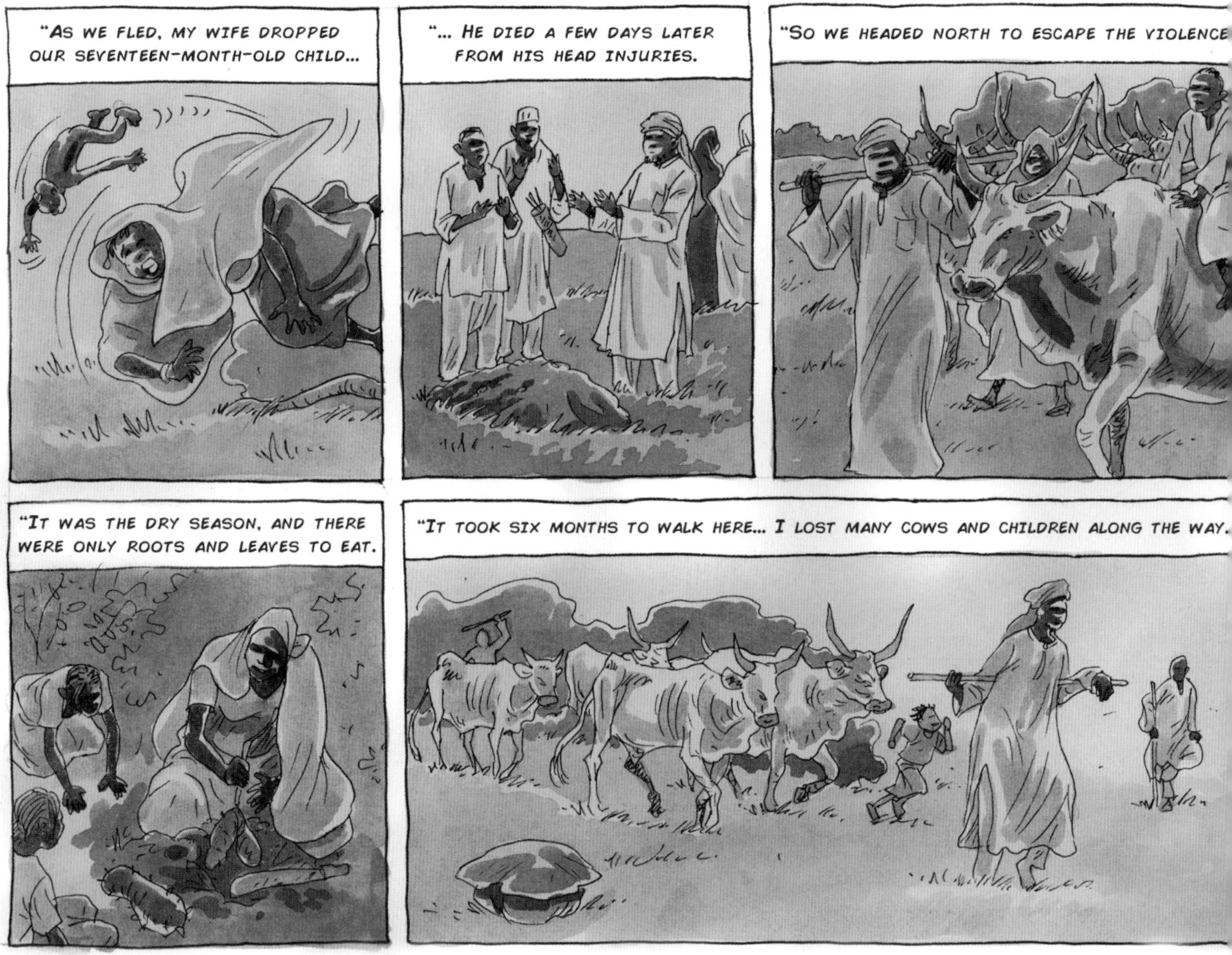
"AS WE FLED, MY WIFE DROPPED OUR SEVENTEEN-MONTH-OLD CHILD...
"... HE DIED A FEW DAYS LATER FROM HIS HEAD INJURIES.
"SO WE HEADED NORTH TO ESCAPE THE VIOLENCE
"IT WAS THE DRY SEASON, AND THERE WERE ONLY ROOTS AND LEAVES TO EAT.
"IT TOOK SIX MONTHS TO WALK HERE... I LOST MANY COWS AND CHILDREN ALONG THE WAY.

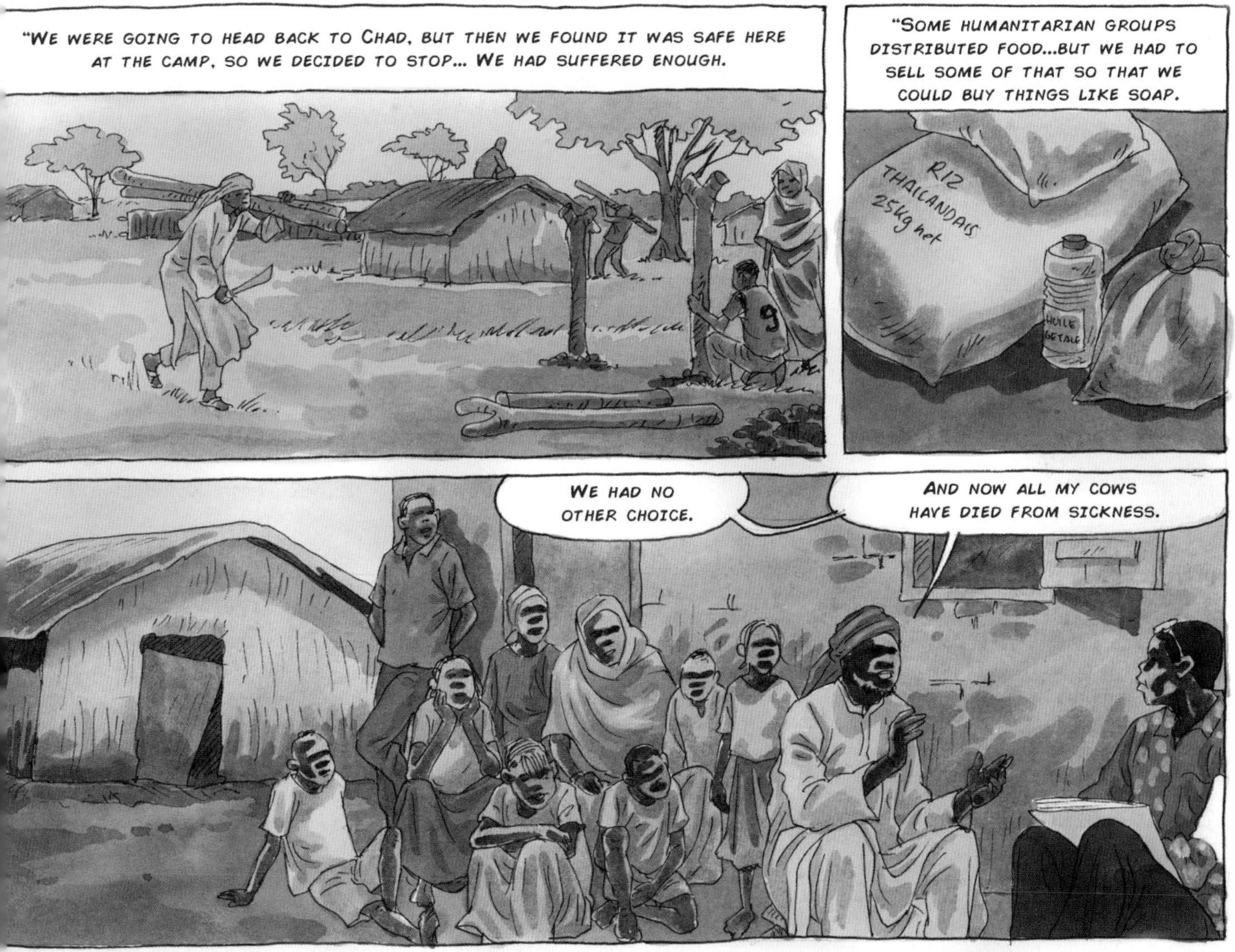
"WE WERE GOING TO HEAD BACK TO CHAD, BUT THEN WE FOUND IT WAS SAFE HERE AT THE CAMP, SO WE DECIDED TO STOP... WE HAD SUFFERED ENOUGH.
"SOME HUMANITARIAN GROUPS DISTRIBUTED FOOD...BUT WE HAD TO SELL SOME OF THAT SO THAT WE COULD BUY THINGS LIKE SOAP.
RIZ
THAILANDAIS
25kg net
HUILE
WE HAD NO OTHER CHOICE.
AND NOW ALL MY COWS HAVE DIED FROM SICKNESS.

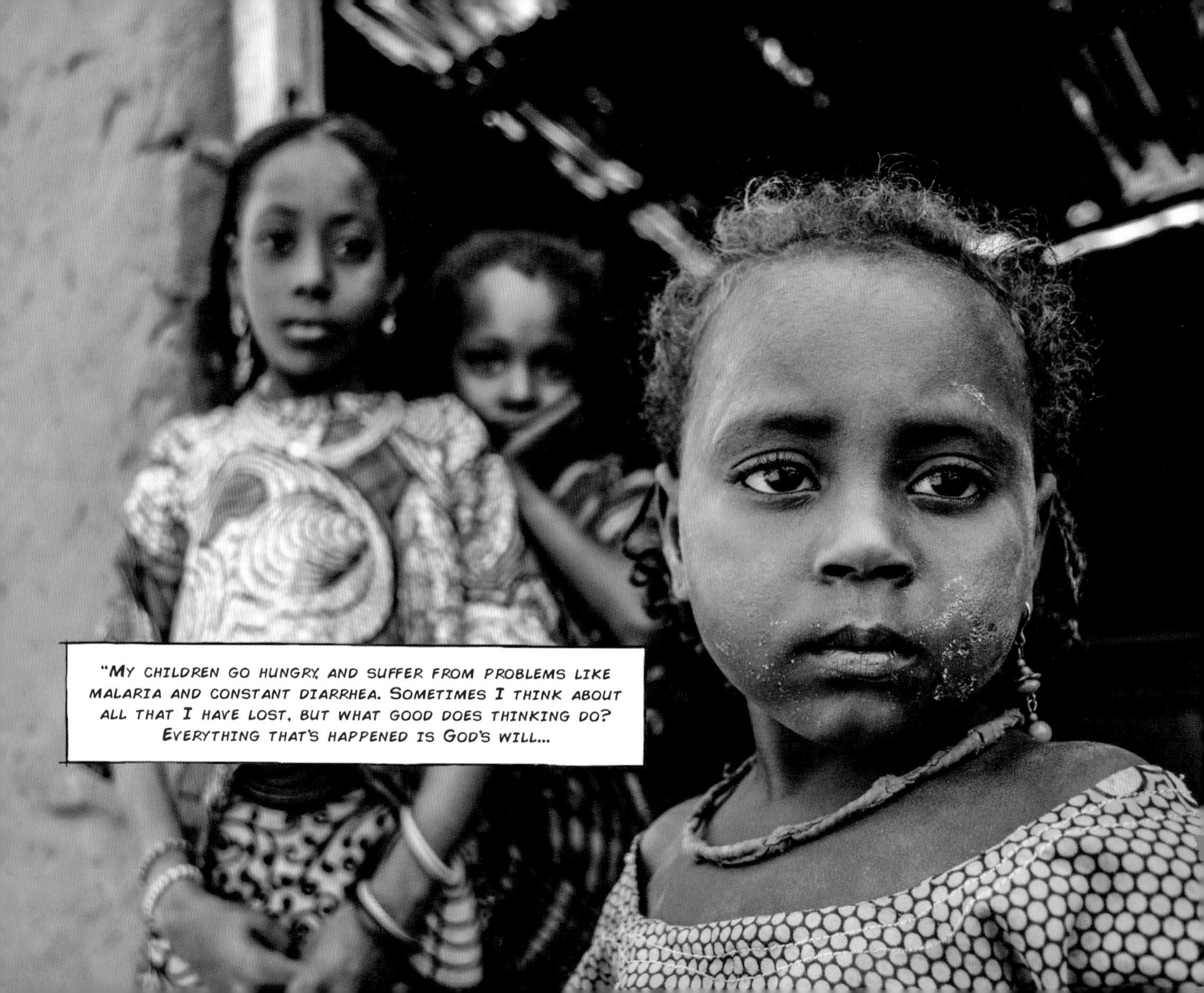
"MY CHILDREN GO HUNGRY, AND SUFFER FROM PROBLEMS LIKE MALARIA AND CONSTANT DIARRHEA. SOMETIMES I THINK ABOUT ALL THAT I HAVE LOST, BUT WHAT GOOD DOES THINKING DO? EVERYTHING THAT'S HAPPENED IS GOD'S WILL...

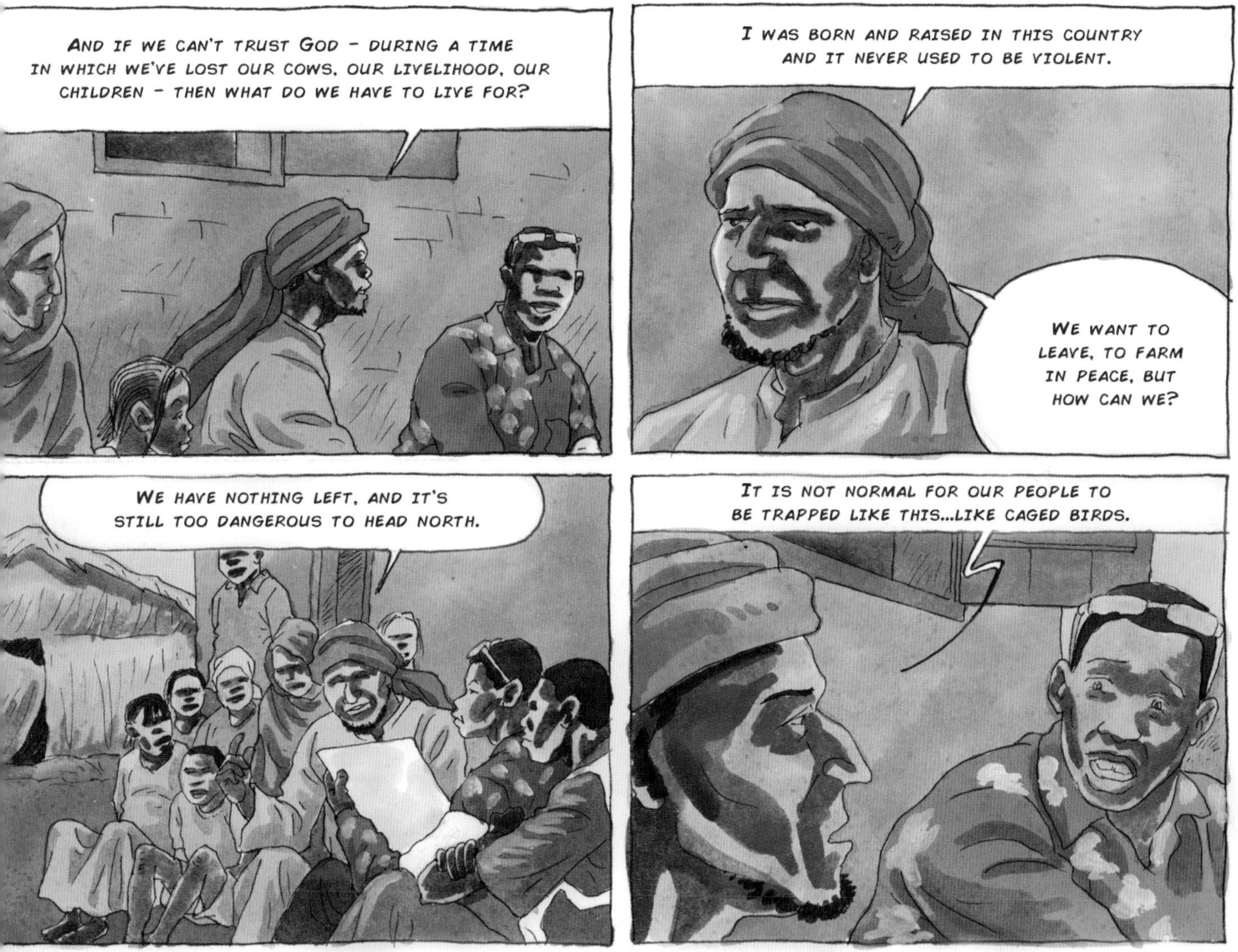
AND IF WE CAN'T TRUST GOD - DURING A TIME IN WHICH WE'VE LOST OUR COWS, OUR LIVELIHOOD, OUR CHILDREN - THEN WHAT DO WE HAVE TO LIVE FOR?
I WAS BORN AND RAISED IN THIS COUNTRY AND IT NEVER USED TO BE VIOLENT.
WE WANT TO LEAVE, TO FARM IN PEACE, BUT HOW CAN WE?
WE HAVE NOTHING LEFT, AND IT'S STILL TOO DANGEROUS TO HEAD NORTH.
IT IS NOT NORMAL FOR OUR PEOPLE TO BE TRAPPED LIKE THIS...LIKE CAGED BIRDS.

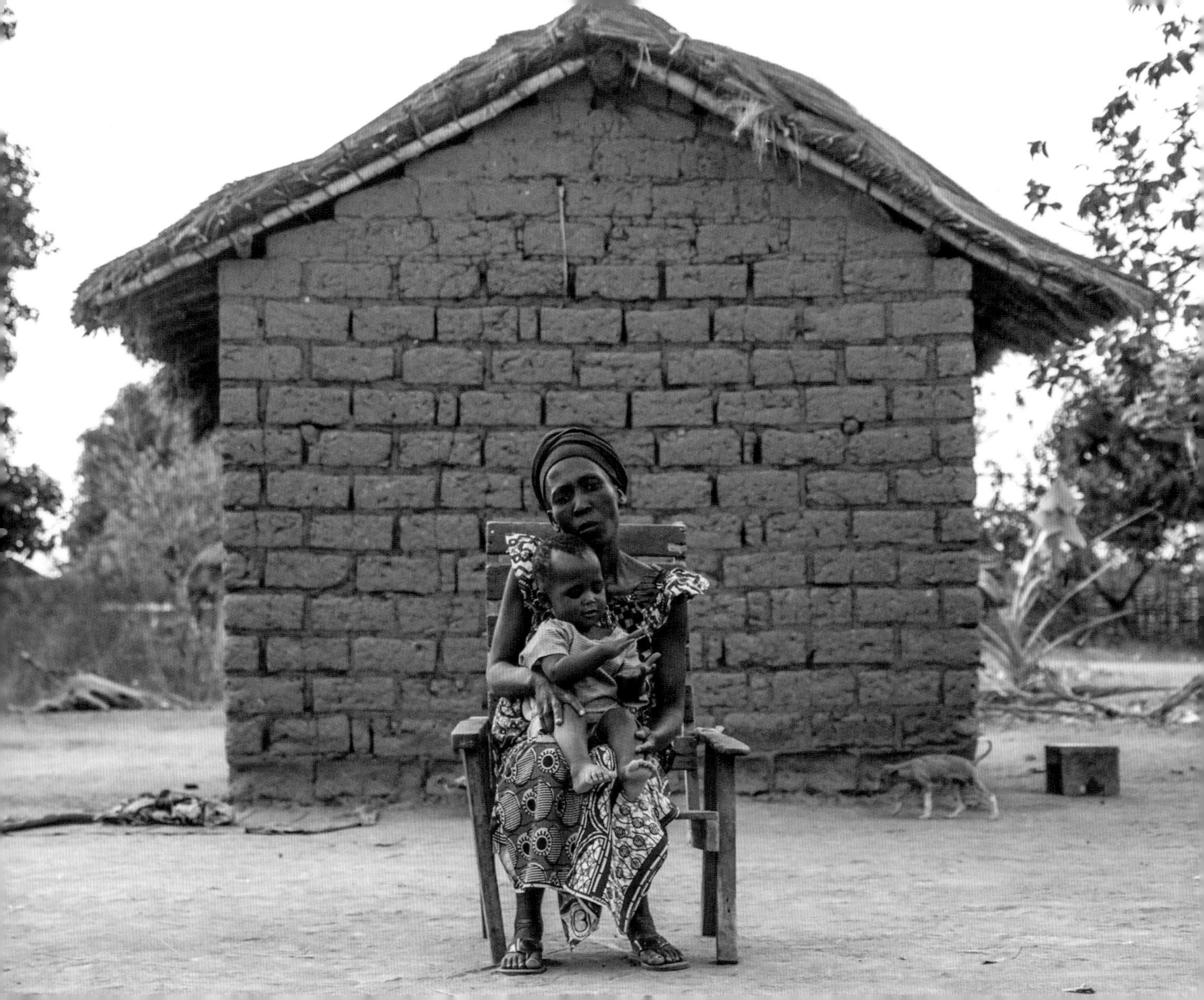

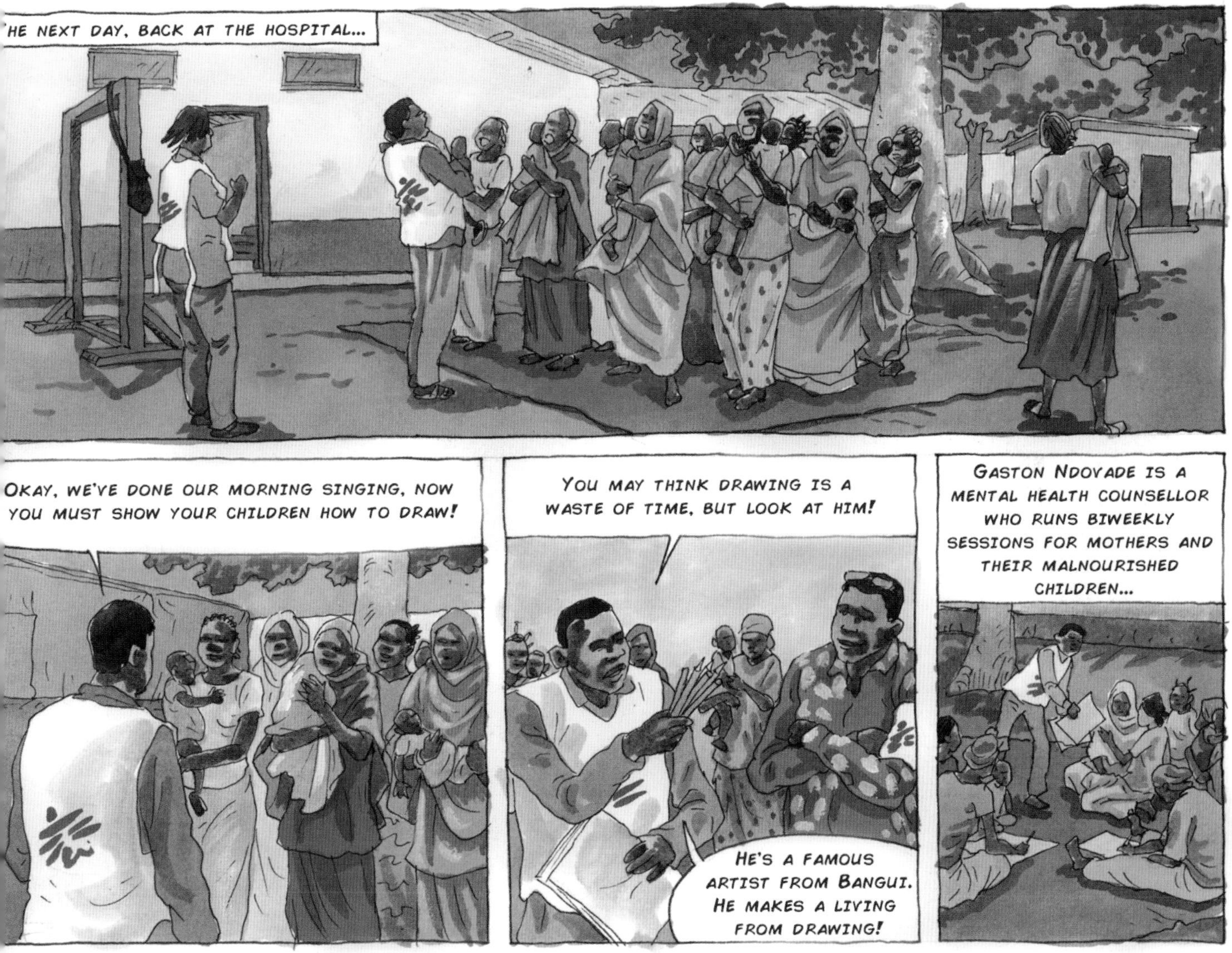
HE NEXT DAY, BACK AT THE HOSPITAL...
OKAY, WE'VE DONE OUR MORNING SINGING, NOW YOU MUST SHOW YOUR CHILDREN HOW TO DRAW!
YOU MAY THINK DRAWING IS A WASTE OF TIME, BUT LOOK AT HIM!
HE'S A FAMOUS ARTIST FROM BANGUI. HE MAKES A LIVING FROM DRAWING!
GASTON NDOVADE IS A MENTAL HEALTH COUNSELLOR WHO RUNS BIWEEKLY SESSIONS FOR MOTHERS AND THEIR MALNOURISHED CHILDREN...

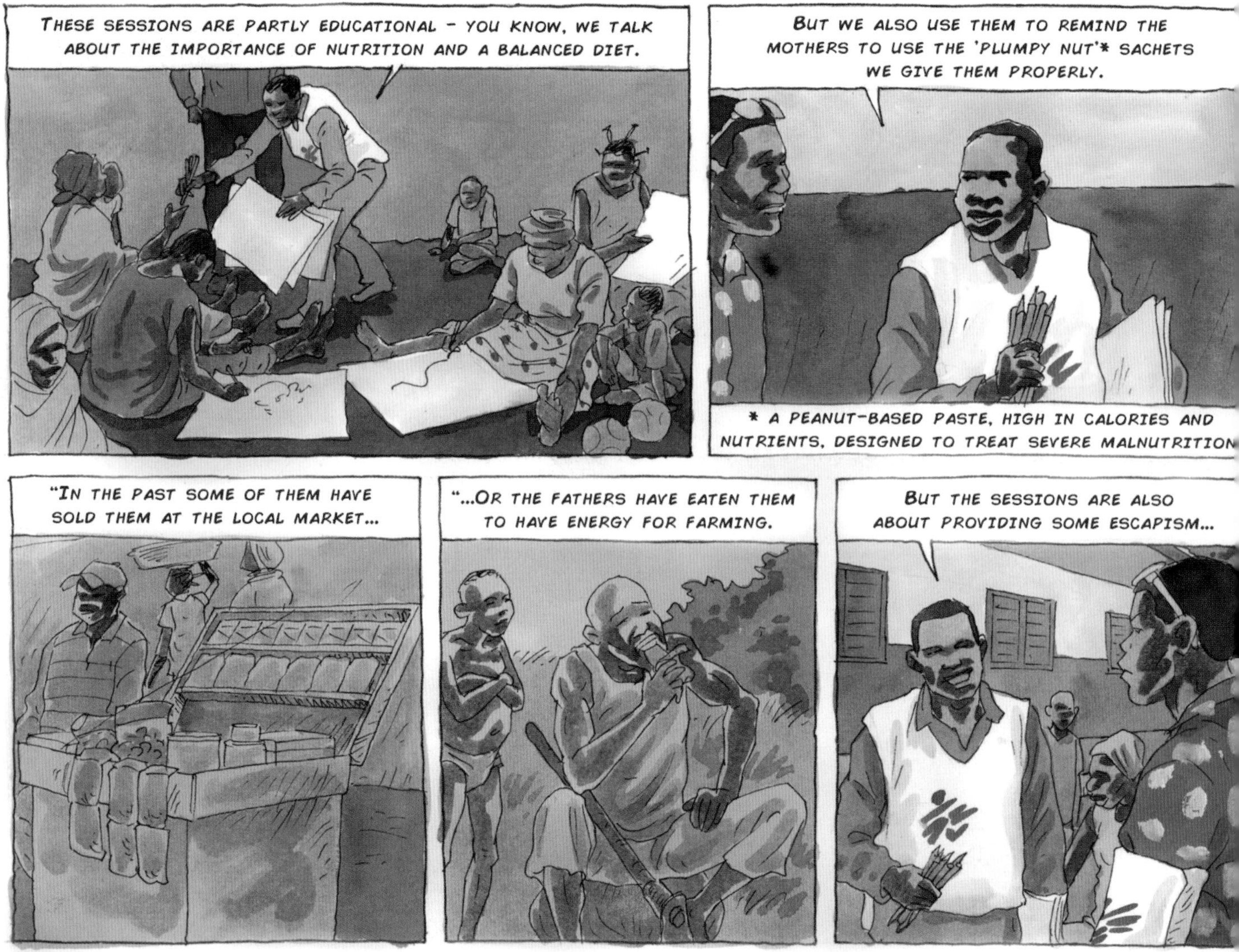
THESE SESSIONS ARE PARTLY EDUCATIONAL - YOU KNOW, WE TALK ABOUT THE IMPORTANCE OF NUTRITION AND A BALANCED DIET.
BUT WE ALSO USE THEM TO REMIND THE MOTHERS TO USE THE 'PLUMPY NUT'* SACHETS WE GIVE THEM PROPERLY.
* A PEANUT-BASED PASTE, HIGH IN CALORIES AND NUTRIENTS, DESIGNED TO TREAT SEVERE MALNUTRITION
"IN THE PAST SOME OF THEM HAVE SOLD THEM AT THE LOCAL MARKET...
"...OR THE FATHERS HAVE EATEN THEM TO HAVE ENERGY FOR FARMING.
BUT THE SESSIONS ARE ALSO ABOUT PROVIDING SOME ESCAPISM...

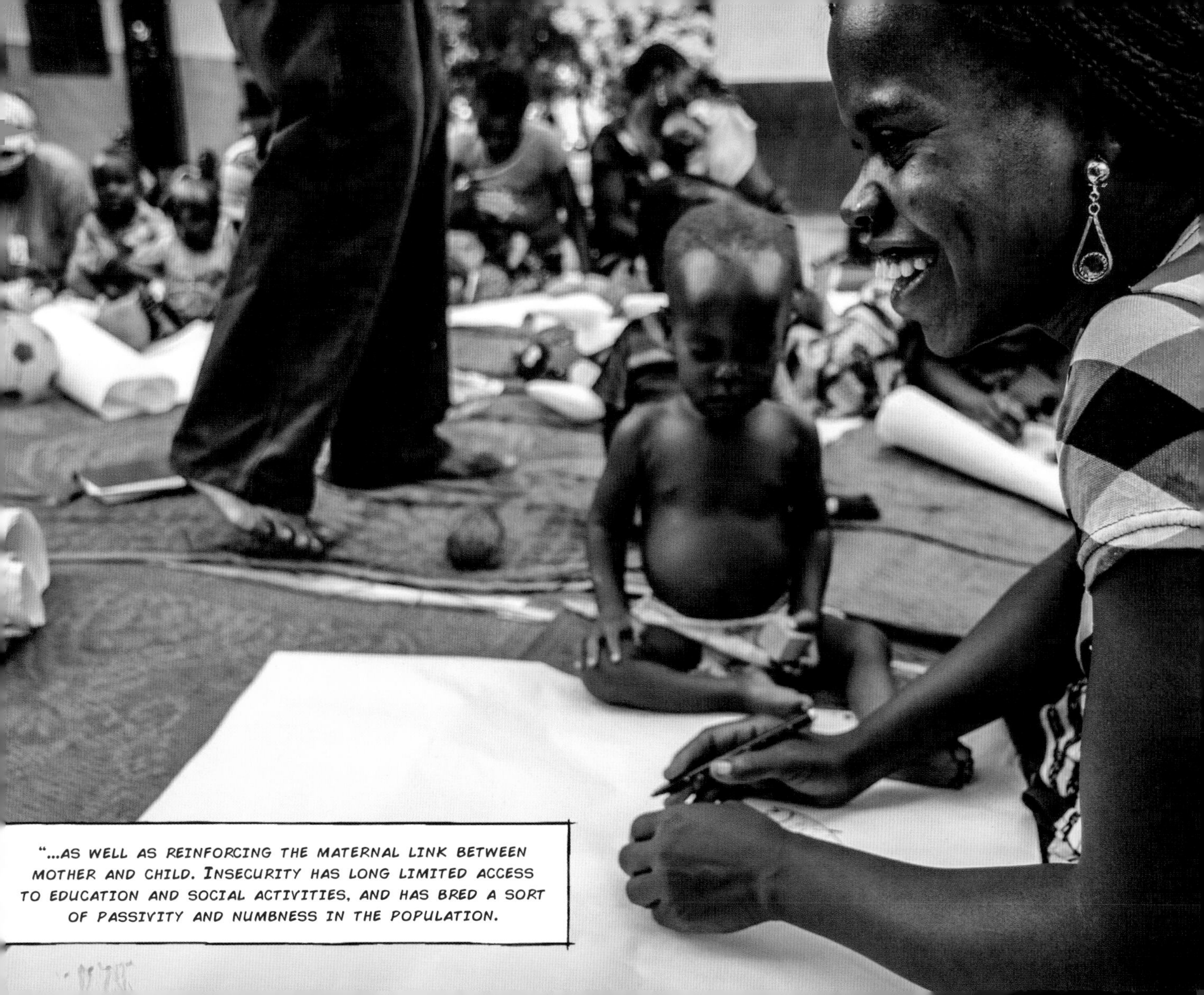
"...AS WELL AS REINFORCING THE MATERNAL LINK BETWEEN MOTHER AND CHILD. INSECURITY HAS LONG LIMITED ACCESS TO EDUCATION AND SOCIAL ACTIVITIES, AND HAS BRED A SORT OF PASSIVITY AND NUMBNESS IN THE POPULATION.

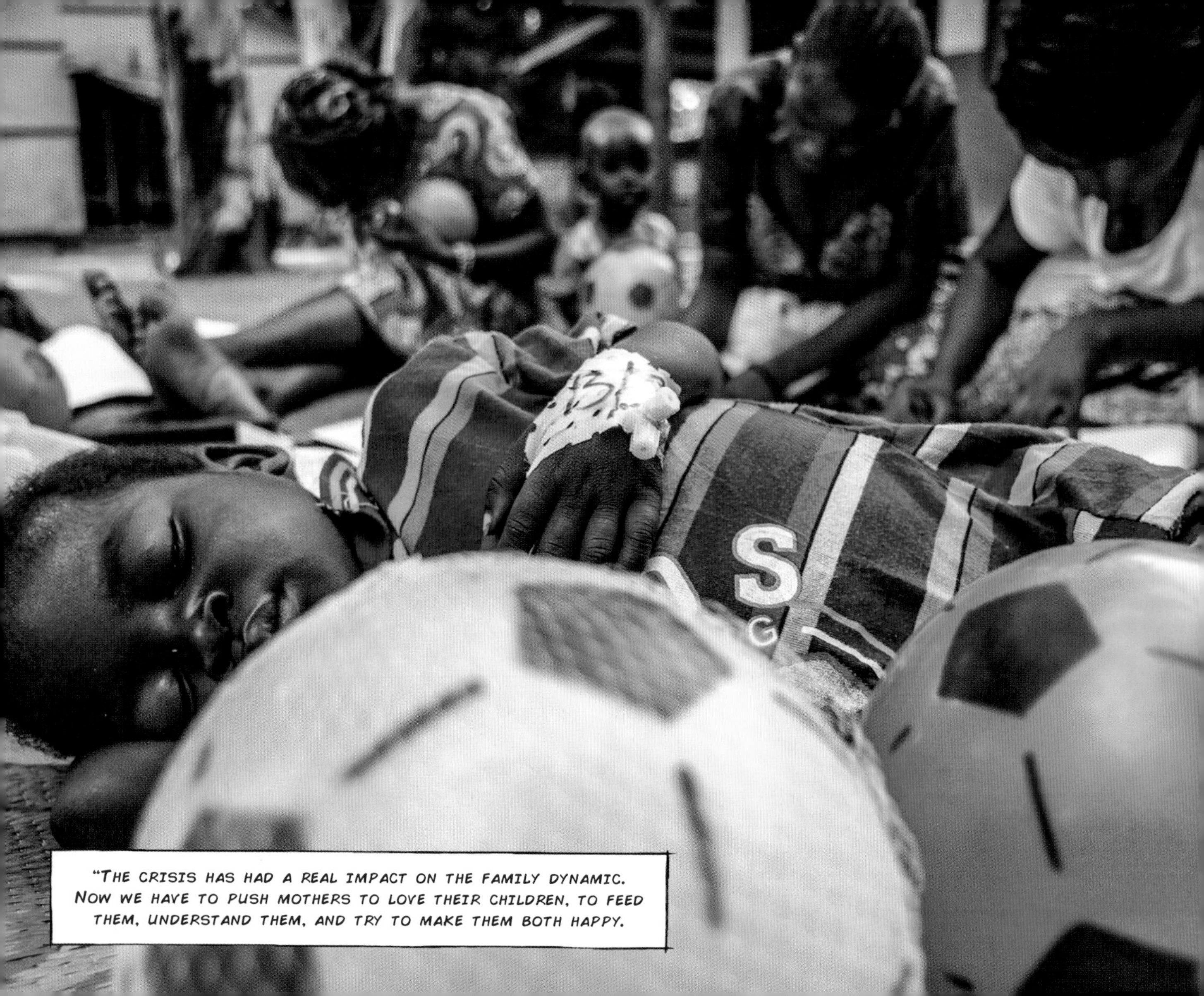
"THE CRISIS HAS HAD A REAL IMPACT ON THE FAMILY DYNAMIC. NOW WE HAVE TO PUSH MOTHERS TO LOVE THEIR CHILDREN, TO FEED THEM, UNDERSTAND THEM, AND TRY TO MAKE THEM BOTH HAPPY.

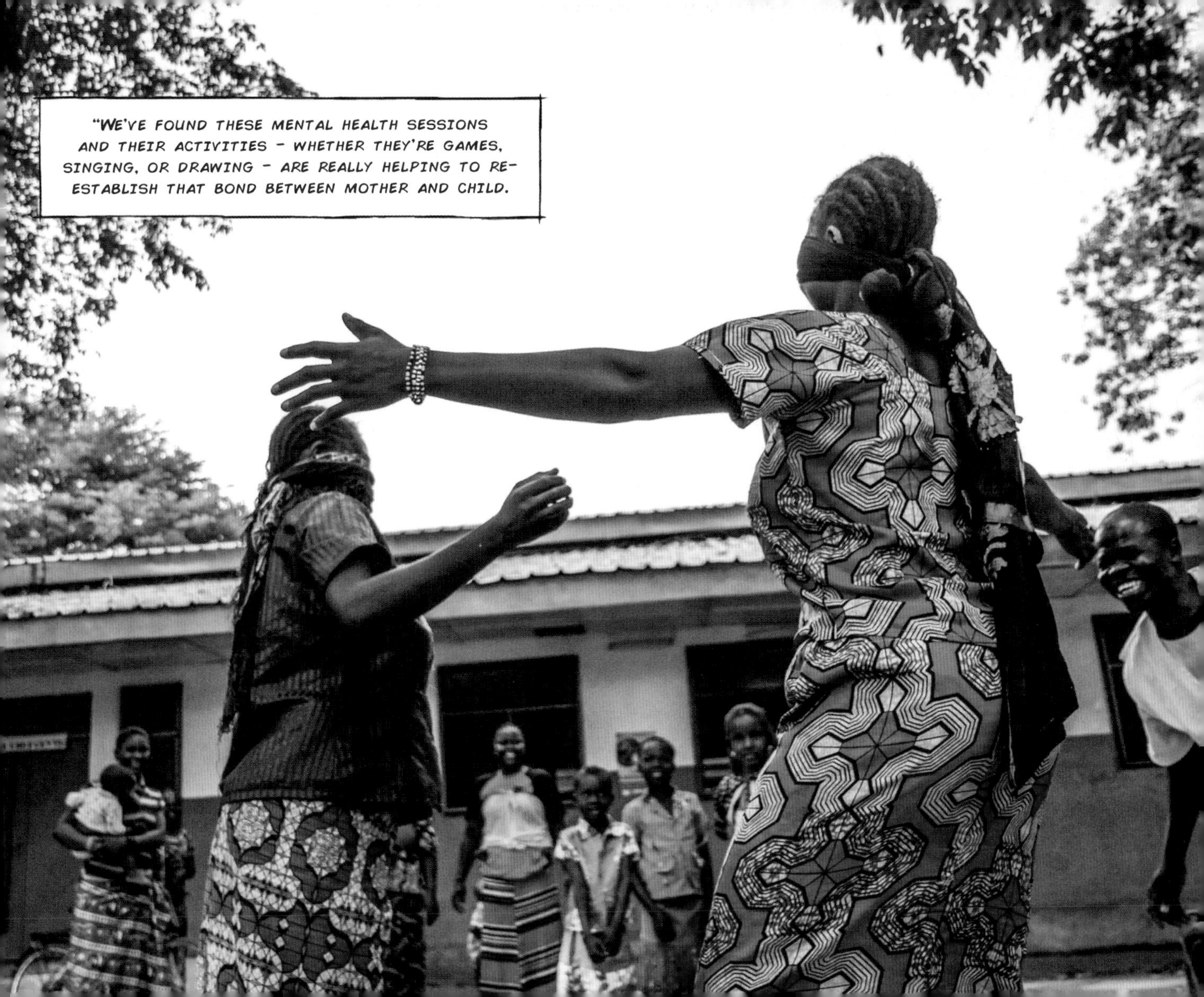
"WE'VE FOUND THESE MENTAL HEALTH SESSIONS AND THEIR ACTIVITIES - WHETHER THEY'RE GAMES, SINGING, OR DRAWING - ARE REALLY HELPING TO RE-ESTABLISH THAT BOND BETWEEN MOTHER AND CHILD.

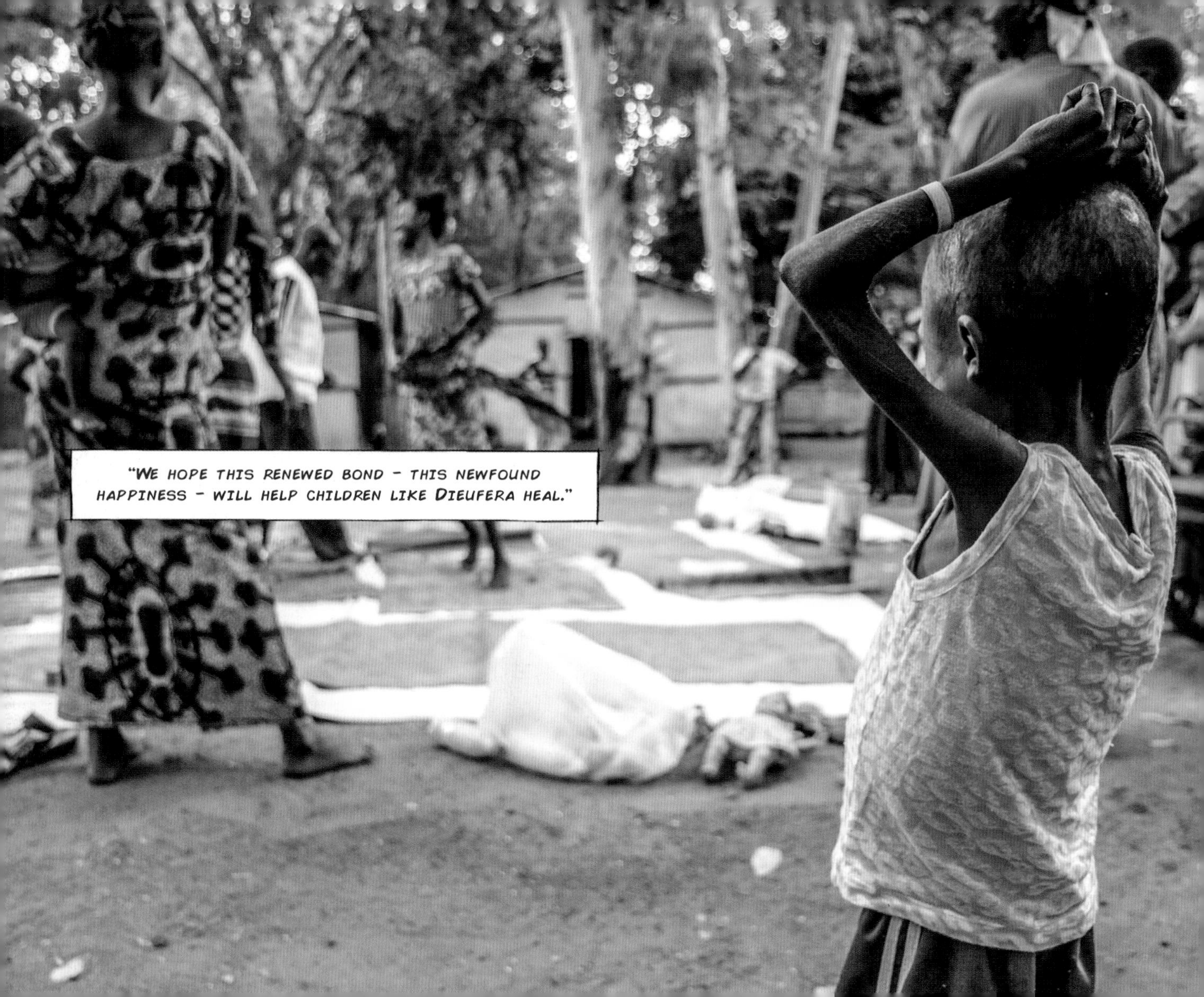
"WE HOPE THIS RENEWED BOND - THIS NEWFOUND HAPPINESS - WILL HELP CHILDREN LIKE DIEUFERA HEAL."

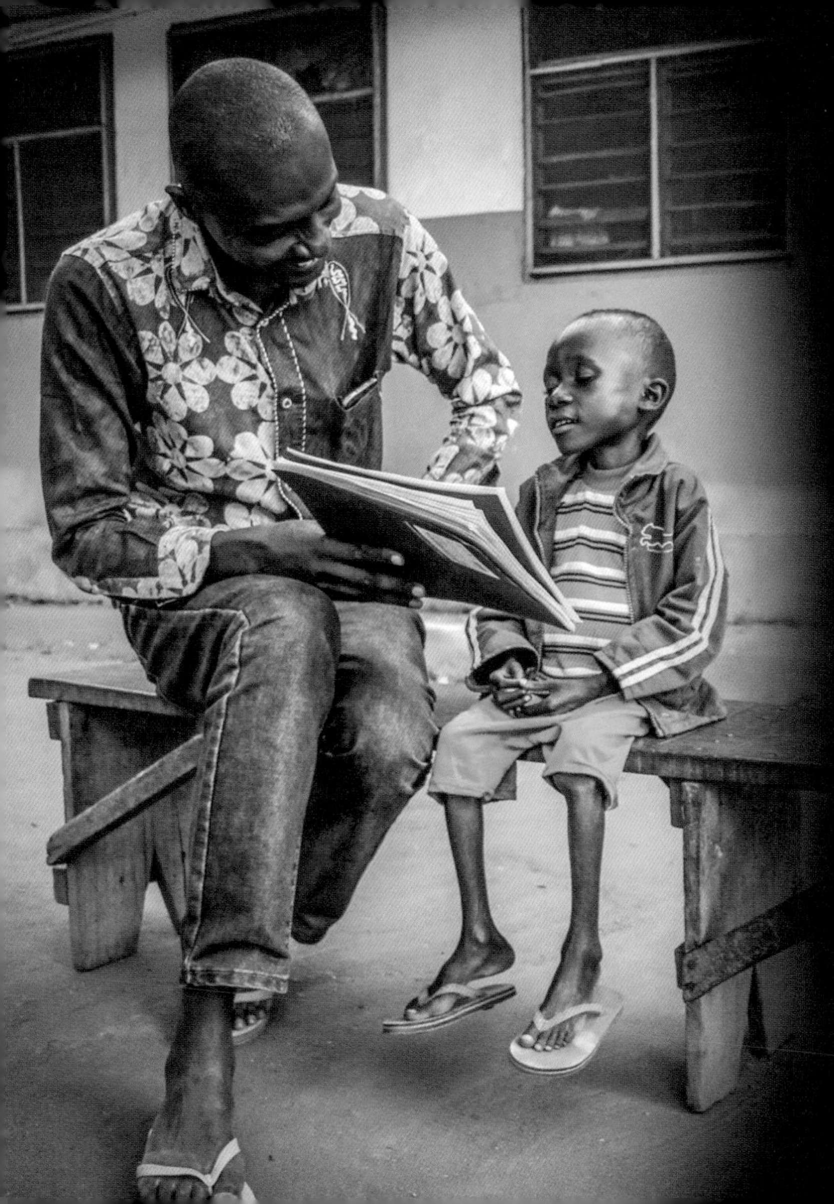

ACKNOWLEDGEMENTS

I stood on the shoulders of giants to complete this project—giants to whom I owe a massive debt of thanks.

Thanks first must go to the European Journalism Centre and their Innovation in Development Reporting grant which made this project possible.

To my partners in crime—Didier Kassaï and Crispin Dembassa-Kette—who were with me every step of the way on this journey.

Thanks to the organizations and their amazing staff who were instrumental in guiding me in the field: Fondation Hirondelle, Médecins Sans Frontières, the Norwegian Refugee Council, Radio Ndeke Luka, Triangle Génération Humanitaire, Unicef, and Voix Du Coeur.

To Donaig Le Du, Maureen Magee, Lewis Mudge, Marieke Hopman, and Louisa Lombard, who offered invaluable pre-departure advice and background.

To an ever-supportive and understanding Monkey who let this guy go cowboy one more time.

And most importantly thanks to all the incredible children—the Dieuferas, the Adamas, the Jacks—who bravely agreed to share their stories with me...

...this project's for you—may it provide a much-needed window into the challenges you all face.

—Marc Ellison
Glasgow, May 2020

ABOUT THE AUTHORS

MARC ELLISON IS AN AWARD-WINNING PHOTOJOURNALIST CURRENTLY BASED IN SCOTLAND WITH TWO CATS AND A MONKEY. *A HOUSE WITHOUT WINDOWS* IS HIS FOURTH GRAPHIC NOVEL. HE HAS PRODUCED WORK FOR *60 MINUTES*, *AL JAZEERA*, *BBC*, *THE GLOBE AND MAIL*, *HUFFINGTON POST*, *THE TORONTO STAR*, AND *VICE*. HIS WORK CAN BE SEEN AT MARCELLISON.COM.

DIDIER KASSAÏ IS A SELF-TAUGHT ARTIST WHO STARTED OUT BY DRAWING ON THE WALLS OF HIS FAMILY HOME IN SIBU WITH CHARCOAL. YEARS LATER, HE BECAME A COMIC BOOK AUTHOR, INTERESTED IN CARTOON REPORTAGE. HE DOCUMENTED THE PAINFUL DAILY LIFE OF HIS FELLOW CITIZENS IN HIS GRAPHIC NOVEL *TEMPÊTE SUR BANGUI*, PUBLISHED BY *LA BOITE À BULLES*.

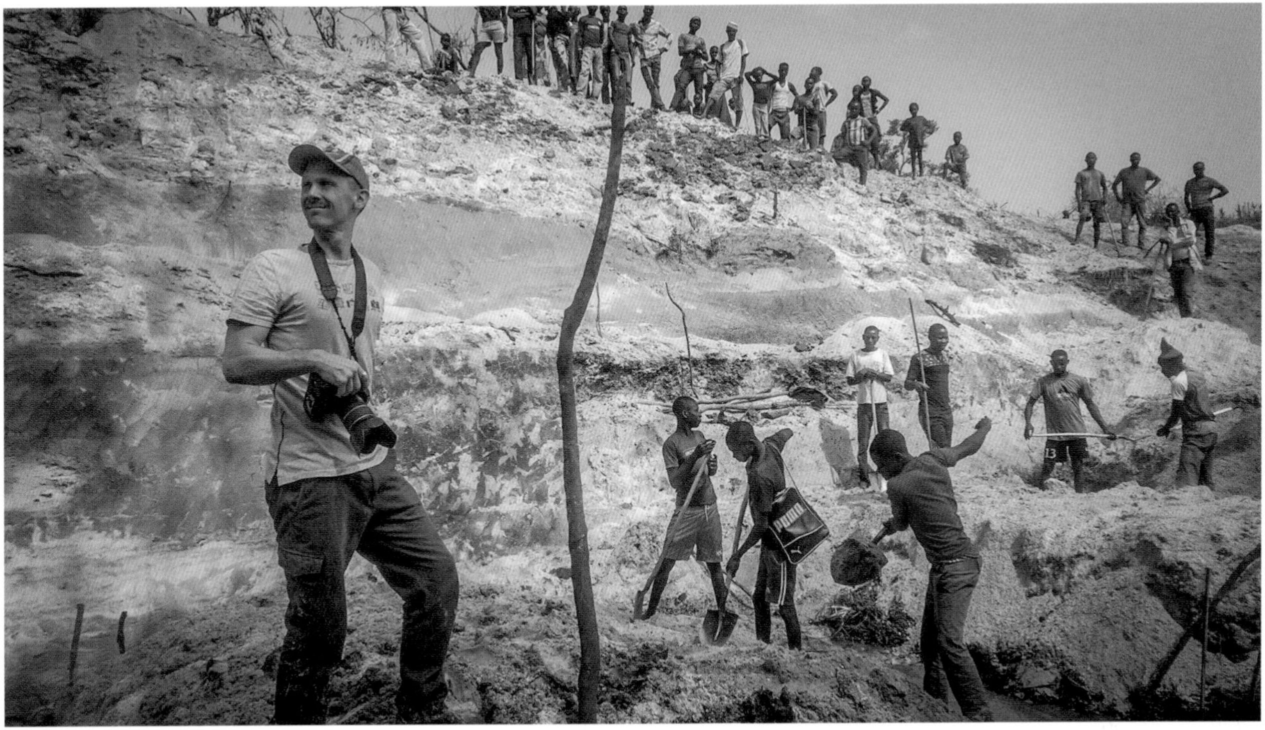
PUMA

Author Marc Ellison standing in open diamond mine. Photo by Didier Kassaï.

AFTERWORD

I have been to the Central African Republic several times as part of my work with Doctors Without Borders (Médecins Sans Frontières, MSF). My first visit was in June 2007, during a dramatic period for MSF. Elsa, a young logistician based in Paoua, had been shot and killed by rebels[1] near Ngaoudaye during a trip to the brush to check the results of distributing tarps and blankets to villages that had been completely burned down by the loyalist army. Having already experienced repeated attacks while treating patients in the brush before this killing, the team was traumatized. A new team, which I was part of, replaced them. Before resuming our aid activities, we had to renegotiate with different armed groups for the safety of our teams and patients. Thus, I stayed on as head of the mission for a year.

I found a country in disarray. The state was failing to take care of its basic functions of safety, justice, education, and health. In 2006, rebellions, which were violently repressed by the country's armed forces, had exploded throughout the northern part of the country, demanding more resources and infrastructure from the government. The rebels in the northwest, the People's Army for the Restoration of Democracy (APRD), were farmers equipped with arrows, machetes, and locally-manufactured hunting rifles. They were backed by former soldiers who were scarcely better equipped. There was also a well-established type of crime: "highway robbers" plundered the northwest by kidnapping hundreds of farming families for ransom, which the families raised by selling their herds. The people lived day to day, managing with great difficulty to make a farm or business yield a profit due to the insecurity. The rich land, conducive to agriculture and animal husbandry, was little used.

Yet this country—one of the most unstable on the African continent—was also one of the most neglected by international organizations and institutions. This resulted in very limited, barely effective support. Even today, in many respects, Central Africa remains that blind house that Didier Kassaï and Marc Ellison speak of: attacks take place in areas that are hard to access, and only rough estimates of the number of dead filter out, let alone the number of wounded.

During this period and the following years, MSF was primarily involved in supplying and managing hospitals in the towns and health posts in the brush. MSF held refresher courses for the country's medical personnel and trained First Aid nurses in basic health care at the health posts. Free care allowed patients to move towards receiving sustained health care. Malaria, infectious childhood diseases such as measles, respiratory infections, diarrhea, and complicated childbirth, as well as HIV/AIDS and tuberculosis, seemed to us to be the principal killers in the country. This abnormally high mortality rate from illnesses that were nonetheless preventable and treatable was confirmed in a number of epidemiological studies that MSF carried out between 2010 and 2011.[2] These studies were conducted in several of the country's prefectures and found a greatly elevated rate of mortality, often rising well above t[...] emergency thresholds that one might expect to fi[...] in countries at war and in acute crisis. For exampl[...] in the town of Carnot in the southwest of t[...] country, which was relatively unaffected by arm[...] violence, the overall mortality rate for childr[...] under five years of age shows that on average[...] children died every day in this area during 201[...] With this context, I returned to the country in Ap[...] 2012 for three months. Peace seemed to ha[...] returned and we were able to focus our work [...] health care needs.

At the end of 2012, however, a new rebellion (t[...] Séléka) appeared in the northern part of Cent[...] Africa; I was already in another country when t[...] Séléka took Bangui in March 2013. The progressi[...] of this armed group across the land was devastatir[...] Looting and general violence reached areas that h[...] been unaffected by the conflicts up to then. T[...] international media finally relayed informati[...] about this country I'm so deeply attached [...] Anti-Balaka militias—also called "self-defense"[...] counterattacked and responded to the Sélék[...] extortion with that of their own as internatior[...] forces, particularly the French army, stepped in[...] action with the stated purpose of protecting t[...] people in a climate of extreme violence and reprisa[...] This was a disaster. The nation was paralyze[...] hundreds of thousands of people were displac[...] inside the country or sought refuge in neighbori[...] lands. In Bangui and the western part of Cent[...] Africa, members of the civilian population—Ch[...] shopkeepers, Fulani, and Central African Muslir[...]

---

[1] Press release, "Clarifying the Circumstances of the Death of Our Colleague Elsa Serfass in the Central African Republic," MSF, April 4, 2008.
[2] Report, "The Central African Republic: A Silent Crisis," MSF, November 2011.

o has been assimilated into the former rebel ...lition by the anti-Balaka—became the targets ...systematic reprisals for a number of months. **An ...estigation carried out in Chad by MSF reported ...00 deaths in three months³—the number of ...d and wounded throughout the entire country ...2014 remains difficult to estimate, since they ...re seldom reported.**

...travels brought me back to Central Africa ...the third time in 2014; I stayed for a year. ...F organized emergency operations and we ...pped up our activities. International aid groups ...lly arrived, and emergency aid was organized ...rywhere. It was difficult for everyone: attacks ...the roads affected humanitarian workers as well ...the general population. Incidents increased— ...ticularly theft, rape, and murder—which directly ...cted our MSF teams.⁴

...ry day, our national colleagues told us about ...ir homes being ransacked, their lives in the ...placement camps, and their family members ...ng killed. Some of them chose to flee the country, ...sent us their news later on from refugee camps ...Chad, Cameroon or Congo. They worked daily, ...pite the danger presented by traveling from ...ir homes to our office or the hospital. Some ...ed and slept on our premises.

...er decades of political and military turmoil, the ...mage from this new period of extreme violence ...enormous and lasting. Families were weakened and torn apart, no longer trusting each other.

Over the course of my travels, I encountered familiar figures, in particular my Central African colleagues, to whom I must pay tribute for their resilience and friendship. They shared their observations, their questions, and their hopes with me. We encountered each other "under fire," in difficult situations.

Today, four years later, the situation is once again degenerating: neither the presence of peacekeepers nor negotiations between the armed groups, the elected government, and various international mediators have been able to hold back the cycle of violence. The latest escalation primarily affected the southeastern provinces at the start of 2017, but from there, most of the country...

The conflict also centers on predation—of diamonds, herds of cattle, and anything of the slightest value. A large part of the population no longer trusts foreign interventions to solve the crisis, whether via armed troops under the aegis of the United Nations or, to a greater extent, international organizations in general, including NGOs.

It was well after my return to France that I read Didier Kassaï's *Tempête sur Bangui* (trans., *Storm over Bangui*). I started following Didier Kassaï's posts on social media. I have a great deal of respect for him: simultaneously engaged, funny, fair, and benevolent, he shows us not only the war but also scenes of daily life in Central Africa and its culture. He lets us share the times when he returns to his village, where life continues according to the seasons. He opens its windows, reclaims its history, and tells us about it.

In so doing, he becomes an active participant and problem solver to recover its history: in my opinion, Didier Kassaï's and Marc Ellison's work is part of the essential dynamic in Central Africa. By putting the subject of children at the center of their work, they show the social, political, and health problems as well as reminding us of what needs to be done. Analyses of the peacekeepers' powerlessness, the underfunded humanitarian response, and the latest developments in the games of alliances and rivalries between the different armed forces often make us forget the people who live in this country —and their potential. This book brings them back to the forefront.

Delphine Chedorge
Head of Mission and MSF Medical Coordinator
In CAR in 2007, 2008, 2012, 2014
Currently writing coordinator for the MSF
guidebook, *Burn Care.*

...e the reports, "Central African Republic: A Year of Endless Violence Against Civilians," MSF, March 2014, and "Central African Refugees in Chad and Cameroon: The Suitcase and the Coffin, ..., July 2014.
...ess release, "Central African Republic (CAR): 16 civilians, including 3 MSF Employees, killed in a Boguila Hospital," MSF, April 28, 2014.
...eadly escalation in the CAR: For Thousands of Central Africans, War Is Once Again a Daily Reality," MSF, September 2017.

MEDECINS SANS FRONTIERES
DOCTORS WITHOUT BORDERS

Doctors Without Borders is a medical humanitarian organization founded in Paris in 1971 by doctors and journalists. For over 40 years, Doctors Without Borders has brought medical assistance to people whose health or lives are threatened, primarily in situations of armed conflict but also during epidemics, pandemics, natural disasters, and exclusion from healthcare.

MSF is independent of all political, military, and religious powers and observes complete impartiality after evaluating a population's medical needs. MSF's independence of association rests on the generosity of its private donors.

MSF reports on its operations based on its activities and the reality observed on the ground. The organization communicates publicly in order to bear witness to the fate of the populations it works with, and to inform others about the aid it provides.

MSF has worked in the Central African Republic since 1997 and today runs about fifteen projects in the country, the province, and Bangui. The project that the authors visited in *A House Without Windows* continues to operate in Kabo.

In 2016, the organization carried out 1,000,000 medical consultations, vaccinated 500,000 infants against various diseases, performed 9,000 surgeries, and attended the births of 21,000 babies in the country. Following the escalation of armed conflict during 2017, MSF adapted some of its programs and ran emergency interventions to respond to the needs of those directly affected by the return of violence.

. . . .

To learn more visit www.msf.org.